EARLY MEN OF HOLY CROSS

"To Sustain Each Other until Death"

GEORGE KLAWITTER

EARLY MEN OF HOLY CROSS
"TO SUSTAIN EACH OTHER UNTIL DEATH"

iUniverse books may be ordered through booksellers or by contacting:

iUniverse
1663 Liberty Drive
Bloomington, IN 47403
www.iuniverse.com
1-800-Authors (1-800-288-4677)

ISBN: 978-1-5320-0965-5 (sc)
ISBN: 978-1-5320-0966-2 (e)

Library of Congress Control Number: 2016917559

Print information available on the last page.

iUniverse rev. date: 10/19/2016

TABLE OF CONTENTS

for

Thomas Maddix, CSC

INTRODUCTION

Every history of the Congregation of Holy Cross must begin with the French Revolution's devastating effects on the country's education system. From 1820 to 1835 the need for teachers brought to the little town of Ruillé-sur-Loir hundreds of young men eager to become Christian educators there under the care of the pastor Jacques Dujarié. After a rudimentary training period, they went out singly or in pairs to run parochial schools in French villages. Although their work as "Brothers of St. Joseph" extended over fifteen years, we have given short attention to these hundreds of generous religious because Holy Cross historians are anxious to get to 1835 when the group moved lock, stock, and barrel to the city of Le Mans. There they trained under the new direction of a vibrant, intelligent, energetic leader, Basile Anthony Moreau, who has received the lion's share of Holy Cross research and acclamation. Dujarié as well has been acclaimed.

But such leaders cannot succeed without religious lieutenants and foot soldiers. It is these latter men whom I focus on for this book. Memorialized in these pages are seven teachers, one businessman, one carpenter, one commissioner, and one priest. I want to bring into the light some of the early great men of Holy Cross who served well but who have been overlooked or relegated to occasional footnotes. For example, there would be no Holy Cross today if it were not for André Mottais, the first Brother to persevere in Dujarié's Ruillé group. Dujarié directed the men from his rectory while it was André who educated the young men, gave them spiritual counseling, visited them yearly out in their little schools. It was André also who facilitated the transfer of the Brothers into Basile Moreau's care.

Dujarié entrusted the day-to-day direction of his Ruillé Community to four of the Brothers: André Mottais (named the Primary Director), Leonard Guittoger, Henry Taupin, and Vincent Pieau. Three of these men remained to their deaths in Holy Cross, only Henry being sent away from the group (in 1834). Thus three of these men will get here some of the credit they have long deserved for their apostolic work: André for keeping the Brothers together, Leonard for fighting to preserve their identity, and Vincent for his long missionary service to establish Holy Cross in Indiana.

Other heroes from the early years include Hilarion Ferton, who led the Brothers back into Algeria two years after they had been abruptly recalled to France, Lawrence Ménage, who served the fledgling Notre Dame as its first financial officer, and Francis Xavier, who outlasted them all, dying four years before the nineteenth-century became the twentieth-century. At the same time, we cannot overlook younger men. Thus Anselm appears in this book because he represents the best Holy Cross had in youthful American generosity. I include young Gatian too because even though he did not die in Holy Cross his brash enthusiasm must never be slighted or omitted from the Community's history. I include Theodulus because he served generously in multiple locations. And I include Alexis Granger, the lone priest selected for focus in this book, because it is my hope that the distinction between priest and brother in Holy Cross will quietly erode, their separation based on a mismatching of ministry and life-style. The book ends with a chapter on a peacemaker, Brother Rémi, who opposed separatists like Brother Leonard and remained faithful to the idea of Holy Cross as envisioned by Basile Moreau.

The appendices at the end of the book contain primary documents. One appendix is a translation of the important 1831 piece that the Brothers of St. Joseph created to hold their members together at a crucial moment in their history. That document contains the plaintive hope that the remaining members will "sustain each other until death." Another appendix is the last letter André Mottais wrote from

Africa. It is a testament to his faith and courage. An entirely different tone informs Hilarion Ferton's upbeat (and bantering) letter from Africa to young student Brothers back in Le Mans. Appendix V is a sad document, important in the unfortunate demotion of Leonard Guittoger. The final appendix is a sermon by Alexis Granger.

In the preparation of this book I owe thanks to three Holy Cross archivists: Kevin Cawley at the University of Notre Dame, Christopher Kuhn, CSC, at the United States Province archives, and Lawrence Stewart, CSC, at the Midwest Province archives. Their kind assistance was always forthcoming, and I thank their respective archives for the permissions granted to reprint documents in this book. The translations from French are my own, except where otherwise noted. Some of the material on André, Vincent, Anselm, and Gatian is reprinted here from *After Holy Cross, Only Notre Dame*. Much of the research was done through generous grants from St. Edward's University in Austin, Texas. I thank the Holy Cross History Association, especially James Connelly, CSC, Walter Davenport, CSC, and John Kuhn, CSC, for stimulus to write these lives. I also thank Joseph McTaggart, CSC, for proofreading the manuscript. I thank the Brothers at Columba Hall, Notre Dame, and the Brothers at the Brother Vincent Pieau Residence in Austin, Texas, for their encouragement.

CHAPTER ONE

André Mottais, the Second Founder: "Remove my name every time it appears"

The two giants in the history of Holy Cross have always been Jacques Dujarié and Basil Moreau, but what if a third man were so important that without him Dujarié's Brothers would have fallen into the footnotes of history and Moreau's mixed Community would never have seen the light of day?

What if this man were schooled in religious spirituality more formally than Dujarié and supervised more classrooms than Moreau ever set foot in? What if such a man had a humility so ingrained that after fifteen years of running the day-to-day operations of a religious organization, he accepted demotion and the humblest of tasks because he knew that the future of his Brothers depended upon his unconditional submission?

What if such a man has been sidelined more or less in the history of Holy Cross while Dujarié and Moreau have advanced in stature and renown, the latter well into the process of canonization? Such a man, we would say, deserves resurrection: his indefatigable energy, his uncanny foresight, and his overpowering virtue need to be better acknowledged than they are.

Most Holy Cross members when they think about Brother André Mottais, if they think about him at all, may consider him a kind of "secretary" to Father Dujarié[1] and dismiss him as a somewhat important, if marginal and shadowy, cog in the early wheel of the Brothers of St. Joseph. They probably know that of the three young men earliest to arrive at Ruillé in 1820, he was the only one to persevere, answering Dujarié's call to rescue children from the ignorance left in the aftermath of the French Revolution. But when André arrived, the Revolution was actually a generation previous, and Napoleon's Concordat, which reconciled Church and State in a form still pretty much extant today, was seventeen years old. André is often lost in the patter of history and survives only in a paragraph of Holy Cross history here and there as a man of some importance to the fledgling Community at Ruillé. It took the brave archivist Philéas Vanier, however, to proclaim André the "second founder of Holy Cross." Today we are wary and incredulous that a non-ordained person could wear the title of "second founder of Holy Cross." Some smile at the title and accept it as a pious metaphor, a kind of testament to a man who lived with Dujarié and worked beside him for fifteen years. Others are content to skip over the title as a historical gesture of no religious or practical significance because, after all, in the last years of his life André worked in a clerical society, and his vocation was narrowly based on the humility and obscurity of St. Joseph himself. But metaphor or not, the title reflects the actuality of André's work. In the words of Vanier:

> Four directors had been established to head the Institute [at Ruillé]: but the last three are more assistants than equals. Brother André directs everything: he rules on everything and is the judge of last resort. He is responsible for formation of subjects; he is master of novices; he presides over all exercises including meals; he gives all permissions; he resolves all difficulties between religious; he harries the lukewarm; he encourages the zealous; he gives direction.[2]

It is obvious that André was the visible head of the Brothers of St. Joseph, Dujarié being distracted by his parish duties and his increasingly problematic supervision of the Sisters of Providence. It is André who makes the annual visits on foot to the scores of little schools run by the Brothers in towns around the diocese. It is André who supervises day by day and year by year the ups and downs of the Community. He is the front man for most decisions, even as Dujarié remains titular head of the Brothers.

Born André Pierre Mottais in Larchamp, fifty miles northwest of Le Mans, the man who was destined to help forge Holy Cross came of solid farming stock.[3] His parents were Jean Mottais and Jeanne Blot, who were married May 14, 1793, seven years before André's birth. The father was born in 1768 and the mother in 1773 making them 24 and 20 at the time of their marriage in the bloodiest year of the French Revolution.[4] Jeanne Blot and Jean Mottais had four children that we know of: Jean François (born September 16, 1794), André Pierre (born February 21, 1800), Jeanne Julienne (born August 10, 1805), and Joseph (born June 17, 1811).[5] For generations the Mottais family lived at Pontperrin, a farm-estate in Mayenne near the town of Larchamp, fifteen miles east of Fougères. The property had been in the family since the sixteenth century. Before the French Revolution it comprised over two hundred and fifty acres. Today it has a single manor house owned by the de Blic family, who also own four surrounding farms. The Mottais farm-estate is located just southeast of Larchamp, off the intersection of Route 799 and Route 523, and its name "Pontperrin" suggests that the family property may have been named for a bridge over a small river on the eastern edge of the property. The Mottais home, with its fine-weathered brick, indicates a family of some wealth. Stone steps lead up to an entrance on the second level, suggesting that originally the lowest level was probably used for storage. The living quarters would then be confined to the two upper levels, and the orderly placement of the windows suggests two or four rooms per floor, the middle level for living and dining, the top floor for sleeping. A barn next to the house is equally old and is used by the de Blic family to this day. Its walls are twenty feet high, and its roof peaks to thirty feet. At one end a high shuttered window indicates a grain loft. The other end appends a smaller building still used as living quarters.

André Pierre Mottais came from a family with deep roots in the area going back several hundred years. As a second son, he was not christened with the name of his father, grandfather, or great-grandfather, nor would he have inherited the family farm. Born in the winter of 1800, André was welcomed into a country chronicled by a new calendar: Revolutionary France records André's birth as 2 Ventose in the year 8 (February 21, 1800). His birth announcement in the Larchamp parish records begins, "Today, the second Ventose," indicating that the Revolutionary Calendar was duly regarded as official in this small French town. In its fourteenth year (1805), however, the calendar would revert to the Gregorian style. The parish church in Larchamp dominates the town and remains much as André would have known it. The bell tower is the highest structure in the area, its old dark stone already hundreds of years old when André was carried into the church to be baptized. The baptistry, where the Mottais family had their son baptized in February 1800, is a separate little room at the back right of the church, a small room that can accommodate a dozen people. The stone font in which he was ritually brought into the Larchamp faith-community is still used today to welcome the infants of the parish into their ancient religion. The interior of the church is dark, although some stained-glass windows let in welcome light. The foot-thick walls would give a little boy the sense of a fortress, affording him security in his religion, albeit tinged with gloom.

The school André attended in Larchamp has only recently been torn down, but André, like the sons of other farm owners, would have learned the basics of reading, writing, and numbers before giving himself full time to work on the family farm, awaiting whatever destiny would come his way. How did he enjoy farm work? We have no record left of his early life on the farm, but later letters written from Africa demonstrate a keen sense of farming. We presume that this virtuous young man worked with a willing back and a cheerful heart, but at some point there definitely resonated in him a call at the age of twenty to leave his family and travel south to the little town of Ruillé where Dujarié was beginning to gather young men into his

Brothers of St. Joseph. André would have walked, or perhaps ridden in a cart, south to Ernée, then further south to Laval, the largest city he would have seen in his life so far. Then he probably would have headed southeast to Sablé and farther to La Flèche where he would have encountered the Loir River—not the mighty Loire of famed chateaux, but the little Loir that runs east-west joining the Sarthe River (from Le Mans) just north of Angers. From La Flèche, André could have simply headed east, following the little Loir as it rambled toward him, past Le Lude, Château-du-Loir, and La Chartre-sur-le-Loir to little Ruillé-sur-le-Loir, where the pastor of the parish either expected him (possibly apprised of his arrival by letter) or was pleasantly surprised by the young farmer's appearance.

Jacques Dujarié had been nudged by Bishop Pidoll of Le Mans as early as 1818 to begin a community of brothers who would teach in rural schools because Dujarié's community of Sisters of Providence had been a growing success during the previous decade. By 1820 the Curé of Ruillé had begun to accept young men into his rectory. The first, Pierre Hureau, arrived on July 15, the second, Louis Duchêne (Dujarié's nephew), on August 20. The former left a year later but returned for six years in 1824. The latter left in 1825. Dujarié's third arrival was a prize: André Pierre Mottais arrived on October 22, 1820, persevered, and eventually became the first Brother to profess perpetual vows of poverty, chastity, obedience, and stability (August 25, 1836). These young recruits slept in Dujarié's attic with the rats, and as the numbers of young men grew, the Brothers eventually flowed over into the laundry room, the bakehouse, the barn, and even the stable.[6] Three months after André arrived, Dujarié told him to start a school at Ruillé. Such was Dujarié's impression of André's promise and talents. The young man had just come from a farm and had no training as a teacher. Then, since Dujarié felt he himself did not know how to train male religious, in spite of his successful guidance of the Providence women for sixteen years, the priest consulted Abbé de Lamennais, founder of a successful community of brothers, who advised him to study the spiritual practices of the Christian Brothers. Their founder, John Baptist de la Salle, had

had noteworthy success with a burgeoning community of religious teachers. Thus a few months after André had started his little school in Ruillé, Dujarié sent him north to Le Mans where the young man had to be reviewed for military conscription, was exempted, and then lived for five months in 1821 with a priest named Lamare and took classes from the Christian Brothers.[7]

The experience with Lamare was a kind of active novitiate by which André blended the pious direction of his priest-mentor with the practical classroom know-how of his Christian Brother directors. In fact, as we read between the lines of André's praise for Father Lamare, we can discern the origins of André's own life-long sense of piety. Lamare was a man of fixed routine, André tells us in his 1833 sketch of the man: he slept no more than five hours a night, prayed two hours before Mass, and left promptly for St. Julian's Cathedral at 6:30. After lunch, the priest heard confessions, sometimes until midnight on the eve of great feasts, breaking away only for a hurried supper. He ate little, subsisting on soup and vegetables, and he never touched wine. During meals he was usually interrupted by poor people begging alms at the door: he never turned them away and listened to all their troubles. In these acts of a saintly man, it is easy to see what André himself picked up for his own life in religion: he became an indefatigable supervisor of new teachers, both in their training at Ruillé and in their little parish schools around the region. He was also an especially prayerful man whose good sense rooted in him a firm and unwavering belief in the viability of the Brothers of St. Joseph, even in their darkest hours. He was as practical as Lamare, and eventually, once his supervisory duties were taken away from him, he exhibited the same calm and ascetic piety that Lamare had exhibited when André was a malleable twenty-one year old young man.

The books that Lamare gave André to read in that five-month period tell us much about what André valued. First there was the life of Vincent de Paul and a history of his foundations. Here André would have seen witness of the great charitable works of the Hospitalers. Secondly, Alphonsus Ligouri's book on the love of God which André characterizes as the work of a "faithful soul." Thirdly, that bedrock of religious meditation right up into the twentieth century, Thomas à Kempis' *Imitation of Christ*. Fourthly, the *New Testament*, and finally the *Exercises of the Presence of God*. Most of André's reading, therefore, was of the quieting kind, just the sort of material he needed to balance the intellectual foot race he was running with the Christian Brothers, learning all he could to help him return credibly to Ruillé as a master-teacher of those young men, many of them teenagers, who would be sent out by Dujarié to teach in schools with even less of the rushed preparation that André received in Le Mans. The practice among religious communities in the nineteenth and twentieth centuries of sending out young men and women with astonishingly little formal preparation to run a classroom lasted for over a hundred years, yet most of these religious did surprisingly fine educational work. Many, of course, failed themselves and their students, who were often almost as old as their religious teachers. André later questioned the wisdom of this practice, but under the protection of Lamare, he was well prepared to assimilate a hasty education from the Christian Brothers, and André recalls with great appreciation Lamare's "wise counsels during my critical troubles."[8] André does not specify what these troubles were, nor does he specify when they occurred. They may have arisen while he lived with Lamare, but as he kept in contact with the old man for another dozen years until Lamare's death in 1833, he may be referring to any number of crises that arose in the little Community at Ruillé. A maxim sent to him by Lamare is most telling: "Let us work always while we are on earth; we will rest when we are in heaven."[9] By today's standards André became a workaholic, yet he credits Lamare with "level headedness and humor that still charm me when I remember them."[10] These twin qualities of common sense and humor would make André a highly valuable member of Dujarié's band of men. In fact, it is not farfetched to conclude that without such qualities André would have folded like scores of other young men in Dujarié's Community. Undoubtedly, he arrived at Ruillé with sound virtue instilled by his Larchamp family, but Dujarié's foresight and Lamare's wisdom also helped André root his own potential into the bedrock of a solid religious spirituality. It is often a wonder that one or two single influences can determine a human being's formation: a generous and wise novice master can make all the difference in the world when adolescents make crucial decisions about their own destinies.

When André returned to Ruillé at the end of November, 1821,[11] with Brother Stephen,[12] who had apparently been sent to Le Mans to retrieve André, the two men were met by Dujarié outside of Ruillé at the foot of a cross and vested with a religious habit designed by the bishop.[13] The habit was simple:

> It was decided that they would wear a kind of black robe or soutane without a train, buttoning down to the waist and buttoned inside from the waist to the bottom, of ordinary cloth, and descending to six inches from the ground; a hat flat in the middle, that is, five and a half inches, and the edge three and a half inches; a small black and white collar, a cloth skullcap, and short pants. Several weeks after, a white band was added to the collar with two branches, resting on the top of the chest, and sewn together halfway. Each branch was about two inches wide, and the length from the neck to the end was about four inches.[14]

At this time in Ruillé there were five Brothers, the first recruit (Pierre Hureau) having left in June. Only two were given the habit, possibly because they were considered "novices." In December, four more recruits would arrive, the same month that Dujarié sent André away for a second time, this time to Paris to live for six months (until June, 1822) at the Christian Brothers' novitiate.[15] In all, André spent almost a year in training (five months in Le Mans and six months in Paris), not a bad educational experience when one compares it to what was afforded most of the Brothers of St. Joseph.

It is difficult to establish precisely how many men came and went at Ruillé in the early years. Record keeping was good but not precise. For example, the *Chronicles* note that in 1822 twenty men arrived and three left, but the "Matricule Generale" assembled by Brother Bernard Gervais in the twentieth century lists for that year only fifteen arrivals and no departures. It could be that men who stayed for only a few days were not officially recorded. If a young man came, for example, just to test the waters, so to speak, he may have been regarded as an overnight visitor rather than as someone serious about devoting his life to religion. In 1823 one man is listed as arriving in April and leaving sometime that same year, but we do not know how long he stayed. It is not until 1824 that the "Matricule Generale" lists a young man (Jean-Pierre Chabrun) who arrives at age fifteen, takes the name Brother Alexis, and leaves two days later. We must remember that for the last half of 1821 and the first half of 1822, André was not in Ruillé and record keeping was probably in the hands of the over-extended Dujarié. When André did get back to Ruillé, he was totally responsible for the instruction of the young men who came, one as young as twelve, to be Brothers of St. Joseph. As for those men who went into the field, the *Chronicles* note: "Those of these novices who had grace of state studied in their establishments and little by little they made themselves useful teachers."[16]

The loose federation of men that constituted the Brothers of St. Joseph was united by a single vow (obedience), which they could take annually. The formula was simple and read in part: "I submit fully to the rules and statutes of the said Congregation, promising to observe them exactly; and consequently I renew for one year the vow of obedience to the superior of the said Congregation."[17] This vow was enough to hold the group together: defections in the first decade of the Brothers of St. Joseph numbered 171 out of a membership of 241. There were, of course, never 241 members at any one time in those first ten years. The peak enrollment was 106 in 1827.

Defections were either unusually low for this fledgling Community or under-reported. Either way, they had to be expected: when young people decide to change the course of their lives, they often have second thoughts. André himself was not without temptations to leave, not at Ruillé where Dujarié kept him busy and important, but rather in Le Mans where he was a little fish in a big pond. A note by André in the *Chronicles* maintains that without the encouragement of Lamare, he may have abandoned the Brothers of St. Joseph. One incident in particular is very important. A seminarian André counted as a friend came to the carriage which was about to carry André back to Ruillé. The seminarian "made the last efforts to make him lose his vocation in forcing him to change his determination, but Brother André saw the snare which the demon held out to him, rejected his perfidious advice, and entered the cart on the field, detesting the conduct of this pretended friend."[18] What exactly was the friend's advice? It was apparently not the first time he had attempted to influence André's vocation. Did he want André to become a seminarian in Le Mans? André's strong reaction and references to "the snare which the devil held out to him" and "perfidious advice" and "pretended friend" suggest something stronger because, after all, the temptation to enter a seminary is not "perfidious." It is a rather noble calling. The last minute appeal, the dramatic appearance at the carriage, all suggest that the friend did not want to lose André's company and, suspect or not, he wanted whatever bonds they had to continue. The scenario can be recollected by any number of religious who made similar decisions against last ditch temptations of whatever nature.

Of the thirty-seven letters we have by André Mottais, all but two of the first thirty were written at Ruillé, and most of them concern business relating to administration of the Brothers of St. Joseph. In the first letter (to Brother Adrian at Hardanges[19]) André gives sparse directions for settling in: the Brother's belongings will soon be sent to him, and the pastor owes the Community for books and supplies. The Brother is to bring the money to Ruillé in one week. Apparently to assuage Adrian's fear of being separated from the Community, André tells him that Hardanges is not far away from the town where Brother Francis teaches:[20] "You can see each other from time to time."[21] What little affection we can discern here is cradled in business. Eight months later, in another letter to Adrian, the formality is still evident: "I'm obliging you, my dear brother, to follow as much as possible the Rule Book for the schools, because those of our Brothers who use most of what it prescribes are also those who succeed the most in their classes."[22] The advice is almost formulaic, and one wonders what comfort it would have brought to a young man living with a parish priest who is, we are told, in bad health. Adrian was only three years younger than André and had been sent out to teach within seven months of his arrival at Ruillé. He received a teaching license one month before André's first letter to him, one of the fortunate young men sent out to teach with an actual license.[23] Such a license, easily obtainable by simply showing the local authorities a letter of obedience from Dujarié,[24] would have been a sign of willingness to teach more than an ability to teach.

Appointed by Dujarié to serve the little group as novice master, spiritual director, and supervisor of instruction (both in Ruillé and out in all the parish schools), André must have been disheartened at times by the rate of turnover among his young Brothers. Of the first fifty men to come to Ruillé, thirty-eight eventually left or were dismissed. Only twelve persevered to die either in the Brothers of St. Joseph or the Brothers from Holy Cross. But as is still true today, the work that André did in affording young men an opportunity to live a prayerful life and acquire the rudiments of a teaching career must have at times convinced him that parishes were much enriched by the men who returned to their homes better for their having lived in a religious community for however short a time. In the first of André's circular letters (dated July 17, 1826), André reminds all the men to think somberly of the coming retreat as it may be the last for some of them: two men have died since the previous year's retreat, the first two men lost to death within a Community which already had over eighty-five members.[25] As early as 1825, André each year visited all the schools, even the most remote ones, scattered across fifteen departments.[26] Dujarié thought the visitations would be a good thing, but he himself attempted to make the visits only twice and gave up both times soon after he left Ruillé because of his health,[27] delegating the trips to André who travelled on foot because most of the roads could not be used by carriages.[28]

André was a careful supervisor and very particular in what he expected of his young teachers. Among his early letters is an inventory of goods for the school at Milly. Every door, window, and stick of furniture is inventoried. Even the number of bolts and hooks in the shutters is set down. Linens are inventoried down to dishrags. In the dormitory are four little beds for the Brothers. The library has fifty-five books. The date of the inventory is May 1829, near the end of the first year the Brothers ran the school. Two years later the school at Milly is thriving and André pronounces it "the best and most agreeable in our Congregation."[29] One can imagine the joy and pride the men and students must have felt when the Brother Supervisor made a visit: since he would inquire after every imaginable detail pertinent to good teaching, everyone would be on his best behavior. The establishment at Milly was not founded without problems, however. In a letter dated November 11, 1929, André indicates step by step what had to be done via the mayor and the local prefect in order to get the Brothers sanctioned for the Milly school. The process began in September 1828 with a request from the mayor to the prefect. Five months later the project was approved by the commune, and three copies of the contract were requested. They were sent within three days to the mayor who signed them and forwarded them to the prefect, who refused the documents because they were written on the wrong kind of paper! Two months later the Community still waited for approval to teach at Milly, but the Brothers were already working there: a letter from André to Brother Stanislaus in September 1830 indicates Brothers had been in Milly for a full year teaching 110 students.

As foundations increased and money matters grew complicated, Bishop Carron of Le Mans thought it necessary to disentangle the finances of the Sisters of Providence and the Brothers of St. Joseph. The Sisters, established by Dujarié a generation before the Brothers, were solid financially and legally, but the Brothers continued to struggle for the legal recognition that would facilitate their financial health. To understand the dynamics of this separation, one needs to appreciate the character of the mother superior of the Sisters of Providence at the time. The Sisters began their history more amorphously than the Brothers, as a group of a half dozen pious girls living two miles from Dujarié in a small house ("La Petite Providence") he had built for them on the outskirts of Ruillé. Financed in part by a loan from Marie Lair, the first woman Dujarié asked to teach the local children in 1804, the establishment encountered problems when she proved to be mentally unstable and irascible. It took years to get rid of her. Meanwhile, Dujarié's pious women saw to the needs of the local poor and trudged into Ruillé every Sunday to receive spiritual guidance from their director. By 1811 they numbered ten, and Dujarié relied on a superior named Sister Félicité (her family name is lost) who lasted but a short time before she left the group. In 1813 more stability came with the arrival of Madeleine Beucher, who directed the group for seven years until the saintly Zoé du Roscoät was elected first Superior General (1820). When Zoé arrived, the Sisters numbered eighteen. Four years later she died, having been with the Sisters of Providence only a short time but leaving an indelible mark on their history. A woman of great virtue and sweet personality, she came from an aristocratic background that heightened the generosity of her selfless dedication to Dujarié and his little Community.

Her successor was decidedly different: Perrine Lecor was a Breton peasant who grew up on an isolated peninsula in northern France and spoke only Breton, no French, until the age of twenty. Madame du Roscoät had hired her as a teacher aide back in Brittany, and Perrine followed Madame to Ruillé, succeeding her as Mother General in 1822. Where Mother Marie-Madeleine was diplomatic, Mother Marie Lecor was brusque. Where the former venerated Dujarié, the latter confronted and circumvented him, not afraid to recognize that the aging priest was losing his ability to direct. Marie-Madeleine had put the person of the founder primary in her concerns, but Marie Lecor barged ahead with Providence as her single concern. Before being elected Mother General, Marie Lecor judged herself to have "a cold temperament,"[30] to be undereducated, and to be without virtue. The Cattas dub Mother Marie-Madeleine the "Angel of Providence." Mother Marie Lecor, on the other hand, was anything but an angel.

Thus when the separation of finances surfaces in 1831 as a necessity in the eyes of Bishop Carron, it is against the backdrop of a tough Mother General, the only one that most of the Brothers would have known because the gentle one had died in the second year of the Brothers' foundation. André, for example, would have known Mother Marie-Madeleine, but she died when there were but a dozen Brothers in Dujarié's new little religious group of men. What the Brothers therefore had to deal with for most of their religious lives was the strong minded Breton Mother Marie Lecor. If the separation of finances was effected in an atmosphere of paranoia and gloom, the onus lies on Marie Lecor who wanted what was best for her Sisters and was not particularly concerned with the future of the Brothers, whose future was darkened by more defections than arrivals in the three years previous to the financial separation. Some of the bad feelings must, of course, be traced to Dujarié himself. He alienated himself from Marie Lecor by refusing to deal with her. On one occasion when she visited his rectory to see him, half a block from the Providence motherhouse he had built for the Sisters, he refused to see her, and when she then wrote him a letter, he sent it back unopened.[31] The pettiness that grew over several years between two very strong personalities nowhere reflects itself in André Mottais who, as primary director of the Brothers, was in a position to become as rancorous as the other two players in the scenario but who remained, like Bishop Carron, fair and above the fray.

André, however, was no match for Marie Lecor's grit, and Dujarié, plagued by gout, often confined to bed, no longer enjoyed the deference of the mother general, her council, or the Sisters in the hinterlands who barely knew him. If anything good can be said for Marie Lecor, it is that she exerted a tremendous amount of power at a time when women were quite powerless both in the Church and in society generally. Once she found her foothold, there was no stopping her, and the last thing she wanted was any financial co-dependence with a group of men who had declined in numbers for two years and showed no signs of any restructuring. Although the intrepid Moreau was waiting in the wings, Dujarié was still in charge, and Marie Lecor wanted less and less to do with him. She should be admired surely for her tenacity in promoting the Sisters, but the bad chemistry between her and Dujarié was as much her fault as his. The old man expected things to go on as they always had under his kind and generous eye: she looked to the future and saw a wonderful opportunity for women to assume their own direction. What she thought of André Mottais we do not know. She probably considered him a well intentioned and harmless drudge who was linked by gender and domesticity more inextricably to Dujarié than she was. Her energies were employed to cut off Dujarié: André was simply one of his adjuncts. Enjoying the ear of the bishop, she was unstoppable.

The document in André's handwriting for the financial separation of the two communities is dated April 21, 1831, which would be the final day of the bishop's three-day visit to Ruillé. André sets out in detail the Brothers' financial status from November 1826 up to the day of the document. He notes that peak enrollment for the Brothers came at the annual August retreat in 1829 (almost 105 men by his count) from sixty-six foundations, but "since that happy time the number of Brothers, and establishments, has declined a lot."[32] He does not here specify reasons for the decline, but various historians have attributed the decline to two reasons: the political unrest leading up to the July, 1830, mini-revolution when old embers from 1789 were rekindled for another revolutionary outburst, and the lack of a solid formation for the young Brothers before they were being sent out to teach in parish schools. André then lists twenty-five schools taken on since 1826 (some of which were operated by the Brothers for only one school year) and fifty-three schools which have paid or failed to pay annual salaries. Some items include benefactors who bankrolled the schools: e.g., the Duchess of Tourzelle who gave 900 francs a year for the Larchamp school and M. de la Porte who gave 10,000 francs to construct classrooms at Sablé and repair the Brothers' house. One of the most poignant entries is the one for the Ruillé boarding school that was under André's direct supervision and existed legally under his name, not Dujarié's, so the Brothers could count on some property: it was sold for 7000 francs to a contractor employed by Moreau to build Holy Cross in Le Mans. Although it has always been known that Moreau was involved in the spiritual guidance of the Brothers as preacher and confessor as early as 1823,[33] that is, within three years of the first vocations at Ruillé, it has generally been assumed that Moreau's involvement with the Brothers' physical properties did not begin until 1835.[34]

The Brothers were not exactly dirt poor at the separation from the Sisters of Providence. They owned and enjoyed the income from the Grand Saint-Joseph (eventually sold for 11,900 francs), the Ruillé boarding school, several vineyards, and some farm property.[35] The *Chronicles* note that the boarding school brought in revenue from its twenty boarders, and the salaries of Brother carpenters was significant. Moreover, various benefactors continued to be generous.[36] The Sisters, of course, had developed their Ruillé motherhouse rather grandly, some of the work being done by the Brothers. The women were, however, established sixteen years earlier than the Brothers and had as their leader for nine years that intrepid mother general who fought aggressively for her Sisters.

About this time someone, probably André, came up with an idea for the Brothers to swear an oath of allegiance to the Community (and to Dujarié). The oath is mentioned in a letter to Brother Adrian dated July 20, 1831, and was conceived as a way to show support for the elderly priest, support much needed after his clashes with the mother general. It is dated September 1831, indicating that it was probably administered and signed during the annual retreat, that one time of year when all the Brothers were expected to come to Ruillé.

We pledge ourselves by the present act of the strictest obligation that we can make so that violations will constitute sin:

1) to live attached to our holy Institute

2) to sustain each other until death

3) to remain united in the body of the Congregation and the Community as long as possible, following the same practices and rules that we have practiced up to now

4) and in case we have to dissolve, to remain united in heart and affections, sustaining and assisting each other reciprocally

5) to assemble as a body in Community as time and place permit.

6) We Brothers of Saint Joseph will continue our submission to and dependence on Father Dujarié ...

7) Conforming to the dispositions of the preceding article, he will be able to innovate and abrogate in our rules and customs everything he judges necessary for the time and circumstances.

8) Near our superior we have our rallying point

9) and if we have the misfortune to lose him, we will rally around the bishop of Le Mans.[37]

It is signed by only twenty men, but some whose signatures do not appear on the document did sign a vow formula binding them to a vow of obedience to Dujarié for one year. The oath of allegiance is striking for several reasons. First of all, it is in André's hand and therefore indicates his primary workmanship. Secondly, it swears a fidelity to each other, even if the institute should dissolve. The bonds forged by many of these men over a decade were considered valuable enough and enriching enough that the men would want to stay supporters of each other even if they were no longer financially or organizationally a unit. Thirdly, the document lists the four directors (up from three of previous years), all but one of whom would die in the Community.[38] Thus the Brothers did enjoy a modicum of self-governance even if Dujarié remained ostensibly their superior. (See Appendix II)

The next few years for André were relatively quiet. Although the decline in numbers continued, membership hovered around sixty Brothers, not a bad enrollment but nothing like the more than one hundred enjoyed from 1826 to 1829. André may have come to realize that the vocation fields had been reaped for the region: there are only so many vocations to any one profession that can be gathered from one demographic area. The few letters we have from him for 1832 and 1833 concern business matters with the Sisters of Providence. In the summer of 1834, however, André wrote the first of three remarkable letters that had enormous impact on the future of his Brothers.

In a letter marked "private" to the bishop in Le Mans just before the beginning of the 1834 August retreat, André points out that the Community is being demoralized by one of the four directors, Brother Henry, who does not follow the rules and gives permissions indiscriminately to those who wish to circumvent André. Secondly, the Community has been trying to sustain two novitiates, one at Ruillé and one at Esclimont, and the latter is draining them and shows little hope of attracting many recruits in that region. Thirdly, the matter of Dujarié's ability to direct is becoming problematic: the elderly priest weakens both physically and mentally. André closes with eleven points he would like the bishop to discuss face to face with three of the four Brother Directors (omitting only Brother Henry from the interview). The eleven matters are substantial and include matters of property as well as matters of administration and formation. Recognizing that Dujarié's group of Brothers is disintegrating, in spite of all the effort that Dujarié and André had put into revitalizing the group at each summer retreat, André asks the bishop to push Dujarié for reforms.[39] Among the eleven points he makes to the bishop is the need for an administrative structure with specific attention given to the number of officers for the Brothers. More importantly, André asks for a chaplain for the Brothers at Ruillé, admitting for the first time in print that Dujarié was unable to minister to the spiritual needs of his own Community. André closes his letter by saying "with these matters on the table for the Bishop, it will be impossible for our Father to refuse to deal with them."[40] The implication is that Dujarié has been approached about the crisis, but the aged priest has been unwilling to face reality and deal with it. With this letter André puts two mechanisms into operation: the rescue of the Brothers and his own eventual replacement as a leader. (There is no mention of Moreau in the letter, only a remark that a chaplain is needed for the Brothers at Ruillé.) We do not know if this letter actually resulted in an interview with the bishop. In hindsight we wonder if the bishop had considered appointing simply a chaplain (as requested) for the Ruillé Brothers, letting André become in effect the leader of the Community. Since he was already doing the lion's share of the work, such a move would not have been impractical. The Brothers, however, were used to having a priest at the helm. We should continue to wonder, however, if André could have saved the

Ruillé Community on his own energies with, of course, the support of the Le Mans bishop.

A lengthier letter in November to the bishop has a more upbeat tone than André's previous letter. In fact, the November letter is downright jubilant. In the course of this letter he uses Moreau's name twice so even if the bishop had not already been thinking of Moreau as a replacement for Dujarié, he may very well have been nudged in that direction by this letter.

> The existence of the Brothers of Saint Joseph being quite precarious up to this time, I feel the need to set forth the means which my mind considers proper in order to consolidate, enlarge and make perfect its real end. These means involve the creation of three societies in one. The first would be the priests under the title of the Sacred Heart of Jesus; they would exercise the duties and tasks of superiorship in the Congregation: thus the Brothers of Saint Joseph with that support would have clear and firm direction and government. The goal of the entire Society would be to be an asylum for people in all conditions, to put them at the service of God, to work for his glory, to work for their own salvation and that of their neighbor, while holding themselves away from the dangers of the world. The secondary goal would be to give a Christian education, one suitable under all conditions of our times, to all classes of society.
>
> The Institute of three societies in one, or of the Holy Family, could establish houses everywhere in a manner that I am going to explain. The Priests of the Sacred Heart would maintain houses where, at the same time, they would have a novitiate for the Brothers of Saint Joseph and a normal school in which to train lay school masters, these however living in separate quarters. The Brothers of Saint Joseph would continue to expand in the villages and countryside, several Brothers together or alone in the pastors' houses; they would live dependent on the Order or Institute. The lay

teachers, once formed, would be free to establish themselves
and live as they wished, except that they would be given
protection, good advice and counsel, and any of them who
found themselves closer to the spirit of the Order as a whole,
by their zeal, good morals, piety or celibacy, could form a
branch with a rule, one like to or shortened from the rule of
the Brothers of Saint Joseph or a short form of the rule of the
Sacred Heart Priests. This rule of the Priests of the Sacred
Heart would be a reflection of the teachings and conduct of
Jesus Christ, of Saint Joseph and the very holy Virgin. But
since they would later have more extensive functions to fulfill
(as I will explain), they would accept the rule of Saint Ignatius
for the Jesuits, whatever is suited to their condition.

The Priests of the Sacred Heart of Jesus, aside from the
functions which have just been assigned, will themselves
maintain boarding schools or colleges for the upper class.
There they would teach Latin, rhetoric, etc. They would also
do the work of diocesan missionaries; they would conduct
annual retreats for the Brothers of Saint Joseph and the
masters of the lay schools, in the novitiate and normal schools
during vacations. They would be able to do the same for
people in the outside world and even in their houses like the
one in Brittany. The three societies in one would have to
contribute to this, at least by their prayers and alms. Helping
the souls in Purgatory would always be the object of their
zeal; to this end they would gain a number of indulgences
each month; that is, every member would strive to gain such
indulgences in harmony with their duties. Briefly put, saying
everything in a few words: the Congregation would bear the
name of the Holy Family.[41]

Thus André elaborates a totally new idea for the Brothers: he suggests
that they be amalgamated into a new tripartite Community of priests,
Brothers, and lay men. André obviously does not consider the
Brothers to be "lay men" in the canonical sense and envisages them

as ecclesiastically median to priests and non-ordained men, the new Community named for the Holy Family. There is ample evidence in the letter that André considers the priests will be the elite members: he reserves to them the instruction of children of the "upper class"[42] while the Brothers will continue to work with poor and ordinary children. He does allow for some fluidity among the priests, Brothers, and lay men in that "the two lesser societies would be able to rise into the society of the Sacred Heart,"[43] but the "elevation," André cautions, would have to be watched carefully because few men would be capable of moving upward. As tasteless as this hierarchical nonsense of higher and lower vocations is to us today, what is remarkable in André's plan is that the vision for a mixed Community of priests and Brothers of St. Joseph, often attributed to Moreau, actually originated with André. We cannot say, however, that the plan was entirely André's since he mentions in the letter to the bishop that he has bounced his new idea off one other person: Moreau. If the two men had a conversation in which they probably reviewed the problems of Dujarié's Brothers, Moreau may have mentioned that he was starting a group of priests who would serve as auxiliaries to the diocese. André may then have mused in private on amalgamating Moreau's priests and Dujarié's Brothers, thus germinating the Congregation of Holy Cross. Such an explanation, however, leaves an important person out of the process: Dujarié himself had planned on starting a group of priests devoted to parish missions as early as 1823, eleven years before André's letter to Bishop Bouvier. Dujarié even planned to dedicate his auxiliary priests to the Sacred Heart. André would have known about all of these plans since he was Dujarié's right-hand man during all the years that Dujarié dreamed of his association of auxiliary priests.[44] Although Dujarié never founded such a group, his plans were intended to bind priests to his Brothers and Sisters. Once the Sisters were on their own (by 1831), André could dream of a different tripartite Community, a dream he confided first to Moreau and then to Bouvier. André was not given credit for his plan, however, for over a hundred years. Finally in the 1940's, Philéas Vanier, CSC, archivist for the Congregation of Holy Cross, wrote a note to Albert F. Cousino, Superior General at the time:

> The confidential letter of Brother André (November 14, 1834) greatly influenced Father Moreau in the organization of the Community; this is a very important point to study, which can explain many things; it should be done without taking sides, slowly, etc. Please excuse the candor of this remark.[45]

It is obvious from this note by Vanier that André's plan had fallen into the cracks of history.

Moreau's original plan (in 1831) was for an association of auxiliary priests alone. With the death of Bishop Carron in 1833 and the accession of Bouvier, Moreau had in his new prelate a man who had himself long recognized the value of an auxiliary group of priests in the diocese.[46] It was not, however, until June 1835, a year after André had written to the bishop, that Moreau formalized his plans to found an association of auxiliary priests. Two months later he took on the direction of the Brothers of St. Joseph in a touching ceremony at Ruillé when Dujarié officially ceded authority over the Brothers. Immediately, Moreau began to clean house: he dismissed some Brothers and insisted all teachers keep careful financial records. Older Brothers who were showing signs of ebbing academic fervor were shifted into manual labor.[47] André began to lose power. When Moreau went to spend three days at La Chesnaie consulting with the founder of the Brothers of Ploërmel, Moreau took Brother Leonard Guittoger with him, not André,[48] and when Moreau opened his new boarding school at Saint-Croix in November 1836, it was Brother Vincent who was put in charge, not André.[49] Catta suggests that Vincent was chosen because he had a teaching license,[50] but André's license predates Vincent's by one year. Of course, André may very well have been left behind in Ruillé to look after the boarding school there in its waning years, but when Moreau moved the novitiate to Sainte-Croix, there were but five or six students left in the Ruillé boarding school.[51] Yet when Moreau called upon the Brothers to signify their fidelity to his organization by pronouncing vows, it was André who came forward first at the end of the 1836 retreat, surely not just because of his seniority, but also because he had worked hard in 1833, 1834, and 1835 to keep the Brothers viable as Dujarié slipped farther and farther away from an ability to inspire and lead. The vows would show his unfaltering faith in Moreau's leadership because André's were the first perpetual vows pronounced in the Community.

In his third and final letter to Bouvier, cosigned by Leonard and Vincent, André begs the bishop for a secret meeting without Dujarié's being aware of it. André is concerned that the rules he has been designing for the Brothers would irk Dujarié because the old priest was not in on their making. This April letter makes no mention of Moreau and gives every indication that the Brothers were convinced they themselves could salvage the Community. But four months later they were turned over to Moreau's control. Clearly the matter of leadership was evolving, if not being outright challenged by men anxious to be governed by one of their own. André, of course, lacked the panache of priesthood, links to hierarchy, and links to priests in the region. André's final memo as head director is dated June 28, 1835. It is a simple notice that he has received fifty francs, which the Sisters of Providence owed on a year of rent. His days as the central administrator are about to end.

In three major crises, it is André who weathers the storms with Dujarié: one political, one economic, and one organizational. The petit revolution of 1830 threatened to destroy the Brothers of St. Joseph by reintroducing unrest reminiscent of the 1789 horrors. The Brothers survived. Then one year later Mother Marie Lecor engineered, with the help of the bishop, the financial separation of the Sisters of Providence from the Brothers of St. Joseph, a separation particularly hard on Dujarié because he had used his own patrimony to float the Sisters and had counted on their success to float the Brothers. Lecor wanted no part of such a plan and forced the separation. She was the only mother superior of the Sisters that most of the Brothers had known: the saintly Mother Marie Madelaine had died two years after André arrived at Ruillé so André had to watch first hand the machinations of Marie Lecor, that hard-nosed Breton woman, as she gradually maneuvered the Sisters into independence. Although today we can praise her courage as a laywoman facing off clerical control, at the time she must have seemed almost cruel and ungrateful to the Brothers who, after all, had done much of the carpentry work at the Grande Providence motherhouse. The third storm weathered by André was the deteriorating of the Brothers as Dujarié himself deteriorated. Three years after financial disengagement from the Sisters of Providence, it was obvious to André that Dujarié was no longer physically or emotionally capable of directing the Brothers. Confined to his bed for weeks at a time, Dujarié lost more and more sense of what was happening to his Brothers of St. Joseph. Thus André in the autumn of 1834 contacted the bishop about forming a tri-partite Community of Brothers, priests, and lay teachers. Then in the following spring, he again contacted the bishop about a private meeting with the four brother-directors, the chief of whom is, of course, André. But within four months, the bishop would transfer the Brothers of St. Joseph to the care of Basil Moreau, Ruillé would begin to crumble as a headquarters for the Josephites, and André himself would eventually move to Le Mans to take up his duties as novice master for the Brothers at Sainte Croix.

Why did Moreau demote André Mottais? Thomas Maddix has analyzed at length Moreau's understanding of a brother's vocation and concluded that it differed radically from Dujarié's understanding. Under Dujarié, all brothers were equal and shared one apostolate, the evangelization of children.[52] When Moreau shifted some Brothers out of the classroom into manual labor, he created two tiers of membership in the Brothers. Some of the men may have, in fact, welcomed the opportunity to leave a profession for which they had no taste or talent, an opportunity that allowed them to remain within the religious society doing some kind of work. It was, nevertheless, a big shift in the basic dynamics of the brother's vocation and worked against the very sense of democracy that Dujarié and André had fostered. Under Moreau, men who could not handle classroom duties were given manual labor to do: hierarchy, implicit possibly under

Dujarié, became full-flowered under Moreau. Did André confront Moreau on this shift in paradigm? Did Moreau react negatively to any questioning of his decisions and sideline André? We do not know. What we do know is that once Moreau assumed control of the Brothers, André began to fade from administration, in spite of his fifteen years' experience, in spite of his being a man of enormous talent and virtue in the prime of his life. Moreau was only one year older than André (they were born in the same month one year apart), and in 1836 one's star continued to rise and the other's started to fall.

As the Brothers began to look to Moreau to save their Community, it is curious that we have no records of letters from André to Moreau. Brother Leonard, however, did write to Moreau in June, 1835, and Moreau responded with an offer of the house in Le Mans "which would be perfectly suited for you, and where I would gladly set you up, in preference to another foundation which I plan to get underway."[53] It is obvious that Moreau is eager not only to assume direction of the Brothers but also to move them to his own territory. He adds, "Nevertheless, I want to wait some time yet out of consideration for your own interests, and you can inform Brother André accordingly." A reader today wonders why Moreau was not communicating these very important sentiments to André himself who, as primary director, was really the person who should have been consulted. The tone of "you can inform Brother André accordingly" is slightly ominous, indicating that Moreau may have little concern for the Primary Director's prerogative. Finally, Moreau delivers a coup: "If you speak to the Bishop, tell him only that I would consider to revive and develop you, provided that I am given full freedom of action." By "full freedom of action," Moreau could mean freedom from restrictions by the bishop or diocesan authorities, but the phrase could also be the triumphant call of a person who already senses victory. There is no deference in this letter to André, Dujarié, or even the bishop. Moreau knows what he wants to do, and he wants it on his terms. There is no room in his scheme for a Primary Director who may be bringing old baggage with him into a new situation.

Is it to André's credit or discredit that he knuckled under? If he had engineered a break from a priest-director as Mother Marie Lecor had done, would the Brothers have survived? They had scores of hardworking men, some property, and the promise of a set of rules (yet to be written). Would these assets have been enough to float them under André? They had, however, grown up tightly enmeshed with a priest at their head, and when they had to rethink their organization, they quite naturally would think about revitalizing their Community under a structure similar to the one that had brought them great growth in the years before the 1830 political unrest. They knew Moreau would not be Dujarié, and André was one of their first sacrifices to the new order. It is important, of course, that organizations get new blood from time to time in administrative posts. It probably was a good idea for Moreau to replace André after the latter had served fifteen years as novice master since subsequent growth attests to the excellence of the novice masters who followed André. André did keep his position, however, for four years after the amalgamation.

As the Brothers at Sainte-Croix saw Moreau's auxiliary priests beginning to infiltrate the teaching apostolate, they grew concerned that their assets would be swallowed up. Moreau summoned all the men together (fifty-one Brothers, ten priests) and outlined the Brothers' assets. Then he drew up the "Fundamental Pact" (March 1, 1837) which served as a stepping-stone to the eventual joining of the two societies, just as their two properties and schools physically adjoined in Sainte-Croix. Moreau really believed that if the Brothers were to survive, they would eventually need priests to be responsible for "the direction and government of their society."[54] Here could be the source of André's fall from power: he was not a priest. Did Moreau really believe Dujarié could have held the Brothers together for fifteen years without André's help? Probably not, but Moreau did believe that his priests should hold the major positions of leadership over the Brothers.

Moreau was a well-educated man who had connections to ecclesiastics and government officials, but as we look back at history, we know that Mother Marie Lecor was not ordained and succeeded very well in governing the Sisters of Providence. Why did Moreau believe that only priests could govern Brothers? Moreover, why did the Brothers let him proceed with his clerical imposition? Were they that demoralized by the defections of recent years, the lack of a working set of rules, and the sad state of their academic preparation for teaching careers? Was Moreau the only answer to their crisis? He certainly came with excellent credentials: assistant superior of the local seminary, proven educator, and founder of the Good Shepherd Sisters. He was a man of immense talent. But so was André Mottais who, apparently in the interests of saving his Community, accepted Moreau's theory of clerical governance. If André had had some of Mother Marie Lecor's vinegar and fighting spirit, the history of the Brothers of St. Joseph would have been much different than it came to be.

Ages often tell us much. When Madame du Roscoät arrived in Ruillé, she was forty. She died four years later. Perrine Lecor arrived at age twenty-eight, a hardened peasant woman. Softened somewhat by association with Madame du Roscoät and the du Roscoät family, she never lost her original toughness. André arrived at Ruillé at age twenty and lived alongside Dujarié for eighteen years, always deferential to the man who had nurtured him spiritually. André was only a year younger than Moreau, but no match for the priest's education, position, and tenacity. It is easy to see how André, accustomed for half his life to clerical rule, would naturally slide from under the authority of one priest to another. He knew no other local pattern—except for the example of Mother Marie Lecor, but the separation in 1831 surely left him with a distaste for the direction that the women so determinedly set out for themselves against his priest-mentor. Dujarié was a friend whom André possibly hoped to find replicated in Moreau, but one should never count on finding a spiritual clone, especially in a person one's own age. André might have been in a way a threat to Moreau's vision, and the Brother had to be controlled if Moreau's vision were to strengthen,[55] a vision that would strengthen on the backs of the Brothers. Moreau was, after all, only bringing to realization the paradigm of a mixed Community that both Dujarié and André had dreamed about.

A curious assumption by some historians is that the Brothers of St. Joseph were incapable of governing themselves or did not want to govern themselves. Catta writes, "Like M. Dujarié, he [Moreau] was persuaded that the frail little tree had to be grafted on to a stronger trunk, which would be the Society of Priests which the Founder had thought of but which he had been unable to realize."[56] In other words, a "frail" organization of some sixty teaching Brothers had to be put under the control of a non-existent group of religious priests. The lack of logic is bewildering. At the end of the same summer that Moreau assumed direction of dozens of seasoned Brothers, he had attracted exactly two secular priests and two seminarians to his auxiliary band, who were apparently already superior to the established group of Brothers. Seminarians superior to veteran teachers? Clericalism at its extreme. Furthermore, the Brothers were kept in the dark about their future. When they assembled for the 1835 summer retreat, they had no idea what was going to happen to them. Finally, on the third day, in the presence of the bishop, in a well-recorded ceremony, Dujarié in the chapel officially handed control of his Community to Moreau. The three ministers at the altar, flanked by the three Jesuit priests who had preached the retreat, presided over the scene, and in the pews sat fifty-six grown men oblivious of what had been determined for them. They had, of course, suspected Moreau would be their new superior and may have hoped it would be Moreau, but did none of those present ever think to wonder if the Brothers under André could have controlled their own destiny as successfully as the Sisters of Providence had controlled their own?

We know little about André's new life at Sainte-Croix. We do know that he was novice master up to 1840[57] and sat on the council with Brother Vincent, Brother Léopold, Father Marseul, and Father Chappé.[58] One happy chore he was given was to travel back to Ruillé in October, 1836, to help Dujarié move to Sainte-Croix.[59] A little over a year later, Dujarié died (February 17, 1838), having been able to live his final year in the same home as André, who had been his stalwart religious helper for fifteen years in Ruillé. He was buried on the grounds at Sainte-Croix, then transferred in 1849 to the new Community cemetery. In 1873 he was brought by the Sisters of Providence back to Ruillé and buried in the crypt of their motherhouse chapel. His old nemesis Mother Marie Lecor was still alive, having retired two years earlier (1871) after forty-three years heading the Sisters. After the interment ceremony in Ruillé, she said, "Now I can die."[60] Even in death the priest was no match for the Breton nun.

The Community began to thrive under Moreau's strong leadership, but André was not destined to stay in Le Mans very long after Dujarié's death. In April of 1840, Moreau announced that missionaries would be sent to Algeria, and André was being sent along to supervise the Brothers in the schools to be established there. In addition to André, named to go were Brother Louis (Victor Marchand), Brother Alphonsus (Francis-Mary Tulou), Brother Ignatius (Theodore Feron), Father Julian Leboucher, and Father Victor Drouelle.[61] Later added to the group were Brother Eulogius (Antoine Boisard), Brother Liguori (Louis Guyard), and Father Haudebourg. André at age forty was not the oldest Brother in the group. Alphonsus was forty-two. Victor was twenty-eight, as was Louis. Liguori was twenty-one and Louis twenty. Leboucher had been an assistant to Dom Guéranger at Solemnes before he joined Moreau's group of auxiliary priests so he came with excellent credentials and seemed perfect to run the seminary in Algeria. He had been with Moreau's Community only six months and would leave the Community in 1843, within two years of the Algerian mission's collapse.

André, waiting at Lyons to embark, writes a long letter to Brother Vincent Pieau, who had been chosen by Moreau to go on the new American mission. André tells Vincent to ask Moreau to write up the chronicles of the Brothers, using himself (Vincent) as chief witness to the events. Vincent had come to Ruillé two years after André, had been one of the Brother Directors under Dujarié, and was a dear friend to André. André tells Vincent to give Moreau everything André had already written on the history of the Brothers up to 1826. Then André adds a most interesting and important phrase: "tak[e] care to erase my name anywhere it is found, because I don't wish to be named anywhere."[62] What prompted this supreme act of abnegation? It is symptomatic of some who suffer humiliation in a cause to which they have devoted themselves generously to experience a sudden twinge of anger and frustration with which they wish to disassociate themselves from the project. It is a way of saying, "You do not appreciate me, and therefore I do not want to be remembered or associated with you." The sentiment is a mixture both of admirable self-abnegation and not so admirable resentment born of frustration, but it is sometimes the only recourse for someone who has lost a battle: to be disassociated from any part of the humiliation.

As André watched Moreau control the Brothers, he may have felt some resentment at losing the premier role he had enjoyed under Dujarié, especially the increment of power that gathered to him as Dujarié grew old and sick. When he had the chance to distance himself from Moreau by going to Africa, he might have felt relieved of the daily reminders of his own loss of power. Moreau, ever a wise judge of character, probably sensed in André a need for a change, and so the obedience to go to Algeria was a blessing for both men: for Moreau it removed a rival in the affections of the older Brothers, and it gave André a dignified way to use his talents in a new venue, albeit still under obedience to a priest.

What stands out in this Lyons letter are the careful instructions André gives to set his affairs in order. It is almost as if he were writing his last will and testament. He asks Vincent to preserve carefully the notes on the financial separation from the Sisters of Providence. He notes how that event hurt Dujarié deeply. He wants the narrative of Dujarié's final illness preserved. Everything is to be attended to with the utmost care. André cautions, "I'm holding to this in my final wishes. Let it [the Dujarié narrative] be read to the Brothers at the retreat and let them have the liberty to speak their feelings and make their observations with total honesty, prudence, civility, and submissiveness."[63] It sounds like an order rather than a request. Underneath André's desire to preserve the memory of the father-founder is a desire that the Brothers air honestly their feelings about the transfer of authority. He then turns his attention to his present state of mind, and he remarks that at long last, away from the milieu he has known for twenty years, he is at last able to have a novitiate experience, become a new person. The former André Mottais is dead and the new André is emerging. He tells Vincent that he has learned that the house the Brothers were destined to live in half a league from Algeria has been besieged by the Arabs. The man who knew only the calm beauty of Ruillé and Sainte-Croix is heading into hell. His farewell to Vincent, whom he had worked beside for so long, is touching: "Good-by then my very dear Brother Vincent. Good-by for eternity undoubtedly, because you are bound for America, we for Africa. Good-by—I embrace you with all my heart."[64] At last the man has time for himself, time to assess his own situation and feelings. Almost from the day he arrived at Ruillé, his concern had been for others. Now there is only himself. Even the three Brothers with him will be the responsibility of the priest superior. André is free. But his purification is only beginning.

Africa is a land rich in tradition and culture, but for the ancient European world, it was a land of mystery, beyond the pale of most geographers. For medieval and Renaissance Europe, it was a land of exotic riches, and for nineteenth-century colonists, it was a land to be carved up and exploited. Algeria, on the northern edge of the continent, had done brisk trade with France since the Middle Ages, and after the French Revolution the great African country seemed like an easy place to expand French ideals. King Charles X, looking for a way to enhance his reign, thought a foreign invasion was just what was needed to bolster his popularity. Waiting for an opportunity, the French found one in April 1827, when the Algerian dey struck the French consul at Algiers with a ceremonial fly swatter. The French had their provocation, blockaded Algerian ports for three years, and finally invaded the country in 1830 with 34,000 French troops.[65] The invasion, however, proved unpopular back home, and Charles X was deposed and replaced by Louis-Philippe, the "citizen king."

Unfortunately once mired on the African continent, France found it difficult to extricate itself and stayed until 1962 when an Algerian rebellion finally forced the French to leave. France had intended to use Algeria as a dumping ground for its useless citizens and as an outlet for French manufactured goods.[66] Thus its relations with the Arab and Berber populations were poisoned from the beginning. Religious communities in France, however, saw a two-fold need in Algeria: the natives needed conversion to Christianity and the conquering French needed schools and churches for their growing colony. Both motives were hardly praiseworthy, but the reality of ministry was such that heads of religious communities responded to the call of the Algerian bishop in the late 1830's to help in the country.

The religious climate in Algeria was anything but predictable for the Church in 1840. On the one hand the French military authorities were reluctant to antagonize the indigenous Muslim population by seeming to encourage the rooting of a foreign church. They went so far as to insist on approving all pastoral assignments and even on occasion submitted outlines to the bishop for sermons.[67] On the other hand, local Muslims were scandalized by the irreligiosity of the conquerors. One emir remarked, "The French have no religion, since they have neither priests nor churches."[68] Needless to say, the few apostolic works the earliest French missionaries did establish often went unfunded by a government that insisted on direct control of all institutions but all too often failed to force local authorities to direct funds to the religious establishments for which the money was intended. It was a matter (as often with the revolutionary French government) of the ideal being unable to match reality. While national control of churches seemed a way to keep Vatican hands off French institutions, inevitably the little people entrusted with administering funds proved incapable of doing the right thing when simple greed or the temptation to redress old wrongs proved too strong for their provincial minds.

When Bishop Anthony-Adolph Dupuch wrote to Father Moreau in October 1839, he already sensed that Moreau was inclined to send men to Algeria. Formerly bishop of Bordeaux, Dupuch had known

Moreau at Saint-Sulpice where both studied in the early 1820s. Thus Moreau received one of his first mission requests from someone he had known for a generation, even if the two had gone in two different directions, one into the hierarchy, the other into seminary work and eventually into the guidance of several religious communities. For all of his status, however, Dupuch lacked Moreau's practicality and promised the priest at Sainte-Croix things he could never deliver—like free boat passage for the missionaries and stable foundations in major Algerian cities. In his circular letter #9 (January 1, 1840), Moreau reprinted in its entirety Dupuch's exuberant letter (dated November 17, 1839) in which the bishop specified the following: "We shall be responsible for all the expenses of the three Brothers in Africa so that your valuable Congregation will be put to no expense whatsoever for them."[69] Dupuch would, of course, not be the only prelate to promise Moreau more than he could deliver, and for a man in the early years of heading his religious congregation at Sainte-Croix, Moreau can perhaps be forgiven for not seeing through hierarchical hype.

The bishop suggested that the three Brothers he was requesting be initially set up at an orphanage (not yet existing) on the outskirts of Algiers near St. Augustine Seminary. Dupuch felt that about twenty-five orphans would surface from the Moustapha neighborhood where French colonists had either died of disease or had been killed by local tribesmen. No mention of a specific building or specific stipend to maintain such an orphanage is made in the bishop's letter, yet Moreau saw no danger signs on the horizon. He did, however, elicit from his Community their reactions to the bishop's proposal. It would have been difficult undoubtedly for anyone to brook the founder's and the bishop's enthusiasm, although hardheaded realists like Brother Henry Taupin might possibly have had misgivings about the enterprise. Moreau's was not the only religious Community to respond to Dupuch's enthusiastic promises: at least five other communities, mostly communities of nuns, heeded Dupuch's call.

The three letters we have from André in Africa show us a person we had barely known up to this point. Finally at age forty, freed from the cares of running the day-to-day operations of a community, he is free to look inside himself and reveal a character we before had to reconstruct basically from events and duties. The Africa letters are the most important letters André wrote. Surely his letters to Bishop Bouvier were extremely important for the history of Holy Cross, but nothing is more valuable to the history of André Mottais the person than the letters from Africa. In one way, André's demotion was good for him because it afforded him at last the opportunity to make an extended retreat—just himself and his God. The three letters are, in this way, amazing.

The first letter, written from Moustapha on July 11, 1840, is directed to his parents. He tells them he arrived on May 27 and lives with orphans in a building adjacent to the seminary that his superior directs. One can only imagine the emotions that Jean and Jeanne Mottais would have felt on receiving the letter and sharing it with their children Jeanne and Joseph. (André's older Brother Jean was already dead.) The crossing was not easy: his five companions were all seasick. Since they had only four beds among them, André gave up his share of a bed and slept on deck "wrapped in a cloak among the soldiers."[70] They passed by Minorca and Majorca, stopped briefly at Mahon, before arriving at Algiers on a Tuesday evening. On going into the city, they met two sons of King Louis Philippe, young men returning to France after military duty in putting down a revolt against the French colonists.[71] The sounds of war are everywhere. André calls the cannon shots that start the day at 4 AM and end the day at 8 PM "the sound of the Angelus in Africa." André tells his parents that on first arriving, the Brothers were placed by the bishop in a hospice where they had to help care for two hundred and fifty sick and mentally ill people, under the supervision of the religious of St. John of God. He comments on the various nationalities that have converged in Algiers, the language, patois, and jargon that dominate the streets. He comments on ceremonies that the bishop presides over, and he notes the prospects for evangelization in a war torn country. André has an eye for detail: native clothing (or lack thereof), sleeping habits, modes of transportation, local cuisine. He comments at great length on the crops and livestock, the Larchamp farmer coming back to life in him. Finally he mentions his own health: he is so weak he can hardly write. During a two-week period he suffered terribly. Before the days of vaccinations and vitamins, one can only imagine the multiple germs and diseases that would meet a European coming to a dirty village where hygiene was primitive and food preparation less than sterile. Something from Africa would, in fact, eventually kill André Mottais.

André tells us that only Father Leboucher lives at the seminary proper where Leboucher is to be rector: the other five live in an adjacent building with the orphans who have been gathered for their care. The two institutions share the same chapel and kitchen staff. There is but one church in Algiers proper—the cathedral which has been made from a former mosque. (To the victors belong the spoils.) The violence to Muslims does not seem to bother André: in fact, he writes that "the Mohametans have their mosques where they go to pray, or rather make their grimaces."[72] The city seems a hodge-podge of Muslims, Christians, Jews, and what André calls "pagans," presumably native Berbers from the interior who have found their way to the city. The missionaries are confounded by a dozen languages, and they begin to learn some basic Arabic, but the learning is rough. As far as Christian liturgy is concerned, Bishop Dupuch does what he can to impress the locals. He, in fact, has had an organ built in the cathedral, a first for Algeria. A procession with the Blessed Sacrament gives calm assurance to the newly arrived that religion can work its graces anywhere:

> What goodness we felt in our hearts! Singing beautiful French hymns, and seeing the triumph of Our Lord on territory where he had not been carried for a long time. Yes, this one event made up greatly for the sacrifices that we made in leaving our homeland.[73]

Such were the first reactions of a forty-year old man to religion in a new country. What his companion, the young man named Brother Ignatius, just out of his teen years, thought of the country we can only guess because none of his letters, if he wrote any, survive. But if André at twice Ignatius's age so thrilled to Algeria, we can imagine that Ignatius too was delighted at the daily adventures of new sights and sounds in an exotic atmosphere that most French schoolboys only read and dreamed about.

There is no evidence that the first colony of Holy Cross religious questioned any aspect of their homeland's great quest: they came to Algeria to abet the French conquerors with religion because Algeria needed, they believed, European civilization. Before the invasion, for example, there were no roads, André notes, so Algeria was progressing toward an advanced civilization. We should not be hasty, however, to condemn what today we would question as chauvinistic zeal. Historically the French did invade Arab territory, but the Arabs had formerly invaded the same territory then held by the Berbers, and who knows what peoples the Berbers may have overrun. What history can say, however, is that the French did treat the Arabs as well or better than the Arabs had treated the Berbers, not that less persecution justifies any persecution, but the mindset of European politicos and their counterparts in Christian churches armed with messianic creeds afforded history but little choice to watch the attempted transplantation of European values into a culture that did not invite them but may have been eventually enriched. Algeria has never repudiated the French language nor has it torn up French-laid roads.

If anything, the transplanted Holy Cross men were awed by their new surroundings. Vegetation, animals, and foodstuff came under André's scrutiny:

> We see olive trees in great quantity ... the wild cotton tree, the acacia, the elm, the banana tree, the palm, the cypress, the orange tree, the citrus tree, the pomegranate, the Barbary fig which covers the hedges and the fruit of which is rather good ... we're still eating grapes. Two months ago natives ate fresh almonds ... for good reason they brag that small Arab horses go faster than the wind. The camel is an ugly beast that

is half as high as a house. It has a great hump in the middle of its back ... and when it has had a good meal, you can lead it along for five or six days without drinking or eating.[74]

But the strange country took its toll on the Holy Cross men, especially on André Mottais who suffered terribly almost as soon as he arrived. In this letter to his Larchamp relatives, he notes that he trembles so much he can barely hold on to a pen to write.

The second letter from Africa is addressed to Father Moreau and dated August 1, 1840, several weeks after the letter to the Mottais family. We learn that after six weeks the Brothers were given charge of an orphanage. To date there are only fourteen orphans, eight of whom board. Where the "six external" orphans slept is anyone's guess. Since the Brothers cannot get authorization to open a school, Brother Louis is studying arithmetic, grammar, and history as he bides his time. The novice Ignatius is not a very good student, so the priest superior has put him in charge of the refectory and food purchases. Brother Alphonsus works as a joiner. André takes care of the orphans from 10 to 11:45 each morning and from 4 PM until supper. Louis takes care of them at the other times. André sleeps in a dorm with the littlest ones, Louis in a dorm with the biggest. André's bed, we learn later, is a mattress on the floor. The orphans can stay until they reach the age of twenty.

André comments on the orphans that he and Brother Louis are taking care of, one as young as three years old. Although there are but half a dozen presently, André anticipates that the number of orphans will grow to sixty or eighty soon. Unfortunately, he is very sick. Father Leboucher had taken him to a doctor who prescribed baths for his rectal hemorrhaging. In spite of his weakness, he keeps up with his spiritual responsibilities:

> I do all my spiritual exercises faithfully and in the spirit of the Rule, I believe, except that I do not regularly recite the Office of the Blessed Virgin; I henceforth hope to be faithful to it. I don't watch over the conduct of my three confreres, and I

don't tell you about them since my confessor told me that I
was dispensed from supervising them. That makes me happy
because I no longer have any responsibility on that matter,
and anyway I already have too much to watch over myself. I
wish I had time for recollection, which I've missed for a long
time. In spite of myself since the retreat the thought that my
death is imminent is no longer bothering me.[75]

Naturally in these comments is not only André's quiet acceptance of
the possibility of death, but also his evident relief at no longer being
responsible for the spiritual direction of the other Brothers. For a man
who had worried for a generation over the development of hundreds
of young men, he is now relieved to find himself unburdened with the
care of others, but his sickness has apparently so concerned Leboucher
that the priest gives André more time to convalesce. Although his
first six weeks in Africa found him in good health, André attributes
his present diseased state to a sea bath, which induced intense
diarrhea, possibly from bacteria. He apparently never considers that
diet may be more the culprit than seawater. André attributes his
sickness to a hemorrhage, loss of appetite, and a weakness that has
led to fainting. A local doctor prescribes "sitting baths," a procedure
which suggests that André was suffering from anemia brought on by
untreated hemorrhoids and loss of blood. André has a relapse every
third day. When one of the Brothers tells André that he may be sent
home, André is surprised and tells Moreau: "1) All who come to
Africa are customarily sick for three to six months or gravely ill. 2)
The doctor made no decision when consulted about me six weeks ago.
3) Numerous people have the same sickness, and it will continue, they
say, until the end of September."[76] These remarks are not so much
the remarks of a man quietly assessing his situation as they are the
remarks of a man plagued by sickness inducing spiritual trauma.
Then André claims that nothing he has ever done has borne apostolic
fruit. His confiding in Moreau is poignant:

I beg you on my knees to see here God's plans, which are evidently to cure my folly and my pride, as well as to convince me of my lack of ability in everything and everywhere, because God out of His goodness lets every job and every country vomit me out as soon as it gets a taste of me. So I beg you, if you recall me to France, in the name of charity give me the last and the lowest job in the Congregation. Dressed in a shirt, if necessary, rather than the religious habit, which I now believe I am unworthy of, I will clean shoes, wash dishes, etc. I have but little time to repair my unworthy life.[77]

How could a grown man drop into such a poor self-image? He has been convinced that nothingness means saintliness, and he craves oblivion. He clearly does not want to return to France where God "allows every job like every country to vomit me out as soon as it gets a taste of me." Where did he get the idea that he is unworthy to wear a religious habit, he who was one of the first two to receive the habit of the Brothers of St. Joseph? Where did he get the idea that he is good for nothing but to clean shoes and wash dishes? This is the dark night of the soul when all the good he had effected in twenty years seems erased by his being "vomited" first out of France and now out of Algeria. Thankfully, the sentiments passed away: two weeks later he adds two paragraphs that are joyous and upbeat. He looks forward to spring (coming at the end of September) when the planting is to begin. He will need vegetable seeds. Possibly a return to health brought him out of gloom or possibly the fear that the despair he expressed earlier would prompt Moreau to summon him back to France. The latter explanation is probably not true because, after all, he did not destroy the dark paragraph before mailing the letter to Moreau. He welcomed anything but a return to the work that had rejected him in France: better to live meagerly and die in a foreign land. So he changes his tone and ends the letter upbeat.

The third and final letter of André from Africa is dated December 1, 1841, fifteen months after the second letter. In the previous spring André had set out to open a school in Philippeville, a town the French had established in 1838, named in honor of the French king, on the site of an ancient Carthaginian ruin. The town sits on the Gulf of Stora of the Mediterranean, one hundred miles east of Algiers and is today called Skikda. By early May he was in his new location. Catta sings the praises of the pastor at Philippeville, but Catta selects only a few sentences near the end of André's long December 1841 letter to Moreau, neglecting to convey the real tenor of André's letter, which is full of details about the parsimony and nastiness of the pastor. Here, first of all, is what Catta gives us:

> There was work in abundance for the new teacher, who had to teach six hours of class every day for twenty-five or thirty pupils ... He was often the go-between for those who wished to contact the pastor, and they came to him during his classes to give him requests for the good curé, while the latter was busy with his ministry ... Their life was one of dire poverty. The food was frugal: a bit of bread in the morning with some dry fruit and "a cup of soup" at one of the meals, which were often cold meals with nothing very substantial. Their clothing was wretched: a habit worn to threads and shoes all worn through.[78]

Catta gives the impression that the pastor shared equally in the hardships, but that is not what André says in his letter. Here is André's real appraisal of the situation:

> I have about thirty-six inscrutable students. I meet with from twenty-two to twenty-eight of them for each class ... I believe a teacher should meet with only eight to ten of them ... we have no beginning book, not even catechisms ... Everything is spoiled in this classroom by the dust and water which falls from the parish priest's bedroom ... More and more I'm obliged to sleep in it ... I can't sing a hymn because the parish priest is bothered by it ... There is no bathroom: for my calls of nature I have to leave town and go into the mountains. The

parish priest has a bedpan that the maid empties at night … In the morning I eat a piece of bread and what I can grab … some dried fruit or a small piece of sugar. The parish priest has his coffee or chocolate.[79]

This does not sound as if André is at all happy with the parish priest, and it is apparent that the two men are not living on the same scale of comfort. Elsewhere in André's letter we learn that the priest has denied André new underwear so André has to wear the same garment for three months. He wears the same shirt for three weeks. He cannot get clean towels. These are humiliations that would try the patience of a saint.[80]

This is André's final letter from Algeria, and in it we learn another sadness: three months earlier Brother Louis had died. No one in Algeria bothered to tell André that the young Brother was gone, a Brother for whom technically speaking André was the "director." André learns of the death when he receives a circular letter from Moreau in November. Louis had drowned in the Mediterranean where he had taken some of the Moustapha orphans to go swimming. Moreau was so upset by the death he says he simply cannot give details in his letter. He adds sentiments from Father Drouelle:

> Brother Louis performed his obedience with such zeal, devotedness, and humility that, by his death far away from his native country, he must have been favored with a speedy entrance into his heavenly home. His conduct, which was ever as simple and unaffected as his soul, always measured up to the requirements of his sublime vocation. His mind was as noble as his heart, and I shall never forget how often his Superiors spoke to me of their hopes for one so gifted with talent and virtue.[81]

Louis was 29 years old. Moreau took the deaths of his young Brothers very hard. Four years later when Brother Anselm would drown in the Ohio River at age 20, Moreau was equally inconsolable. Moreau's was a genuine heart, and one can only imagine how he had to approach the parents of these lost youths with news that the sons they had given to the Church and Holy Cross were gone in their prime and promise.

In this letter, following Moreau's request, André assesses the suitability of each of the Brothers, something André does reluctantly. He then remarks that his hemorrhoids are worse than ever. Moreover, the water is putrid and teems with "little critters." He teaches computation, spelling, and penmanship but receives no salary whereas the public school teacher, who has only ten students, is paid by the government.[82] André's students do not work hard, and the classroom is poorly lit with one entrance which unfortunately opens into a noisy street frequented by soldiers and passersby who often stop to listen in on the day's lesson or to inquire after the pastor. André takes Thursdays off, his only break because on Sunday he has to clean the church, teach catechism, perform baptisms, and wind the clock! All is not bleak, however. During the vacation break from July 15 to August 19, André visits Hippo to see the ruins of the ancient basilica. He remembers that St. Augustine had sat nearby on the beach and had meditated on the Trinity. In spite of deprivations, André is content with his work, but his health continues to deteriorate. Ringworm plagues him, and hemorrhoids cause him to lose much blood three or four times a month. He stops the bleeding with improvised paper compresses. Reporting to Moreau the sad state of life in Algeria, he does not show in this final letter from Africa any of the dark despair that had driven his letter three months previous. A man who found strength in his apostolic work, André seems revitalized in just knowing that he is fulfilling the wishes of Moreau to establish Holy Cross in Africa.

As 1841 ended and 1842 began, some of the Holy Cross foundations had floundered and some had prospered. The situation in Brother Eulogius's school in Blidah had become so bad that he closed the school and returned to help in the orphanage at Moustapha. The French government had actually finally gotten around to recognizing the existence of the Blidah school and had voted a subsidy, but it came too late and Eulogius had already left town. The orphanage began to brighten when a new location was found—a pleasant home that formerly belonged to the consul from Denmark. The place sat on the shady side of a hill near the seminary compound where the orphans, now numbering thirty, could play field games. So pleased was Bishop Dupuch with the work of Leboucher and Drouelle at his preparatory seminary that he changed its name to Notre-Dame de Sainte-Croix. Nevertheless, relations with the bishop soon soured over two episodes. The first actually concerned the treatment of another Congregation (the Congregation of the Apparition) in a dispute that they had with one of the bishop's vicars-general. Holy Cross personnel sided with the offended religious. In the second matter, the bishop wanted Father Haudebourg to run the parish in Moustapha, but Haudebourg said (rightly) that he first needed Moreau's permission to assume the pastorship. The bishop was incensed. Moreau volunteered to recall Haudebourg from Algeria in order to appease the bishop, but then Moreau sensed that the situation with the Algerian schools was proving hopeless, and he took advantage of the lapse in episcopal good will to recall all Holy Cross men back to France.

Thus came to an end the first phase of Holy Cross in Algeria. As late as the middle of May, Moreau was still trying to pacify Dupuch and even offered to send more Brothers to replace André and Liguori for whatever reasons. He also offered to shuffle the placement of Leboucher and Drouelle, the former to minister in the military hospital and the latter to head the orphanage. But all six Brothers and three priests left the country on June 5, 1842, without, of course, Brother Louis, who had been lost to the Mediterranean.[83] They were a dispirited group, and at least one of them, the great Brother André, carried in him the seeds of disease that would kill him within two years. His body broken, but his soul strengthened by the African ordeals, he would end his days in peace and love surrounded by his Le Mans confreres who were only too eager to have him back among them. Algeria would not see another Holy Cross religious for over two years. In August 1844, six Brothers would sail to Algiers, with only one of them (Liguori Guyard) from the earlier expedition.

It was surely Moreau's fault that he did not investigate conditions in Algeria thoroughly before sending men there. He did not visit nor send a visitor before shipping André and the others off. One of the harshest criticisms he had for Dujarié and André was their indiscriminate scattering of personnel, yet when it came to his first missionary foray, he showed no better judgment than Dujarié or André had been faulted for. He sent Father Haudebourg to Algeria after the man spent three months in the novitiate, Father Leboucher after five months. It is true that these two men were already ordained and had years of seminary training behind them, but their Community formation was as rudimentary as many of the men under André's care at Ruillé. Algeria was a disaster from the beginning.

When we evaluate today Moreau's vision for Holy Cross abroad, we should always rely on the first person testimony of those he sent to foreign shores. In no other way can we validly assess the strengths and weaknesses of the early Holy Cross endeavors. André Mottais remained throughout his time in Algeria a stalwart son of Moreau, ever grateful that the vigorous priest had undertaken saving the Brothers of St. Joseph in one of their darkest hours. André never questioned Moreau's wisdom. In retrospect from France, he questions only his own inadequacies:

> May the Lord Himself be pleased to choose those who will be used in this laborious mission and ready them beforehand for the sacrifices that they will undertake. As for myself, I believe that I had neither the virtue nor the qualities needed to take part in this happy colony.[84]

He does not mention, however, that Moreau was unable to read André's lack of suitability for this venture. We would expect no other analysis from a man of so intense a humility as André Mottais, a man who writes "I would not have left [Algeria] if my body had let me stay."[85] André returned to Sainte-Croix in broken health. At age forty-three, he was a man near death.

Only two letters remain from his last year, written on May 25 and May 26. The first is a formal greeting on the occasion of the second colony's departure for America. It is a public letter of encouragement from the Brothers at Le Mans to the Brothers in America, signed by twenty-six men. The second letter is a private letter to Brother Vincent signed only by André. How fitting that the final thoughts that remain from him were sent to his comrade of so many years, reflecting a brotherhood that went back twenty-two years to the early days at Ruillé. He tells Vincent that the Brothers are soon to go back to Algeria. As for André himself, Moreau has made him a member of all the councils at Sainte-Croix and given him the title "Assistant."[86] At Sainte-Croix, André reports, there are forty-six Brothers and postulants, not counting another thirty men at the Solitude. André teaches bookkeeping, writing, and reading. He is convinced that the Brothers have turned a corner under Moreau's direction, and that the union of Brothers and priests is solid: "I cannot grow tired of thanking the Lord and praying that He will maintain forever the union of priests with the Brothers."[87] He ends with the hope that he and Vincent will rest together in heaven.

André died at Sainte-Croix at 8 PM on Saturday, March 16, 1844. The chapel was draped in black linen, and the boarding school students, four of them carrying torches, processed with the body up the hill to the Community cemetery. We do not know where he is buried today because all of the graves of the early Holy Cross Brothers and Priests were used for graves of Marianite Sisters, under the direction of Father Charles Moreau, nephew of Basil Moreau. On the back wall of the cemetery one can see today a large attractive panel naming and commemorating all the Brothers and Priests of Holy Cross who lie somewhere in the soil. André is remembered in that plaque. He lies among the scattered.

Thus fades the life of the second founder of Holy Cross without whom the survival of the Brothers of St. Joseph may never have happened and without whom Holy Cross may never have coalesced. The *Chronicles* in noting his death make the point that on his return from Africa, he wanted to be kept in the background: "His conversations and example made him a perfect model of the religious life for everyone."[88] Why has André slipped out of the Holy Cross limelight? Part of his invisibility is a result of his own doing: waiting to embark for Africa, he did write a letter requesting that all references to André Mottais be erased from the Community chronicles of the Josephites. But the time has come (one is tempted to write "again") to rehabilitate the legacy of André Mottais: without him, there would be no Holy Cross as it is known today. He was as vital to the beginnings as Dujarié and Moreau were. May the darkness of historical oblivion never again dim his memory. Espousing St. Joseph's primary virtue, humility, André effaced himself and has become a beacon only at those times when history opens from time to time to reveal him for what he was: a selfless servant, a hard working minister, and amiable founder. History should never again underestimate his importance at Ruillé or at Sainte-Croix. Vanier, the first to name André the "second founder" of Holy Cross, summarized André's contributions to Holy Cross: day-to-day, André carried out the necessities of running a community well for fifteen years. If Dujarié was the heart of the Brothers of St. Joseph, André was the head: without him, Dujarié's group would not have lasted as long as it did.

It is no easy task to convince an established religious community that it has three founders instead of two or one. Part of the problem may be iconographic: we have no idea what André Mottais looked like. We have no photo, no oil painting, no statue. Therefore we have nothing to help anchor an image of the man in our imagination. Moreau, Dujarié, Mary of the Seven Dolors—these people are fixed in our brain from photographic/oil painting images. But what do we have for André? The mind works on image, and for André Mottais we can only fabricate. We do not even know if he were short or tall, fair haired or dark, brown eyed or blue eyed. Only his spirit remains and struggles from time to time to be revitalized in a religious here and there.

CHAPTER TWO

Hilarion Ferton: Apostle to Africa

Apparently Father Moreau never planned on totally abandoning Africa when he withdrew all Holy Cross religious in 1842. He kept up a correspondence with officials pertinent to teaching credentials for Algeria, and the Algerian Inspector of Public Instruction (Lepescheaux) wrote to Moreau on May 23, 1843, saying how happy he was to learn from Moreau that the Brothers had received approval by royal decree to teach on the primary level in Algeria.[1] This letter would have come less than a year after the Holy Cross exodus so clearly good relations were maintained between Le Mans and Algeria. In the letter Moreau is assured that if he were to send his best Brothers, they would thrive in the school system. Given, however, Brother André's terrible experiences the previous year, one wonders what miracles were being worked to make a Holy Cross return more workable than it had proved to be earlier. Possibly Moreau had known he could use total withdrawal as a bargaining chip with the school authorities by showing that he would brook no further nonsense in either the licensing of schools for the Brothers or the conditions in which they would have to teach. It is obvious that the French were vitally interested in having Holy Cross return to Algeria. At least the Brothers. The priests were another matter. The inspector tells Moreau that life on the frontier would continue to be hostile and difficult for any priests who would emigrate. One can conclude that it was the clash of Christianity with Islam that most concerned the French: native Algerians would be more accepting of new schools for their children than they would be of churches that could attempt to evangelize among the Muslims.

A similar letter to Moreau arrived one day later from the Minister of the Interior who had already been told by the Minister of Defense (Marshal Soult) that royal approval of the teaching Brothers had come through. This official mirrors the enthusiasm of the Education Minister for the teaching Brothers and likewise counsels Moreau to send them without priests. He specifies that the direction of the Brothers should be left to one of the Brothers, leading us to suspect either a current of anticlericalism in the air, not unlikely even this distant from the Revolution, or possibly the ministers were aware of some awkwardness having a priest in charge of teaching Brothers as had been the case with the earlier Holy Cross missionaries. Of course, Brother André had been their "director," but in the last year, that is half of the time Holy Cross had been in Algeria, he was off in Philippeville teaching one hundred miles away from both Moustapha and Blidah where the other Brothers were teaching. Communication, as we have seen in the matter of Brother Louis's death, was not easy. In effect, Father Drouelle had been both the superior and de facto director of the Brothers. It is true he himself was teaching at the seminary and may have been very fine in principles of pedagogy, but he would, of course, have had none of the solid supervisory experience that Brother André had accrued in twenty years of classroom visitations in and around Ruillé and Le Mans. The ministers, perhaps knowing the dynamics of the Christian Brothers, who thrived without clerical supervision, might have seen or heard of the disasters in Blidah and Philippeville and attributed them to bad clerical supervision or lack thereof. When a man is running a parish, often one of the last things on his mind is the quality of instruction in the parish school, and even if it were on his mind, he would lack the expertise of knowing how to remedy bad situations, short of firing people.

Catta claims that Holy Cross priests were not invited back to Algeria because Soult had told Moreau that "the number of ecclesiastics was 'altogether sufficient to meet all the spiritual needs of Algeria.'"[2] Catta does not specify which of two letters he is quoting from, but the minister's comment is suspect for another reason: why would a government official, or any official for that matter, governmental or ecclesiastical, refuse the offer of new help? The answer may well lie in the bad relations between Bishop Dupuch and previous Holy Cross missionaries back in the spring of 1842. There were ostensibly two reasons the bishop had soured on the Holy Cross priests: the refusal of Father Haudebourg to accept the bishop's request to take over a different parish and some matter between the Congregation of the Apparition and a vicar-general, an incident in which Holy Cross priests sided with the Apparition Sisters. Neither of these incidents seem to have involved Brothers. The first case certainly did not, and the second one probably did not for a very good reason: six hours per day a Brother teaches thirty or more students who need to be motivated in reading, writing, drawing, and doing basic mathematics, so at the end of the day he is not inclined to be enmeshed in a local brouhaha with a vicar-general with whom he would have had little contact to begin with. Just as trouble happened between Haudebourg and the head doctor in Blidah at the local military hospital, trouble could certainly have brewed with Drouelle and Le Boucher at Moustapha where the one priest ran the seminary and the other taught in it. The seminary had ten seminarians, hardly a full time job for two grown men. Moreover, the two priests would have had more interest in the battles of a fellow priest (the vicar-general) than a Brother would have. It could very well be that it was the Holy Cross clerics who eroded their own welcome in Algeria. Certainly Haudebourg did because Moreau volunteered to withdraw him before Moreau determined to pull all men from Africa in June 1842, and it could very well be that Le Boucher and Drouelle wore out their own welcome by meddling in diocesan politics. Brothers traditionally have little interest in ecclesiastical squabbles. Moreover, Algeria was a huge country with a growing number of French colonists, most of them nominally Catholic. There would have been a growing need for priests to minister to them in spite of what Soult supposedly wrote to Moreau about the surfeit of priests in the country. After all, when Dupuch was first named bishop of Algiers in 1838, there were already 100,000 Catholics in the country and but four priests. It is more likely in 1843 that the public ministers were aware of Dupuch's run-ins with Holy Cross priests and would not risk losing once again the brother-teachers by incidents similar to the clerical debacles with Dupuch in 1842.

Curiously at the end of his chapter on Algeria, Catta states:

> The activity of Holy Cross in Algeria continued for some time, but on a very reduced scale ... The Superior General had made it possible, even with scanty means, to offer an important contribution to the thankless task of evangelizing Algeria. Richer, more rapid, and more lasting results would have been obtained if, with the same zeal and equal foresight, all those involved in this work had given evidence of the same spirit of union, and especially had the French government understood the Christian mission conferred on France by virtue of its conquest of Africa.[3]

Of course Catta wrote these sentences a few years before the Algerians so ungraciously threw the French out! But two things are rankling in Catta's aborted consideration of Holy Cross in Algeria. The first most obvious insult is that Algeria had no worthwhile religion before the French conquerors came or it had an inferior religion that needed upgrading to Christianity. Secondly, in his remarks is the implication that Holy Cross history in Algeria stops when there are no more priests to write about. One could not find a more clerical conclusion in this most clerical of biographies. Readers, Catta seems to say, will not be interested in what joys and trials various Brothers had in a country which now took a back seat to more glorious enterprises underway in Indiana and Canada.

Moreau continued, however, a strong interest in returning to Africa. In a letter dated August 5, 1843, while Holy Cross was absent from Algeria, Bishop Dupuch notified Propaganda Fidei that he had approved the rules and constitutions of the "Brothers of St. Joseph of Le Mans." This is a significant letter in that it shows Moreau still on very good terms with his old St. Sulpice classmate in spite of the sad circumstances of the 1842 withdrawal. In December of that same year Dupuch writes to tell Moreau that he has already prepared a beautiful school for the Brothers at Oran (a town 150 miles west of Algiers). He also responds to a question from Moreau about the possibility of having a Holy Cross priest do an official visit of the Brothers annually, to which request Dupuch agrees, there being, of course, no mention of permanently reinstating Holy Cross priests in Algeria. That matter was apparently closed.

And so it came to pass that Holy Cross Brothers returned to Algeria, six of them in September 1844, two years and three months since their previous missions there. The leader (director), Brother Hilarion Ferton, came to Le Mans from Calais to join the Brothers in 1837 at age 20. Three years after his profession, he was chosen to lead the Brothers back to Algeria, but unfortunately he was to die there at age 32 in 1849. He was a wonderful letter writer, sending letters full of details and drama. Brother Liguori Guyard had actually already served in Algeria, leaving France as a novice in 1840 and returning to France two years later when Father Moreau recalled all Holy Cross religious. Unfortunately, he would leave the Community in 1846 at age 27. Aloysius Gonzaga Galmard, or Louis Gonzaga as he called himself, was sent to Algeria three years to the day of his first profession. His was to be a long service in Holy Cross. In 1855 he transferred from the Brothers' society into the Holy Cross Priests' society and was ordained. He would die in 1893 at age 75 in Paris. Brother Victor Catala was the second Victor to serve in Algeria, the previous missionary by that name having left the Community in 1842. This second Victor arrived in Algeria still a novice and left the Community within fourteen months, probably without ever taking vows.[4] Brother Basil Gary had already been professed and had received his teaching certificate before he went to Algeria. He worked long in the Community, dying in 1888 at age 76. The youngest member of the group, Brother Marcel Coupris arrived in Algeria at age 19 and stayed until 1853. He too lived long as a Brother, dying at Angers in 1896 at age 71. One can see that Moreau had made rather solid choices of men for this return to Africa: of the six Brothers, only two left the Community, not a bad percentage in years when attrition was often 70 percent or higher. Moreau was a fine judge of character and sent his best to serve. We focus now on Brother Hilarion Ferton, leader of the Holy Cross return to Algeria.

Hilarion was born Louis Ferton on February 24, 1817, at Boulogne, seventeen years after the birth of Brother André Mottais at Larchamp. The location of his birth-town is problematic.[5] His parents were Louis Ferton and Agnes Baguette, and we presume, since he bore his father's first name, that he was a first born son. His parents were probably farmers. He came to Le Mans to enter Holy Cross on May 20, 1837, at the age of 20. Three months later he became a novice (August 30, 1837) and was professed on August 22, 1841, just one year after Father Moreau himself took religious vows. He was only the second man in Holy Cross to be given the religious name "Hilarion," and he appears as #315 in the General Matricule.

At the Le Mans novitiate (La Chabonnière) Hilarion's novice master would have been either Brother André Mottais (the only novice master Father Dujarié used) or one of the auxiliary priests whom Father Moreau would have preferred over Brother André. The assigning of a novice master in the Brothers' Society was sometimes a contentious matter, as we will see later when we discuss one of the last letters Brother Hilarion signed. Whether André Mottais was Hilarion's novice master or not, Hilarion would have known the great man who had engineered the transfer of the Brothers of St. Joseph away from Father Dujarié's care to Father Moreau's. Hilarion would have undoubtedly been inspired by the appointment of André Mottais to be among the first missionaries Moreau sent out in the spring of 1840, intrepid men who would embark on a religious adventure in 1840 that would bring them into history and would stir the hearts of younger religious.

When Brother André Mottais returned to France in broken health, he may or may not have interacted with Brother Hilarion at Le Mans thereafter. The latter was probably teaching in some little town and would have seen the great André only in late summer at the annual retreat of either 1842 or 1843. André died in Le Mans in March 1844, five months before Hilarion would be named for the second mission to Algeria. Of the six Brothers bound for Algeria, Hilarion was the second youngest. At age 23, he was older than Marcel, who was 19, but two men, Victor and Basil, were in their 30's. Liguori was two years older than Hilarion, and Louis Gonzaga was four years older than Hilarion. Clearly Moreau saw something in Hilarion he did not see in the others. Hilarion became the most prolific writer: we have twenty-seven of his letters in the Holy Cross General Archives, all but six of them written to Father Moreau.

Getting to Algeria was no easy task, as we learn from Hilarion in a September letter to Moreau.[6] Since the coach leaving Le Mans for Paris on August 20 was in excess of the allowable number of passengers, the Brothers had to get off before various towns (Nogent le Rotrou, Couraille) in order to avoid inspectors. Brother Basil Gary describes the departure: "It was about 11 PM when we left Le Mans. Our driver was in a bad mood. He was late half an hour and there were two too many for the coach. It didn't take much to make him swear like a devil."[7] At Chartres they did manage to get into the cathedral during the half-hour stopover there, but Hilarion and Basil had to walk a league out of town before the driver would let them back into the coach. Fear of inspectors again. Or maybe a residue of hatred of clerical types by a nasty coachman: the French Revolution with its rabid anti-clericalism was barely two generations behind them. At Rambouillet the same story. At Versailles, finally exasperated, Hilarion took the train into Paris where he discovered the arrangements for travel to Lyon were messed up: he and the others faced a week's layover. Their only consolation was a chance to spend time with saintly Father Mollevaut at St. Sulpice in Paris. They were then given space on the coach for Lyon on August 25, but in Lyon, Brother Basil had a bad spell:

> After finding a hotel and getting a room for all my Brothers
> who were coming that evening, I took a little nap. When the
> time came to get up, I couldn't budge from the bed: a fever

from fatigue had grabbed hold of me. I had to stay in bed. I begged the hotel boy to go wait for the stagecoach and bring back my confreres, and this brave man did it gladly. But since the stagecoach was late, he had fun drinking, and if the Brothers had arrived any later, this man wouldn't have able to talk to them. All the same, he went, did what he could, but couldn't be understood. "Why isn't Brother Basil here?" some of them said. "He's a good-for-nothing," said the others. Finally the station agents, who knew the boy, saved them from embarrassment by indicating to them the house. When they got to the room where I was, I saw that they were going to eat me alive, and when I made excuses by saying I was sick, they barely listened to me … At 4 AM we had to catch the steamship … At 5 PM we got off at Avignon. At 8 PM we took a coach, which went directly to Toulon where we arrived the next day, the 28th, at 4 PM, rather tired but otherwise OK. We went down to the Maltese Cross Hotel.[8]

On August 31 at Toulon they boarded the ship *Acheron* for Algeria. Hilarion weathered the Mediterranean trip well, as did Ligouri. The other four got seasick. On September 2 Hilarion sighted Africa for the first time, and that afternoon at 1 PM he set foot on the continent that would be his home for the rest of his life.

Bishop Dupuch was out of town as was the Interior Minister, but the Secretary General told Hilarion that he would take Hilarion the next day by boat to Oran where Hilarion was to teach. Hilarion, however, wished to stay a few days with his confreres and also attend to business Moreau had commissioned him to do. On Tuesday they all went to the tomb of Brother Louis Marchand, the Brother who had drowned while swimming with his orphans in 1841. Their eventual reception by Dupuch was cordial but not warm. He promised each Brother a letter of introduction to their various pastors, and then rushed them along. So much for the hierarchical euphoria he had expressed in letters to Moreau! Once the sheep arrived, they were merely sheep. From what we know of Dupuch, they were lucky to be rid of him.[9] As first bishop of Algeria, he was anything but stellar. His successor was better, but the third bishop, named a cardinal, was notorious for mood swings and a vicious temper.

On September 3, 1844, Hilarion wrote from Algiers to give Moreau further details of the group's arrival in Africa. They had seven days to wait for transport by boat to their various destinations so they decided to trek to a Trappist monastery at Straouli five miles outside of Algiers in order to make a retreat. Walking the entire way, the group split up so that Hilarion and Liguori could deliver to a priest at Drariah a letter from Father Haudebourg, a hoot of a Holy Cross priest who had served in Algeria on the first ill-fated foray. Unfortunately Hilarion and Liguori lost their way after leaving Drariah:

> We got lost in horrible ravines and sometimes we had to pass over very high hills. For two hours we wandered ravine to ravine, hill to hill, in the worst heat, without meeting a living thing except a little shepherd who gave us bad directions. Climbing on a rock we saw a small road not far from us, and continuing on we were soon pestered by large drops of rain. We encountered a group of Arabs, and Brother Ligouri, already familiar with their way, asked them, I don't know in what language, for the Strouelli road. These Moors, these poor people, seemed very helpful. One of them came away from the others to show us our road.[10]

Being lost in a foreign country may be adventurous for young travelers, but with a forbidding terrain, the fun quickly dissipates. The missionaries were lucky that native people were in the area. At the monastery they were welcomed by the guestmaster, but the Trappists were a mess: half of them were bed-ridden from disease and four had recently died. Brother Basil writes:

> The good Trappists scrubbed their best ones [cabins] for us, but in spite of their solicitude, we slept badly. To compensate

these good Fathers, who in spite of their troubles lavished on us the little they had, we offered to water their garden, which had suffered badly from the heat and the bad health of the gardeners. Those of us who didn't seem robust enough for this kind of work worked in the kitchen under the direction of Father Guest-master. We were quasi-Trappists during our short stay.[11]

At the Sunday Mass one Trappist Brother was anointed and appeared near death. An episode like this would impress anyone, but it took sensitive letter writers like Hilarion and Basil to make it vivid for us.

In the same letter Hilarion notes that he finally got to baptize someone. Back in Algiers at a hotel at 1:30 in the morning, a desperate mother asked Hilarion to baptize her dying infant. Hilaron named the child Jeanne Euphémie. She died within hours, but Hilarion was ecstatic at his good deed: "Fly, little angel, fly—go beg the Father for mercy for the unfortunate who opened the door to heaven for you. My little St. Jeanne, pray for us, pray for the entire Community, both for those who are in France and for those in America and those in Africa, and for all the children to be entrusted to us."[12] Hilarion must have caught the eye of this poor family. The baby's father was a French army officer.

On September 10, Hilarion and Victor saw Liguori and Aloysius off to Philippeville, Basil and Marcel off to Bône. Hilarion at 27 is not the oldest in the group, but he is their local director. He was paired by Moreau with Victor, who at 36 is oldest of the group. Louis at 27 was paired with Liguori who is 25. Basil at 32 was paired with the youngest of the group, Marcel, who is 19. Philippeville, founded in 1838 by the conquering French on the site of an old Phoenician port, had its name changed in 1962 after the Algerian War of Independence. Today, a city of 150,000, it is known as Skikda. Bône, known today as Annaba, was founded near the site of the ancient city of Hippo, but nothing remained of St. Augustine's city by the time the French invaded. That same evening Hilarion and Victor reboarded the *Acheron* for Oran. Today the second largest city in

Algeria, it lies halfway between Morocco and Algiers. No one stayed in Algiers, and thus the original foundation of 1840, the orphanage at Moustapha, was in the hands of another religious congregation. The Brothers at Bône and Philippeville were only twenty miles apart, on the far eastern side of Algeria near Tunisia, 200 miles from Algiers. Oran is 200 miles to the west of Algiers, so the Oran duo would have been 400 miles from the other four Brothers.

At Bône, Basil and Marcel had ready access to the site where the ancient city of Hippo was situated. Basil made several trips to Hippo, about a mile from the pastor's home in which they temporarily lived. At Hippo he found what was left of the monument to St. Augustine: an enclosure about eight meters in diameter, a half meter off the ground. On this platform was a marble wall with an iron grill topped by gold strips. The center was paved with Italian marble, and in the middle was a white marble altar with a tabernacle topped by a bronze statue of St. Augustine half a meter high. Although today there are extensive ruins dating from the time of St. Augustine, including the foundations of what might have been his basilica, there is no evidence that the monument described by Brother Basil still exists. It would be interesting to go to Hippo Regius and try to find it. Basil also noted, "A little below this monument to St. Augustine are the ruins of an old building given to the bishop. Nobody knows what it was. Some think it may have been a prison."[13] Basil was a fine reporter, and he proved also to be an excellent nurse for his housemate Brother Marcel, who had contracted some bug in their new surroundings and had become so weak that Basil had to carry him to and from bed. Marcel eventually strengthened, but by December he was again ailing. Living with borrowed furniture and blankets, the two were promised a house by January 1. Sadly, by year's end neither the Brothers at Bône nor the Brothers at Phillipeville had received their trunks, which were supposed to have come over with them on the *Acheron.*

At Oran, Hilarion ran into a tug-of-war between the pastor and the sub-director of public instruction over a house for the two Brothers (Hilarion and Victor). Neither the pastor nor the local Sub-director of the Interior (Mr. Berthier) had anything ready, and Hilarion ended up sleeping on a sofa in the rectory for two weeks. Although the delay was exasperating, he did take some delight in watching the fray between the pastor and the sub-director: "To an outsider like me, it was delightful to hear these two men hurling epithets at each other, and both believed it necessary to read to me their correspondence before I could judge who was right and who was wrong, although I wanted to remain neutral in this whole affair."[14] Clearly, Hilarion had a nice sense of humor which undoubtedly helped him weather the situation in a country that was more cavalier about commitments and time than France had ever been. It was one of the first lessons Hilarion had to learn in his new homeland. After three days, a suitable house was finally found for the two Brothers: one story, four rooms, a small courtyard. The sub-director wanted Hilarion to use a small apartment at the front of the house as a classroom, but Hilarion rejected the suggestion since the room was poorly ventilated. Hilarion turned this room, with the addition of a stove, into a kitchen. These events took place in late September.

By October 19, Hilarion was negotiating with a cabinetmaker to furnish the house. There was still no decision made about classrooms so Hilarion concentrated on the house and the hassle between the pastor and the sub-director:

> Nothing moves forward. I'm pushing the wheel, little accustomed to this way of living. I'm already tired. If this were France, I would have said good-by to these gentlemen until they had finished their debates and had prepared a suitable house.[15]

Seeing the young missionary's frustration, we can today wonder why Moreau had not learned his lesson from working with Algeria's clerics and bureaucrats four years earlier, but Moreau's patience must have been colossal. Likewise for Hilarion on-site: raised in a well-run country like France, he was accustomed to government and ecclesiastical expedience, in spite of the Revolution that had so devastated the country two generations earlier. He opines: "I was told at Sainte-Croix, and rightly so, that clergy in Africa cannot [complain] or we will be subjected to lots of misery."[16]

As leader of this second expedition to Algeria, Hilarion was responsible for keeping his men in working order, a duty that included confrontation if their character flaws needed correction. That the men did not always accept his corrections graciously is obvious from a letter Louis Gonzaga sent in early October:

> I have waited a long time to reproach you for the comments that in your charity you made about me and you also made about Brother Liguori. On the contrary, I thank you with all my heart. You are not complaining enough about our bad character.[17]

The sarcasm is evident. Hilarion may have sensed that trouble would brew between Louis Gonzaga and Liguori because the two young men at Philippeville were of conflicting temperaments. Indeed, more trouble would eventually arise between them in the two years ahead. But currently Louis Gonzaga seemed happy. In fact, he waxed eloquent to Moreau in a letter penned on the same day as his harsh letter to Hilarion:

> Oh! How you have to love God to be a Trappist! Who can hold on in a place where they are always sick or inconvenienced or working in the lowest and most tiring jobs, where they are badly housed, dressed, nourished, and rested? Ah! How impossible for me to be equal to one of these men of God![18]

So the Trappists held no allure for this young man, but he had plenty to distract himself in Philippeville. Prices were high so food was expensive, Liguori had been sick for a week, and the unfinished classroom was "a miserable hole without air or light." In two weeks classes would begin, and Louis Gonzaga was expecting up to sixty students.

By late October Hilarion had his own troubles in Oran: Victor was racked with dysentery and unable to be of much assistance for the opening of the school, which would happen on November 4. Another distraction involved a small child:

> A month ago a soldier brought me a small Arab orphan about ten years old, whom I kept with me until last Friday because he spoke French, Arabic, Spanish, and even a little German. I hoped that later he could be useful to the Community or even the boarding school, but two soldiers wanted to take him away from us. I asked the little boy if he preferred going with these soldiers or staying with us. Since he did not respond "yes," I let him go. Two days later they wanted me to take him again, saying what the child had and that the soldiers had no way of feeding him. I didn't want him in spite of the entreaties of the king's procurator, who confided his own child to me by sending him to my school, and whose wife took an interest in us. Today they just presented me with another.[19]

Obviously an incipient orphanage seems in the works, as if a school of sixty boys was not enough for young Hilarion! He certainly had a large heart. He confides to Moreau:

> Oh, how I feel when instead of being in the middle of the Sainte-Croix boarders, I find myself around children of different colors, dressed differently, speaking all manner of languages. This really touches me. Help me with your prayers. I hope God will give me the courage to do His will always.[20]

Hilarion is clearly the right young man in the right place: sensitive, considerate, and generous. Soon students were arriving, including that son of the king's procurator. Moreover, the pastor at Mostaganen, twenty-five leagues from Oran, was begging for a Brother to open a school in his parish, and Hilarion favors the idea—if Moreau can send more Brothers.

That Hilarion was basically a virtuous man with solid principles can be demonstrated throughout his correspondence with Moreau, whom he regarded as more than a religious superior. He phrases his devotion to Moreau quite like a son to a father in the most venerable of sentiments the nineteenth-century fostered within religious communities. The bond was genuine, Hilarion seeing Moreau as someone who would bring peace, harmony, and even sanctity to a young missionary off in a distant and unfamiliar country:

> My reverend Father, the more I see myself far away from you, the more I sense in my soul the filial emotions which I had fallen into the first days of my novitiate. Regret, love, recognition spoke to me loudly, "What are my obligations?" Faith and religion will always fulfill me. I know too well that I am not capable of a single worthy act, so I put all my confidence in He who knows all, can do all, who gives to him who asks and opens to him who knocks.[21]

These are the heartfelt words of a sincere person who had sacrificed himself for the promised rewards of spiritual fulfillment that young men hoped to find in Holy Cross.

In the daily world, however, Hilarion was equally successful at his teaching craft. Daily he faced seventy boys in one classroom. They aged from six to sixteen. Such an age-spread is today difficult enough to swallow, given today's educational standards and expectations, but to add to the mixture the fact that Hilarion had no books to work from, his daily work becomes heroic, if not a downright crucifixion. He had, of course, brought books to Africa, but they remained in his lost trunk, which lay, so he thought, in a merchant ship somewhere between Toulon and Algeria. In fact the trunk had never left Toulon. Moreover, his students are a mish-mash of English, German, French, Italian, Spanish, and Arab boys "all speaking a little French." How he communicated with all seventy of them is a wonder. How he survived is a miracle. What a gifted, energetic, and creative young teacher he must have been.

By early January Hilarion was able to report to Moreau that Victor had had some good days, but Hilarion was embroiled in a battle over the types of students who could be accepted at the school. The sub-director insisted that non-paying students who have a certificate stamped by his office could be accepted into the school, along with all the tuition-paying students Hilarion could accommodate. A glitch, however, in the public announcement gave local people the impression that tuition-paying students would not be accepted. The misinformation was soon corrected, and tuition was set at three francs per month.

Hilarion found Oran, a city of 15,000, ugly. Ships had to dock almost a league away (at Mers-el-Kebir) because the channel at Oran was not navigable. Arid conditions made farming problematic: almost everything was imported from Spain or France, making the cost-of-living high. Living in a house so poorly constructed that rain seeped through was only one trial he had to endure. His housemate Victor, besides being chronically sick, had a foul mood about him. Hilarion, being the man in charge, had to put up with much. Victor did not teach—he was their cook—and when he was sick, Hilarion had to do the cooking after teaching seventy boys all day. Things were not running smoothly either in the Louis Gonzaga house. Evidently even before the group split up in Algiers, there was some bad temper from Louis Gonzaga, who apparently showed some reluctance to be under Hilarion's direction. He refused at first to be part of a group discussion, the "minor chapter" as Hilarion called it, until it became obvious Louis and Liguori were in the minority. Then both joined in. Even before getting to Philippeville, these two may have been in league against Hilarion. Both were, of course, older than their religious director and had been with Moreau's community longer. Hilarion suggested in a letter to Moreau that Louis Gonzaga expected to be in charge of the Algerian mission, not Hilarion, so the older religious (Louis Gonzaga) had an early animosity against his younger director, an animosity he took little care to hide. Later, Louis Gonzaga tried to mask his umbrage as "joking around," according to Hilarion's January letter to Moreau,[22] but under the surface Louis Gonzaga continued to seethe.

By mid-January, the trunks had still not arrived. They were back in France at Toulon. The Brothers at all three Algerian locations had no linen (shirts, underwear) and no books for teaching. One man had no pants at all. At Bône Brother Basil had thirty students but prospects for one hundred. His classroom could accommodate, however, only sixty-two. His housemate, like Hilarion's, was often sick: quinine helped Marcel through his fevers but the fevers returned. He undoubtedly suffered from malaria.

But half a year later, in June, things were going so well in Oran that Hilarion requested a third Brother be sent. He even named a possibility: Brother Theotime.[23] Hilarion obviously had a fine working knowledge of Holy Cross personnel if he could request a specific member for the Algerian mission as he did. His request to Moreau also shows him able to work on a level playing field with Le Mans, satisfied with the beginning success, however bumpy, of the Algerian schools and hopeful for their future improvement. The local authorities promised a salary of only 800 francs per annum (not the 1500 Hilarion was receiving), but Hilarion reasoned the two salaries together would nevertheless make a fine income for the three men living together. (Victor, the cook, did not of course receive a salary.) The school was thriving, but Hilarion had heard rumors that the Christian Brothers were poised to horn in on his territory: a second Holy Cross teaching Brother for Oran could expand the enrollment sufficiently to make a Christian Brother foundation pointless.

In July 1845, as the first school year was coming to an end, Hilarion was able to report a favorable start at Oran. So well had the school progressed that he even thought a boarding school could be possible. Of course, the public school teachers were unhappy that he was "snatching" their students away. Apparently sixty or more boys in one classroom did not seem unwieldly to the Brothers at the time. They reveled even in what we today would find an unteachable situation. Brother Louis revealed sadly that Basil in Bône had only twenty students. As far as income, the ratio of non-paying students to tuition-paying students was apparently not so excessive that the Bothers could not manage to earn a decent salary in Algeria, at least in this second attempt at colonizing. Oran in 1845, with a population of 9000 Europeans, 1500 natives, 2000 soldiers, and 3000 Jews (Hilarion's breakdown of the population[24]) got along with three schools, one of them Hilarion's.

Two months into the second school year (fall, 1845), Victor left the Community. Hilarion was thus alone, but anticipated a housemate. Victor never taught in the school. He was expected to cook for the two of them and, we presume, get supplies and tidy the house. He was not overworked. Instead of returning to France, Victor decided to stay in Oran and work in a Jewish restaurant. Thus Hilarion was left alone in Oran to cook for himself after a full day in the classroom. But his spirit did not deflate: he did, however, look forward to getting another Brother from Moreau to replace Victor, and a new church was being built in Oran, its cornerstone laid on October 12. All was not, however, sweetness and light since a local tribal leader named Ab el Hader was terrorizing the province and preventing colonists from working in the fields. The French general Lamorcière arrived to chase the Algerian rebels into Morocco, and another commander, Marshall Bugeaud, with ten thousand French soldiers was operating to the west of Oran. Hilarion either does not seem particularly concerned, or he was a young man quite brave and touched by an adventurous spirit. Both characteristics would make him an excellent missionary. From a perspective of over a century and a half in retrospect, it is not easy for us today to judge the French conquerors. As they continued to flex their muscles worldwide, they can be either dismissed as heartless or valued as harbingers of European civilization. Either way, Hilarion and his confreres played a small but important role in educating children, who are, after all, the innocent victims of conquest, even if they are among the invading people.

As 1846 began, another man defected: Liguori left the house in Philippeville and took a position as sacristan for the local pastor, who promised to teach him Latin and let him teach school. Since Liguori, like Victor, was sent to Algeria by Moreau to cook, not to teach, the situation seemed a little irregular. Liguori had been with Holy Cross for seven years and had been in the first colony (1840) to Algeria. His departure left Louis high and dry with eighty-five students in his school and no help in the school or house. Thus two out of three Holy Cross cooks in Algeria had left in a matter of months. This Brother Liguori must have been a piece of work, but as Louis Gonzaga describes him to Moreau, he does seem to have had good reasons for leaving:

> His reasons for leaving, he says, are: little consideration was taken for his brother at Sainte-Croix: boredom with his life here, having only cooking to do which took him scarcely an hour a day, and an affectionate letter you didn't send him and which he thought you would send him to console him in the troubles that he told you he was going through. To these reasons, I add the following: the attraction of the world, a seductive letter his brother wrote to him, little friendship between him and me, bad advice that he got from people hostile to the Community, bad direction from a confessor, if that is possible, and offers made to him.[25]

Liguori may, in fact, have been temperamentally incapable of living with only one other person in the house. The set-up of the three houses in Algeria (one teacher, one cook, in each of the three locations) was not unlike a husband-wife configuration: the breadwinner left early in the morning to teach school, leaving the housekeeper behind with little to do and no network of other housekeepers of like background in the neighborhood.

With such a brother-cook, things were probably bound to boil over, and boil over they did. In a letter to Father Chappé (February 1846), Louis narrated in great detail the fistfight he had had with Liguori over a mattress that the pastor's cook wanted to borrow:

> Brother Liguori ... told me after the cook left that I was being ridiculous, insensitive, and smug, and that he should have

given the mattress without my permission. I told him that he was insolent, that I forbid him to take anything without my permission, and that since this cook was the cause of my receiving such stupid remarks, I forbid him setting foot in our house. He replied that he would come in spite of me and his brother too [Brother Liguori's brother]. That annoyed me all the more, since he had said nothing on the subject of his brother, and that induced me to tell him that his brother couldn't come any more, and that if he came, I'd have him thrown out by the police. That was the end of the talking. Brother Liguori got up, came around the table, put his fist on my chin, and hit me saying, "You ...!" It was not much longer before I pushed his fist away from my face. Brother Liguori grabbed a chair. But thinking quickly, I returned a blow with a chair on his back and a fist in his face. Then he threatened to leave, and I told him as I withdrew that he could do whatever he wanted.[26]

Perhaps Louis Ganzaga was blessed with Liguori's departure. He surely had some peace and quiet when he remained the only one in the house.

What stress Hilarion had to endure with the defection of one-third of his work force is not hard to imagine. By January 1846, he had ninety students to teach, divided into two sections. How he managed to keep half of the boys occupied while he taught the other half is anybody's guess. Then, as if he did not have enough to do, the "Foreign Affairs Committee" back in Le Mans (probably a subcommittee of the Holy Cross General Council) was pressuring him to submit a report on teaching conditions throughout Algeria. Before leaving France, Hilarion had in fact promised Moreau this information. What he did finally send to Moreau are two remarkably precise documents. The first document is dated February 8, 1846, the second February 24. The first is the longer of the two. In it Hilarion lists the number of tribes and the number of sub-divisions for each tribe in Algeria. He gives a report on the terrain of each city and village. Where he amassed all the data is unknown: he could not have visited all these locales while he was teaching ninety students at his school. He must have relied on local charts or contacts in Oran. One way or another, his information is remarkable and, one would think, should be valuable today to anyone studying the early history of France in Algeria. One small example:

> The actual civilian territory of Philippeville is 8 to 10,000 hectares. Its boundaries are a line which goes from the sea on the West to the blockhouses at Jmges [sic] and ends up in the East at the mountain peaks. It encompasses the whole valley of Zeramma and the lower part of the Safsaf valley. Three centers of civilization are being set up in this territory. Two in the valley of Safsaf, a valley on the right hand riverbank. Darémont on the left bank, one at the top of Zaramma, Saint-Antoine. Mr. Ferdinand staked a claim of 600 hectares near Philippeville. In the village of Valée as of April 1, 1845, there were 77 inhabitants, 15 houses and 17 under construction. Darémont and St. Antoine are in the process of being established. The Safsaf valley was developed on a stretch of 32 kilometers right by the El-arrouch camp.[27]

His lists for the cities are broken down by the number of Catholics, Protestants, Moors, Jews, and Blacks. How curious that he would discriminate "Blacks" as a religion.

By April of 1846 Brother Hilarion had a second man at Oran: Brother Clement arrived to replace Victor.[28] Hilarion's original classroom had been divided to accommodate two classes, each one capable of holding one hundred students. Hilarion had hoped to use Clement as a kind of teacher's aide for the smallest children, but Clement claimed there was enough housework to keep him busy in their house. The number of children at the school was 112, and Hilarion had to teach all of them by himself. Teachers and administrators today would shake their heads at such an unimaginable workload. By June, Clement did help out a bit in the school, but he proved to be a less than satisfactory teacher, and Hilarion, aware that Clement would probably be recalled to France, was further stressed out over the prospect of trying to work without him. By July the enrollment reached 130 students.

What did Brother Hilarion think of the native peoples of Algeria? He never wrote a bad word against them and his occasional encounters in his school with little Arab boys leads us to believe he was an honest teacher of any who came into his care. Yes, he was a member of the French colonizers, ministering to their sons, but his heart was greater than ethnicity or country. He loved beyond bounds of creed or color. He wrote to Moreau:

> My reverend Father, won't you send me a novice for the souls of these poor but interesting children?! The Jews are beginning to frequent our school. I have four in my class. Brother Clement, one. He would have to be initiated a little into the Arabic idiom. I would be comfortable associating with and receiving lessons from a native to whom I could teach French.[29]

So he characterizes the students as "poor but interesting," a kindly assessment without condescension or hostility.

Brother Hilarion loved young people as is evidenced by his very long letter in 1847 to the brother-scholastics at the motherhouse. He had visited Le Mans the previous September, and once he was back in Oran, he wrote in January a very long letter to them with copious details about the boat trip. He jokes with the young Brothers and even narrates his use of snuff: "I slowly introduce my thumb and forefinger into this orbicular cavity, and I lift out a pinch of the best Moroccan tobacco and perfume my hydropic brain."[30] His language is ornate to the point of silliness, just the sort of pedantic filigree young college students delight in. He tells them the sad tale of a cabin boy who was put in shackles and taken down below for not washing properly behind his ears. He talks of businessmen who wile away the voyage drinking, sometimes with the captain. Arriving back at Algiers, he gives details on the Casbah, and he writes a long narrative about a trip with Brother Basil into the interior where they are feted by local tribesmen, removing somewhat, no doubt, the mystery and fear of missionary life for the young men of Holy Cross back in Le Mans.

> At 7 AM we take our coffee. Then we mount on horseback. We do not follow a direct route. Our guides alone know where we are, sometimes on the crest of a mountain, sometimes in deep ravines. It seems we're wandering, but for the Arab one mountain indicates another to him, and in this way we come to our goal. It's 10 o'clock. We halt. Here's an organized camp, officers and soldiers, all at work, soup made. But here's where neighboring tribes of Arabs rush to this new sight, and Chief Ab-el-Kerim at their head greets the general, passing his right hand under his and then kissing it. From all over come chickens, butter, milk, couscous, crepes, honey. Everything goes on the general's table. Then the soldiers go about their business. While we eat, 50 Arabs are grouped around us, delighted to see us. To better entertain us, they bring in some musicians who flay our ears with the horrible sound of a kind of flute and the noise they make knocking their fingers and drum sticks on skin stretched tightly on a cylinder which somewhat resembles a pipe put under our chimneys to stop smoke. They accompany this music with a chant so monotonous that we would gladly have left to go to sleep if the impatient general had not given marching orders. The Arabs make their horses gambol in front of us, and we let them gather up what the soldiers can't carry with them.[31]

The letter was calculated to intoxicate brother-scholastics' brains with zeal for Algeria, and it undoubtedly had that desired effect: there was no lack of men for Algeria during the ensuing quarter century. It is a remarkable letter, very much unlike any of Hilarion's letters to Moreau. It is stylish, almost contrived, yet winning in its exuberance and vivid details. It is a work of art in itself. He must have labored long over it even though it seems written in a burst of adrenaline. Of all the Algerian letters written in the early years, only Father Haudebourg's could rival this Hilarion letter for energy.

Hilarion was a careful administrator, working as he had to between Moreau's expectations and the expectations of the local inspectors in Algeria. He was apparently successful as he notes of one visit in August 1846:

> On July 30, Count Salvandy, the Minister of Public Instruction, visited our classroom. He made me interrogate the students on grammar, arithmetic, and geography, made me dictate a participial phrase and he dictated another one. He looked at the writing notebooks and then some linear drawings. He was agreeably surprised to find primary instruction so advanced. He ended with praise for the students and gave me more than I expected, without a doubt. Getting on his horse, he said to me: "Please tell those two soldiers' children who recited perfectly that they'll be mentioned when I get back to Paris."[32]

The inspector came just two weeks before the end of the school year. Students and teachers got the month of September off, and the Brothers used the time not only to recuperate but also to have their annual retreat. In 1846 that retreat was planned to take place at the Trappist monastery which the men had visited on their first arriving in Algeria.

Hilarion, as generous as he could be, was not perfect, as witnessed by Brother Basil who, in writing from Bône to Moreau, said this about his Algerian superior:

> He's a clumsy oaf who thinks everything ought to go his way. Thus last year when I dared make comments about our trip that he didn't want to grant, I was treated like a beast and imbecile. However, he saw that afterwards all the noise he had made came to nothing. I count all that as nothing, my Reverend Father, and it's not for me to moan, but I'm saying

it anyway. It's only to show that these clumsy oafs don't get the job done any more than others do.[33]

How much of this appraisal is born of frustration near the end of a school year and how much is valid insight is hard to tell, but clearly Hilarion did raise some hackles, not unlike Moreau himself, who was able to alienate confreres even when he had the best of intentions. What Basil's rant tells us about Hilarion is probably not as valuable as what it tells us about Basil.

Meanwhile, Algeria was getting to enjoy a new bishop. Dupuch, who had watched in dismay as Holy Cross had withdrawn in 1842, retired to the Trappist monastery and was replaced by Pavy, a man who visited the Brothers' school, liked what he saw, and got on amazingly well with the Holy Cross men.[34] Their acceptance by another cleric, however, was less than cordial: he tore into Brother Basil over the matter of the cook-Brothers, whom, he thought could be used to share the teaching load. When Basil objected that Moreau had forbid such a move, the priest ridiculed him.[35]

In May of 1847, Hilarion got one of his requests: another Brother for Oran. Unfortunately this new man, Brother Cyprian Ménage, died of typhoid within four months of his arrival and was buried in Oran, leaving Hilarion with 145 students to teach alone and with just Brother Marie-Florentin Verité as cook in the house. Hilarion missed Cyprian and narrated to Brother Zachary a little trip the three Oran Brothers had taken nine months earlier. The details are precious:

> We sat there, then, opening up our little provisions. We mimicked a feast. We had scarcely begun our frugal meal when a crowd of large and small Bedouins, seeing us from their tent and curious to meet us, came down from their mountain with the agility so natural to them and with wild cries one to another as when there is something evil in their tribe. The most brave came forward toward us so the most timid could examine us 15 feet away. Since the reception of the first ones was friendly, the others saw that, and at a signal I didn't understand, they approached and formed a group

sitting oriental style around us. We offered them some of our provisions. They tasted everything, assuring themselves that there was not a bit of pork in it. They tasted everything but our wine, and do you know why the Arab does not drink wine? Their prophet forbade it because it stays 40 days in the belly. Since I wished them to have a good time, I didn't insist on it for fear of causing them terrible indigestion. However, I'll tell you that not all are so scrupulous because I've seen more than one at Oran in the grapevines of the Lord.

We were already rather chummy. Only one small black didn't dare approach us. He sat some feet from us. I had noted it and I wanted him also at the feast. I went toward him, but he ran as fast as he could to the mountains. I kept him in view so he wouldn't get away. I got up to him quickly and filled the hood of his burnous with sugar, almonds, and dried grapes. I made him get over his savage shyness, and I led him back to the interesting group. After the meal, I unwrapped a packet of dried coffee. For the finale, joy radiated on the Bedouin faces. Understand, if wine is our favorite drink, among the Arabs it's coffee, nothing but coffee, always coffee. I arranged three stones to set the saucepan on. Some went to look for wood. The others took care of the rest. I had nothing to do but to watch and laugh heartily at their procedures and to wait patiently for the first boiling of the refreshing liquid that I did not have to taste. Everything disappeared so promptly that I didn't notice the saucepan had been emptied by avid drinkers and that a second had met the same fate. I hadn't brought drinking glasses, and I was not so naïve as to lend them my brass cup that Father Drouelle gave me when I first left. Each drank as he could. The second saucepan being ready, those who couldn't taste from the first one came forward and drank in the same way so it was necessary to boil a third one. I preferred to wash the saucepan and continue my patient role up to the end. Then it was time to leave, and we left our good friends seated oriental style around the fading fire. We passed to the other side of the stream and made our way to Oran, happy to have made some people happy.[36]

At the end of 1848, Hilarion wrote to Moreau in his standard mode as local director in Algeria. He gave a sad report on the tired Brothers in Bône. On a trip with Bishop Pavy, Hilarion also had a chance to drop in on his Philippeville Brothers and found them more dispirited than he had expected them to be, especially Marcel. Hearing that the former orphanage in Algiers had been sold and fearing that Brother Louis Marchand's bones would be lost, Hilarion got permission from the police to retrieve the remains. (Louis had drowned in 1841.) The gardener opened the grave:

> I found the skeleton dressed in a rather well preserved cassock, indicating the position yet that had been given to the body. I found a little leather medal with the effigy of St. Louis Gonzaga, a piece of purple ribbon, and Brother's profession crucifix, everything well preserved. Before leaving Algiers I filled out a ceremonial form that I had Father Brouot and Brother Simon sign, both present at this ceremony. We today finished as much as we could of our project of translating the remains of this poor Brother to Sainte-Croix, saving them from inevitable loss and keeping them in our house until we can transfer them to the Community cemetery.[37]

Hilarion ends the letter with a fond wish to do what he could to be useful to Father Moreau. It is the last letter he wrote to his religious superior, and we can sense in it that Hilarion is tired. The two teaching Brothers at Oran have 155 students, some of whom pay tuition and some of whom have their tuition paid by the city (if the children procure a certificate of indigence).

We have but one more letter by Hilarion, and it is a difficult letter indeed. On October 28, 1848, Hilarion at Oran, Louis Gonzaga at Philippeville, and Basil at Bône sent a letter to Bishop Bouvier of Le Mans. It is a letter highly critical of Father Moreau, enumerating nine areas of concern. First of all, as the French motherhouse had accepted more and more non-teaching recruits for the Brothers, there is a fear that the Brothers will become "servant Brothers" to the Holy Cross priests. Father Moreau, moreover, seems to be trying to scare the Brothers with sermons stressing the secrecy of chapters. Brothers are being required to choose priests as superiors and master of novices, and Father Moreau is becoming a despot in his authoritarian manner of government. The rules keep changing, and nobody seems to know which rules are in effect. The anarchy in the Community is causing pastors to by-pass Holy Cross when they are looking for new teachers for parish schools. These are the last words we have from Hilarion, and we have no way of knowing if he were the primary instigator behind the letter or not. The sentiments do not sound at all like his, and his is not the first signature on the letter so it may very well have been the creation of Louis Gonzaga who signed it first. It sounds like Louis. Either way, Hilarion apparently endorsed its sentiments. Being at odds with the motherhouse is not the nicest way for history to take its leave of the wonderful Brother Hilarion Ferton.

Hilarion died of cholera at Oran a year later on October 15, 1849. He was 32 years old. The previous June Father Moreau had addressed the matter of cholera, which was ravaging France:

> We know not whence or how it came, where it is going, or how it strikes. It deceives the most watchful by the whimsical uncertainties of its progress and its surprising power for destruction. We know not whether it is in the air, whether it comes from the earth or from water, whether it rides on the wings of the wind, or whether it finds its germs already in our bodies. We know only that it strikes its victims mercilessly, regardless of sex, age, or rank.[38]

Moreau had offered, in fact, to the city of Le Mans one of the Community houses (La Charbonnière) to use to nurse the sick and had offered four nursing Brothers to help with the epidemic. Moreau was devastated by the death of Brother Hilarion:

I must recommend to your prayers the one whom I loved most among all the Brothers because of his untiring devotedness to the work of Holy Cross and his great aptitude for various obediences in the Society. This good Brother was to return to Notre-Dame de Sainte-Croix where he had already rendered great service, and whence he had carried away to his far-off mission the esteem and respect of all the priests, Brothers, and students who recognized his unusual talents. I know that he was looking forward to coming home. I was happy over it, too, and could already see myself turning over to him the task of teaching in the Novitiate and training him to handle the administrative details of the Mother House.[39]

For Moreau to refer to Hilarion as "the one whom I loved most among all the Brothers" is high praise indeed and not to be taken as mere hyperbole. Hilarion was really special, and Moreau had already informed him of the new assignment, which was to be effected in the following year.

Hilarion's final moments were related to Moreau in a letter from the Brothers at Oran:

I send you the sad and painful news of the death of good Brother Hilarion which took place on Monday, October 15, at nine-thirty in the evening. That day the good Brother had taught his classes as usual. He had for some time been suffering from dysentery, and the physician whom he consulted advised rest and certain medicines. Brother took the medicine, but no rest. During the morning of the very day which was to take him from us, he assured us he was better, although some bleeding still continued to give him trouble. But he went to the classroom and stayed there six hours.

Cholera was raging in the town and in the outskirts of Oran, but Brother Hilarion was not afraid. He used to say, "Even if I die, I will remain, faithful to the end, at the post God assigned me." His actions confirmed his words. At four-thirty he left his classroom and came to look for us. His face was all discolored and he could scarcely talk. "I am worn out," he said, "I can hardly breathe. I am going to lie down." We were obliged to undress him, and he went to bed. While doing so he said: "I do not know what is the matter with me, but it is not cholera." Then he added: "Please get the Superioress of the Trinitarian Sisters, for I have great confidence in her. Also ask the Superior of the Jesuits to come and hear my confession." I went and on my return found that Brother knew now what his sickness was. The symptoms of cholera were now only too evident. We gave him every attention demanded by his condition. But, alas, it was all in vain! In four hours cholera had done its work. He died in our arms, strengthened by the Sacraments of the Church, which he received with the most tender piety, while recommending himself to the prayers of the priests, Brothers, and students of Sainte-Croix.[40]

Hilarion's reassignment to France and his stewardship of the motherhouse would never come to be.

Sadly, we have no letters from Hilarion in his final year of life. Surely he wrote some, but they are not in the Holy Cross general archives. He was not a minor actor in Holy Cross history, and as we read his letters and come to know his story, we can appreciate him more and more. He was, after all, the man whom Moreau trusted to lead the Community back into Algeria, and he fulfilled his duties as director diligently. He was a hard working teacher, and he was loyal to the ideals of the nascent Holy Cross Community. A man of fervent good will, he gave his life without question in a foreign land that welcomed him, challenged him, and ultimately watched him die. He was a man of common sense, good humor, and unflagging energy. He never stopped working for the good of his mission. He truly was a singularly effective leader.

CHAPTER THREE

Leonard Guittoger: Prophet or Fool?

Brother Leonard Guittoger was born Pierre-François to Pierre Guittoger and Marie-Scholastique Poussin at Terrehaut[1] (Sarthe) on July 13, 1802, the year of Napoleon's much needed and much welcomed Concordat. Thus he arrived when France was settling down into a relative peace following the terrible dozen years of the Revolution and its bloody aftermath, the Reign of Terror. Robespierre, Danton, and Marat would still, of course, be names on everyone's lips, even in remote provinces, but the country by and large began to enjoy the calm of Napoleonic dictatorship, a calm that would last until the next upheaval, the petit revolution of 1830. In the Guittoger family, Leonard would have spent his early years getting a rudimentary education at the local elementary school and thereafter being employed on the family farm or in the family business, but we know nothing precise about his youth until, at the age of 23, he went to Ruillé-sur-Loir in the autumn of 1825 to enter Dujarié's Brothers of St. Joseph. By the time of his arrival, the little band of Brothers, begun only five years earlier, had swelled in number and was serving as teachers in a dozen towns around the diocese. Over one hundred men had come to Ruillé before Leonard[2] and over seventy had remained with the Community.[3]

At Ruillé in these early days, life was regulated by the talented Brother André Mottais who served as Dujarié's right-hand man and more or less ran the community on a day by day basis. André was not only novice master, but he was also supervisor for all the schools making him totally responsible for the academic development and expertise of all the Brothers. Since he was also responsible for the spiritual direction of all the men at Ruillé, one wonders what exactly Dujarié had to do with the little community, aside from his daily Mass, weekly confessions, and correspondence with priests regarding placement of his men in the parishes. Of course Dujarié, a saintly man himself, was never a vowed religious but remained throughout his life a guide to those within the Brothers of St. Joseph. Dujarié, with whimsical respect, would on occasion refer to André as "his Holiness."[4] Having had a formal novitiate and scholastic training with the Christian Brothers in Paris, André shouldered quite properly the daily shaping of the amorphous group at Ruillé into the vigorous community it would eventually become. He and Dujarié made a superb team, although he has been overlooked more often than not, or simply dismissed by Holy Cross historians as Dujarié's "secretary."[5] Like the other young men who came to Ruillé, Leonard would have followed a strict daily routine, rising at 5 AM, kneeling for meditation before Mass, then having breakfast, morning classes, prayers before the noon meal, followed by afternoon classes until 4:30, prayers and study before supper at 7 PM, recreation thereafter until prayers and retiring at 9 PM.[6] There were, however, no games allowed for recreation. The young men recreated themselves with pious conversation. One wonders how young bodies survived without exercise or play.

Three months after arriving at Ruillé, Leonard began his novitiate, or rather became a novice since the term "novitiate" implies a limited time (a year or two) in a semi-cloistered atmosphere. In Dujarié's community, however, the Brothers could remain "novices" for ten years or more, until they felt impelled to take a simple promise of obedience, a step some of them never took. We know, however, that Leonard renewed his vow of obedience on September 11, 1830. We have no record of when he first took the vow. One year later he signed the Pact of Fidelity, the touching document that, following the political turmoil of 1830, the remnants of Dujarié's band of Brothers created and signed as an endorsement of their wish to remain faithful to Dujarié's vision. Noting that they lacked the "hope of expanding or even continuing to exist for any length of time,"[7] nineteen Brothers signed the document. They wished to preserve what they had joined so faithfully, but should they have to disband, they wanted "to remain united in heart and affection, supporting and assisting one another." In the document Leonard is named "Second Director," right after the First Director André Mottais, and before both the Third Director Henri-Michel Taupin, and the Fourth Director Vincent-Ferier Pieau.[8] Thus at the age of 29, just six years after his arrival, Leonard had already risen to a position of prominence and authority, so evident were his talents and his promise as an administrator and leader. He had been, in fact, one of the four directors since 1826 and would remain so named until 1833 when he would be assigned to teach for one year at the school in Esclimont.

As an administrator, Leonard was entrusted with significant responsibility as can be deduced from his January 1833 letter to a priest concerning the ability of the Brothers to acquire property in their own names without legalizing the purchase under Dujarié's name alone. The problem on which Leonard was seeking the priest's advice was the matter of obligation that the community had or did not have to consult departed members on the matter of property disposal. Leonard argues, and we presume he is arguing as a voice of all four Brother Directors, that consultation with dispersed members would be difficult if not impossible in the matter of property the community enjoyed while those members were still legally members of the community. Leonard is trying to argue for an institution's ability to buy and sell property in its own name, not in the name of a specific individual, a matter of intense debate in France at the time. Moreover, five of the Brothers are dead, and consultation with their relatives would be pointless since the latter would have little or no knowledge of or interest in the affairs of the Ruillé Brothers. The addressee of this letter is not known, but he obviously was a canon lawyer since Leonard requests that the priest's decision on the matter be communicated to a notary for legal approbation. Leonard writes an intelligent letter in impeccable French. He writes with authority, deferential but authoritative nonetheless.

By October of 1834, Leonard has returned from Esclimont to Ruillé to be on site as the little community devolved from Dujarié's hands to Basil Moreau's. In 1835 he goes with Moreau to La Chesnaie where for three days the two consult with the founders of the Brothers of Ploërmel. It is curious that Moreau, as he moved to take over direction of the Brothers, did not take André Mottais with him. Instead he takes Leonard. One would think that as Moreau developed his ideas for rules and the direction of the Brothers of St. Joseph, he would keep at his right hand André, the man most responsible for moving the community away from Dujarié's direction to Moreau's care. It was André after all who wrote behind Dujarié's back to Bishop Bouvier about the aged founder's failing health and inability to oversee the group. It was André who for all intents and purposes ran the community, not Leonard. The selection of a companion for the visit to La Chesnaie does not, however, indicate Moreau's lack of trust in André. As of September 1, 1835, Leonard had been made Master of Novices in Le Mans, while André remained at Ruillé to direct the remnants of the community there and oversee the school. From day one Moreau had intended to move the Brothers from Ruillé to Le Mans, a metropolitan area much more conducive to the growth of a community than was rural Ruillé: the bishop resided in Le Mans as well as the government officials to whom Moreau needed access. Moreover, Moreau was an established and respected citizen in Le Mans. It made perfect sense for him to capitalize on his Le Mans contacts to further the growth of his new community of Brothers to whom he intended to attach his little band of auxiliary priests. Moreau would thus leave André at Ruillé to oversee the winding-down of the community headquarters there and where André could be close to his mentor and friend Dujarié.

Moreau eventually did away with the concept of the Four Directors in favor of a government run by a general council and a particular council. As both the Brothers and the priests started to grow rapidly in Le Mans, Moreau saw the need for a more complex system of running operations. The system of four Brother Directors may have worked in little Ruillé, but a more representative system was needed at Le Mans. In 1836 Leonard was third in rank on the Particular Council and held the title "Master of the House" at the new school in Le Mans. Early that year he was elected secretary of the General Council and named Director of the Brothers' Society. One year later, however, he left both councils and was sent to teach in Saint-Berthevin. In this same year he received his teaching diploma. On August 19, 1838, he took religious vows in Moreau's Holy Cross Community, but within a year he supposedly began his attempts to separate the Brothers from the auxiliary priests. It was a cause to which he would be linked, whether he liked it or not, for most of the rest of his life.

That Leonard enjoyed a good deal of respect from Moreau is obvious when one reads Leonard's letters to Moreau. In fact, Leonard had the same "frankness"[9] that Moreau valued as a trait in himself. Writing confidentially to Moreau, Leonard could raise sensitive issues about his own removal from office as well as the assignments of various other Brothers. Moreau had a tranquillizing effect on Leonard's insistence, possibly because he sensed in Leonard gifts valuable to Holy Cross. Thus Leonard honestly submits to Moreau's judgment: "In all these circumstances [just enumerated] and others I am grateful for, I have never acted against you for purely personal reasons, but only for reasons suitable for religion and the Congregation ... I have the highest confidence in you."[10] This is not to say, however, that Leonard did not confide in other Brothers his concerns about the direction the Community was taking under Moreau's leadership.

In a letter to Brother Hilarion dated June 17, 1849,[11] Leonard reveals his concerns about keeping the novitiate where it is: he wants it distanced from Le Mans for reasons unspecified other than for "incessant disturbances." Presumably he wanted novices kept away from community intrigue, or he may have wanted the Brothers' novitiate separated from the priests' novitiate. He asks Hilarion to communicate these views to Bother Louis Gonzaga but not to tell

Louis that they originated with Leonard: "I don't want to be an instigator—I want everyone to have freedom of initiative for the community's needs—I frankly do not want to be behind the others as they write or speak, do not want either to harm nor constrict what may come." Although Leonard here again uses the word "frankly," he is being disingenuous for not being willing to show openly his behind-the-scenes efforts to move action on the relocation of the novitiate: we can learn much about the man from what he may not think he is doing. Furthermore, Leonard is concerned that he is being watched because a long letter to Brother Pascal four months earlier has not elicited a reply from Pascal: "I suspect it has been intercepted," he tells Hilarion. Intercepted or not, a truly frank person would not let paranoia dissuade him from letting his own name be attached to his efforts and ideas. We do not know where Brother Pascal was stationed in the winter of 1849. If he were at Le Mans, the implication would be that Moreau was canvassing incoming mail, something totally out of character for Moreau. If Pascal were not in Le Mans, the implication is even more devastating—that Leonard's reputation for intrigue was such that others besides the Superior General were interested in preventing Leonard's correspondence from reaching its designated addressee. What we should not overlook, however, are two other eventualities: the letter may have been lost en route (a very slight possibility) or the letter may have been received by Pascal but not answered for whatever reason. The important point for Leonard, of course, is that he suspects it had been intercepted.

By the end of the summer in 1849, Leonard had become such a concern to Moreau that the founder wrote to Bishop Bouvier:

> Since Brother Leonard has upset a dozen Brothers by saying you approved of their society's being governed by a Brother rather than by a priest, I beg you to please tell me if this is really your thinking, because it is important for the future of this institute, especially when I will no longer be around, that no one sow seeds of division which would overwhelm it one day.[12]

It is significant in this letter that Moreau does not know if Leonard has actually communicated with the bishop. Moreau was not one to impede his subjects from having correspondence with higher authorities. Nor does Moreau ask Bouvier if Leonard has approached the bishop for an opinion. It would be foolish for Moreau to ask anything about a bishop's correspondence or involvement with religious matters. It was none of Moreau's business whom the bishop corresponded with or what the bishop said to correspondents. Moreau is very careful simply to ask Bouvier if he is indeed in favor of a Brother directing the Brothers' society. Moreau's letter to Bouvier proves how firmly Moreau believed in his system of governance for Holy Cross: after all, by this time he had spent fourteen years creating and refining the rules of governance, and even though his Constitutions were yet six years from papal approbation, they were solidly in place in a Community thriving on three continents.

One month after Moreau's letter to Bouvier, Leonard himself writes from St. Berthevin to the bishop requesting advice on letters that Leonard has received from various Brothers. He wants to know if he can simply summarize the contents of the letters for Moreau instead of turning over the letters themselves. He is most intent on preserving the anonymity of the Brothers who have written to him presumably in confidence on sensitive matters, possibly the matter of the novitiate location. There is no indication that the letters may have concerned the matter of a Brother director for the Brothers' society, but since the matter was probably hot at the time, we might presume that the Brother director matter was indeed touched upon in the letters in question. As harmless as a separate Brother director may seem to us today, it was probably perceived as the first step, a very important step, on the way to separation of the two societies. Moreau undoubtedly would have seen it in that light.

In May of 1853 Leonard writes again to Bouvier. It is getting close to Bouvier's death (1854) and the approbation of the Holy Cross Constitutions (1857), both events having significant impact on the firming up of governance within Holy Cross. Leonard, in fact, remarks in his first paragraph on the movement in Rome towards approbation. Eighteen Brothers and Father Chappé have met at Bouère to discuss confidentially what they might say to Bouvier. Leonard says he could have summarized the meeting to the Apostolic Nuncio but has not for two reasons: the nuncio has recently been changed, and secondly Leonard has great confidence in Bouvier. The telling paragraph follows:

> I told Father Moreau confidentially eighteen months ago when he thought about sending me to Rome that in this case, if I were admitted to an audience with the pope or with some Roman prelate, there would be some question about our society—I would speak in all frankness about our congregational weaknesses and thus the necessity to prolong the [Constitutional] experiments. Good grief! He was offended at my frankness and divulged my confidences—to my great surprise.[13]

The significance of this paragraph cannot be underrated. First of all, we learn that Leonard was still held in such high regard that Moreau actually considered using him in Rome as advocate for the approbation of the Constitutions—at least according to Leonard, and we have no reason to doubt his veracity since he is, after all, telling such to the bishop who could easily confirm the information with Moreau. Secondly, we are confronted with something we rarely see in Moreau—a show of pique, an abrupt loss of face, and most importantly a misreading of one of his closest and most talented Brothers. Moreau would never have suggested sending Leonard to Rome if he were not sure that Leonard was of his mind on the importance of getting the Constitutions approved as soon as possible. After all, such approbation would lend not only dignity to the Community but also a kind of permanence that would attract vocations and reassure prelates and pastors that Holy Cross was viable and worthy of trust. But the most significant insight we can take away from this letter is a softening of our century old evaluation of Bouvier in regard to the Holy Cross Constitutions. We have always believed that Bouvier withheld his approval of the document (a politic if not necessary step before they could be passed by Rome) because of some nastiness that existed between the bishop and Moreau, his former assistant at St. Vincent's Seminary, some nastiness that could never be resolved: Bouvier gave excuses for not forwarding the document (e.g., he had misplaced it, he needed another copy). But in reality his motive may very well have been a valid concern that the document was flawed because a number of Brothers were dissatisfied with the matter of the Brother director. Bouvier would have seen no point in approving a code of governance that might one day explode in Rome's face—as indeed it would a century later in 1945.

It is good to soften our appreciation of former nemeses, and just as Bouvier has alternately endeared himself to or distanced himself from various historians as a Gallican bishop, times change and attitudes toward Rome change. So too in Holy Cross appreciation of Bishop Bouvier should tilt to favorable where it might once have been negative. Bouvier may very well have had the welfare of the Brothers very much in mind as he failed to pass on the Holy Cross Constitutions (right up to his death). After all, he must have had immense respect for men like Leonard and André Mottais. Even though André was more in the confidence of Bouvier's predecessor (Carron) as André helped engineer the transition of the Josephites from Dujarié to Moreau, Bouvier would have known, as rector of the seminary, all of the good work that André was doing in the diocese, at least second hand from Moreau, in the years 1830-1833 when the Ruillé community was falling apart. Then when the novitiate was transferred to Le Mans under Leonard's direction, in the second year of Bouvier's tenure as bishop, Bouvier would have knowledge of Leonard as well as of Vincent Pieau and others. Bouvier was, after all, bishop of all his people, not just his priests. So when one of his prime religious expressed doubt to him in letters about the need to reconsider the matter of a Brother director, Bouvier would have listened, not to block the heady success of his previous assistant Moreau, but simply out of a valid concern that Holy Cross Brothers be afforded justice as they saw it.

After Bouvier's death on December 29, 1854, it was not long before his successor Jean Jacques Nanquette became involved in the matter of Brother Leonard. By the summer following Bouvier's death, Victor Drouelle, the first Holy Cross Procurator General, wrote to the Sacred Congregation requesting that the original character of the Congregation uniting priests and Brothers be preserved as a distinct characteristic of Moreau's vision. Drouelle grounds his argument in a little known fact: Father Dujarié had actually attracted three or four auxiliary priests to his little community at Ruillé, and one of them was still living at Holy Cross in Le Mans.[14] So intent was Moreau on saving the Josephites that he had "radically" reformed Dujarié's group with the result that "within a very few years few of the first Brothers were to be found."[15] Drouelle does not refine "few," but a solid core of the early Brothers actually did remain after the transfer to Moreau, including three of the four Brother directors. Drouelle asserts to Rome that the Brothers benefit most materially from the linkage to Holy Cross priests because if the two societies were separated eight-tenths of the Community property would be held by the priests. Presumably the buildings in Le Mans were the bulk of this "eight-tenths" because the schools that the Brothers ran in various little towns were parish owned.

Father Drouelle's sentiments in Rome were undoubtedly known to Leonard even though Drouelle was living far from Le Mans. In any case, by December of that year Leonard was formally warned of his dangerous attitudes:

> His Reverence [Moreau] expresses the strongest discontent with the conduct of Brother Leonard who, as proven in one of his own letters, persists in a bad spirit; and in particular by not stopping his correspondence with other Brothers, in spite of his being forbidden by his Reverence, showing sentiments contrary to the union of the societies forming the Congregation, vowing to have sent to the bishop copies of letters unfavorable to the establishment; having notoriously encouraged his confreres (in a letter to Brother Zachary) to

govern themselves ... as a result of these grievances, which his Reverence declares authorized [by Leonard], he [Moreau] commands this Brother not to communicate in the future with anyone, either in writing or vocally, under pain of removal from the Congregation.[16]

Thus Leonard has been put on notice officially that he is treading on dangerous and seditious grounds. The warning, apparently, was not enough to keep Leonard from pursuing his conscience. The next month from Vendôme he writes to Bishop Nanquette, and two Brothers sign the letter: one Brother, Leonard explains, has been with the Josephites for thirty years, the other for twenty. Leonard, having been with the group since 1825, would be the former, and the latter is Narcissus, who entered Holy Cross in 1835.[17] Noting that both men consider their Community under the bishop's authority, Leonard wants to bring several matters to Nanquette's attention. Leonard has already consulted several priests in the diocese. His discontent, apparently, was no secret. In sketching for Nanquette the early history of the Josephites, Leonard says that two Brothers, one now in America (this would be Vincent Pieau) and the other dead (probably André Mottais[18]) wanted to move the headquarters from Ruillé to Le Mans because there was no real formation program in place and not even a set of rules to follow. Leonard makes no mention of Moreau's hand in the move.[19] This is an odd omission since history has always understood the Josephites were transferred to Le Mans at Moreau's insistence. It was, in fact, one of his conditions for assuming direction of the group. This is not, apparently, Leonard's recollection: Moreau becomes a bystander to the saving of Dujarié's religious group. Leonard is anxious to share with Nanquette a summary of letters written seven years ago by six Brothers but cannot show the bishop the originals because Moreau has destroyed them. The gist of their complaints is that the new rules are a hodge-podge of prescriptions, many of which go unfollowed. Thus the community is at the edge of a "menacing abyss" from which only the bishop can save them. There is no mention in this letter of separating the two societies. It may very well be that Leonard, under threat of dismissal for any discussion of that question, has chosen to try a different tactic with the bishop, hoping possibly that once the ordinary got involved with the question of rules, the matter of separation could surface naturally. Perhaps. But one would never know from this letter that Leonard is at the heart of the separatist movement. He never mentions it here as a desired goal.

Two weeks later Leonard again writes to Nanquette, this time without Narcissus as a co-signer. The letter is sensitive as it contains gossip that Leonard passes along purportedly from Father Chappé and another unnamed priest (whose name Leonard promises to give the bishop if the bishop thinks it necessary). The latter informant supposedly said to Cardinal Barnabo: "What good is founding a group of priests when there are already so many such groups? And why found a group of Sisters when they are springing up all over and the group Dujarié founded is prospering?"[20] Leonard clearly thinks he has the good will of the bishop. But such wishful thinking gets Leonard nowhere. It was not likely that Nanquette would keep such discontent secret from Moreau, a man close at the bishop's hand in Le Mans. Nanquette did not have the strong hand Bouvier had, nor did he have any reason to trust a religious complaining about a superior. Nanquette was a peacemaker[21] and would have let any community organized under his predecessor manage its own internal dissent. Moreau was, after all, well known around the diocese as a successful administrator, spiritual advisor, and founder of several religious communities. No matter how many years Leonard had in religious life before Moreau, the Brother would never have the cachet of the priest-founder.

More telling than any correspondence with a bishop is Narcissus' letter to Leonard dated 1856 (tentatively so dated on the basis of its contents). Very rarely does correspondence between Holy Cross Brothers survive the early years. Most of their correspondence to superiors was, of course, archived but letters between themselves were generally read and discarded. Narcissus's letter to Leonard bears citing in full:

It seems that the good priests do not like Brother Edward.[22] They want a priest superior for the Brothers' novitiate, the goal of these good priests being to let disintegrate all the little establishments the Brothers have, keeping only the strong establishments, and having priests as superiors. This would be for them a good way to annihilate the Brothers' authority: most of the Brothers would have consented without thinking they were destroying themselves. Father Dujarié's goal was to form teachers for the countryside. If we never forsake that goal, the Brothers will flourish. I am only a poor, ignorant person, but I have always foreseen that things would happen as they are today. You are the only one who has shown courage and steadfastness.[23]

Narcissus is not the most intelligent of letter writers (he pretty much ignores punctuation), but he does voice his passionate concern with appropriate intensity. It was probably to Narcissus's bad fortune that Leonard did not destroy this letter as it eventually found its way to the archives suggesting that Moreau did get it, probably as a result of Leonard's determination to prove that Leonard was not alone in his concern for the direction that authority was taking in the Community under Moreau.

The archived letters of 1855 and 1856 end one chapter in the life of Brother Leonard. Although he continued to write, letters in the following decade are business letters. We can presume, therefore, that somehow Moreau came to grips with Leonard and was able to convince him that the major superiorships would best remain in the hands of Holy Cross priests. At any rate, Leonard did not leave Holy Cross and was not dismissed. But all fire was not extinguished in the breast of Brother Leonard. By the summer of 1866 Father Moreau was replaced as superior general and Leonard would soon have a new nemesis to face.

Edward Sorin was elected Superior General of the Congregation on July 15, 1868, in a chapter which mercifully included the Father Founder, who had been refused attendance at the 1866 General

Chapter where he was denounced (without benefit of formal hearing) for the financial woes of Holy Cross and where Pierre Dufal was elected Superior General. Dufal lasted fewer than two years before he realized he could not shoulder the crises of the Congregation, including the infighting among its members, but his resignation, he should have realized, only added another crisis to the pile. While the Congregation wrestled with its problems in the spring of 1868, Brother Leonard began again his efforts to save the Brothers. Unwilling to let the Dufal dust settle, he may have seen the time as opportune to make a move calculated to revert the Brothers to their structure as envisioned by Jacques Dujarié. By May of 1868 the General Council became aware of machinations Leonard had begun at Easter time. The minutes of the May 8, 1868, General Council meeting indicate that the matter of Brother Leonard needed serious and quick attention:

> Reading is given of Brother Leonard's letter dated April 29 in which he pretends that he and those who signed a piece addressed to the Eminent Prefect of Propaganda [Cardinal Barnabo] did not ask formally for the separation of the two Societies because, he says, "we recognize that we can't nor ought to ask Rome to demolish what it built in 1857, otherwise it would be audaciously foolhardy on our part." But it is not less true that the goal of this step and the sole interpretation to which it is susceptible is to bring about this separation, as is evident from the tenor of the letter and notably its citing the Christian Bothers at Nancy, those at St. Gabriel, St. Lawrence in Vendée, and the Little Brothers of Mary who originally were associated with priests and had gotten a separation to their advantage. This letter, drafted by Brother Leonard, steward at the Flers foundation, dated Holy Saturday, April 10, peddled around Mayenne during Easter week, where it gathered eighteen signatures, was brought to Father Chappé's attention by April 16, but only then through a copy. The author hedged from addressing it to His Eminence,

the Cardinal Prefect of Propaganda. After reading this copy, Father Chappé made some remarks to Brother Leonard who declared himself enlightened and promised not to send the Cardinal the letter in question, adding that Bishop Fillion [of Le Mans], who had been privy to it, had also counseled him not to send it saying that this letter would be in direct contradiction to what he [Fillion] had himself written to Rome about the Congregation.

In spite of Brother Leonard's promise, he has not stopped following his plan as is plain from the following passage in his April 29 letter: "Would you let me add, Reverend Father, that our request has twenty-four signatures and would have sixty more if we were permitted to present it to Propaganda as we asked." Despite long years and many retreats, this Brother followed up by sowing among his Brothers the deadly idea to separate the Brothers from the priests, and in 1855 had proposed the break between the two societies to such a point that the General Council after being made aware of it, found themselves obliged to threaten expulsion from the Congregation if he did not desist.

Today the General Council regrets bitterly seeing one of the oldest members of the Holy Cross family working so assiduously and secretly for the institution's destruction at a moment when the Congregation is passing through a crisis which asks urgently for the most heroic and most selfless devotion from its family members in order to save it. The Council senses so vividly the danger of steps similar to Brother Leonard's, and those of his followers, that the Council believes it has to make known to the said Brother the Council's decision dated December 19, 1855, at the same time that the decision reached by the Council, which neither the old age nor the remembrance of a long devoted life can swerve from a just punishment of he who makes a criminal attempt at the life of the Congregation, the saving of which has to be the goal of all its members during this crisis through which we are passing.

Father [Pierre] Chappé

Father Dillion

Brother Gregory [Henry Leroy]

Brother Bernard [Adolphe-Jean Legras][24]

Although the council does not indicate what exactly it would do to punish Leonard, they are unanimous in their will that he stop his campaign as they perceived it. Father Moreau's vision for Holy Cross remained for the majority of its members the desired structure of their religious institute, and since at the time there were over five hundred priests, Brothers, and sisters serving in ninety-three houses in three different countries,[25] one can assume that the separatists were a minority: only eighteen signatures appear on Leonard's circulating document.

It is too easy to fault Leonard at this juncture in Holy Cross if we simply condemn him for taking advantage of chaos in the Community in order to further his agenda. After all, he was witnessing Moreau's public disgrace at the hands of men far less talented or saintly than the Father Founder. We have no indication that Leonard sided with Moreau's opponents, and given the Founder's care for Leonard, we can presume that Leonard acted in 1868 not to further distress Moreau, but simply to act on what he saw as the imminent demise of Holy Cross due to internal factions. To salvage the originating vision of Jacques Dujarié and the fundamental work of Brother André Mottais, Leonard may have had to pursue "separation" in order to divide the Brothers from rancorous priests who were chaffing under Moreau's reprimands for what Cleary has identified as "administrative irresponsibility."[26] As much is said in a letter dated June, 1868, sent from the Josephite capitulants to Dufal just as the General Chapter convened in Rome: "Brothers Leonard and John-Baptist here present, signers of the petition [sent to Barnabo], have declared they have no other goal than to insure the existence of the Brothers' Society in case the Congregation dissolves."[27] The capitulants are concerned that Brother directors of houses have written to Brother Gregory, a member of the General Council, expressing their wish to keep the Community united. But the Brother capitulants acknowledge that the circular letter informing the Community of Dufal's resignation threw everyone into a panic as far as the future of the Congregation was concerned. Leonard and John-Baptist have both declared that their petition to Barnabo was not meant to separate the two societies. The Brother capitulants, however, are concerned that the "germs" of division are fermenting not just among many of the Brothers but also among the priests. After listening to the dissatisfied, the Brother capitulants list the causes they have identified for the unrest. First of all, some of the priests consider themselves superior to the Brothers. Secondly, some priests have little regard for the Brothers. Thirdly, some priests have not shown good example to the Brothers in matters of poverty and obedience. Fourthly, some priests have attracted gifted recruits away from the Brothers. Fifthly, some priests have made excessive demands on Brothers. Sixthly, there is a certain antipathy evident among some priests for the manual-labor Brothers. In order to address the growing problems, the Brother capitulants propose a novel solution: reunite the two novitiates into one novitiate under the direction of a Jesuit who would be assisted by a Holy Cross priest for the Salvatorist novices and by a Holy Cross Brother for the Josephite novices. Finally, the Brother capitulants suggest that the phrase "of two distinct societies" be erased in the Constitutions from the sentence "The Congregation of Holy Cross is composed of two distinct societies." The Brothers do not suggest replacement wording for the sentence.

It is easy to read in this letter the hand of Brother Leonard or at least his spirit at work. Although the letter is not signed (at least not in the typescript that remains for us) and purports to be written in the name of the Brother capitulants, near the end of the document the phrase "je puis ainsi parler" clearly indicates a single author. If that author were Brother Leonard, we have to conclude that his threats of separation, if there actually were any, were used to get the priests and Brothers to recognize the serious problems that were arising, and are bound to arise, in an organization that defines itself on the basis of cleric and lay.

The amazing document generated by Brother Leonard and dated June 8, 1868, was addressed to Cardinal Barnabo in Rome prior to the opening of the General Chapter summoned to replace Bishop Dufal as Superior General of Holy Cross. The dating of the document is actually the dating of a copy made by Bishop Dufal, probably for use at the General Chapter. In order to accumulate the number of signatures it did accumulate, the letter would have to date back to at least May or even April, that is, soon after the resignation of Dufal had sent the Community into a tailspin. Dufal himself attributes it to Easter week. The document originated at Flers where it was signed by three men: Brothers John-Baptist, Leonard, and Leontien. From there it went to Oisseau where it was signed by Brothers Macaire, Ariste, Elisée, Eulade, Moses, Germain, and Raphael. At Bouère, Brother Francis Xavier signed it. At Gennes, Brother Zachary. At Ernée, Brother Valery. At Bourgneuf, Brothers Sixtus and Basilide. At Anjou, Brothers Adolphe, Frederick, Sosthènes, Julian, and Vincent de Paul. At Rosnes, Brothers Octavius, Claude, Ives, and Matthew. After establishing the credentials of the signers, some of whom, they declare, have been with the Brothers for thirty-five and forty-two years, the writers get to the heart of their grievance: the Holy Cross priests are "suffocating" the Brothers, but a problem with separating from the priests, they aver, would be the matter of debt liquidation. Finally Leonard (and John-Baptist and Leontian) are mortally afraid that the demotion of two Superiors General (Moreau and Dufal) within six years is going to demoralize the Congregation into extinction. There is no overt request to Barnabo for separation of the two societies, but obviously the Brothers are less concerned about the future welfare of the priests than they are about the future of the Brothers. They cite, after all, several examples of Brothers' communities who have thrived without connection to priests. But that said, there is no rabid posturing over division of the two societies, only the wish, as the letter concludes, that the signers "can sincerely continue the association of the Brothers of St. Joseph if the Congregation of Holy Cross cannot subsist."

Rather than think of Brother Leonard as a separatist, that is, someone who wanted to fracture Holy Cross, one should think of him as someone who wanted to save the Josephites should the Congregation crumble. The documents of 1868 make this point clear. One cannot read, of course, Leonard's heart, but the documents come as close to his heart as anything we can get. Once Edward Sorin was established as leader of Holy Cross, however, Leonard was up against a more formidable superior than any he had met to date. He knew Sorin well, of course, but since the priest had been in America for twenty-seven years, Leonard's recollection of the young Edward Sorin would have had to have been radically altered after the priest's heady success first in Indiana and then at the Rome General Chapter of 1868. At the end of the year 1868 Leonard writes kindly to Sorin, but the issue of the Brothers' grievances is not dead. We do not hear of those grievances, however, from Leonard. It is Brother Leon, writing from Dampierre, who tells Sorin on December 31, 1868, that he (Leon) is convinced the Community is so sick it will collapse sooner or later.[28] Leon is convinced that Holy Cross, the sole French religious community formed of lay and cleric members, is inherently unviable. He rues the day that the Brothers of St. Joseph, without being consulted (his words), had their purpose changed. He claims, moreover, that such is the sentiment of the majority of Brothers, offering, however, no proof.

Leonard himself, in fact, was quite reconciled to the state of the Congregation in the years following the 1868 Chapter as he asserts to Sorin in a letter dated August 20, 1870: "I can affirm in good conscience that I have said to no one since our chapter in Rome that I desire and ask for the separation of the Brothers from the priests."[29] He goes on to say that it was the desertion of Holy Cross priests in 1867 and 1868 as well as Dufal's resignation that prompted him to petition Cardinal Barnabo to save the Brothers as a unit in case Holy Cross were to fold. We have no reason to doubt the sincerity of Leonard's remarks. That he would be working secretly behind the scenes while telling his Superior General the contrary would be unthinkable for a religious of Leonard's age and prestige. For example, in a strongly worded letter to Sorin the following May, Leonard regrets Sorin's extended absence from France and the fact that they have not heard from him in eight months. Various matters, some scandalous, need immediate attention and Leonard does not spare details, but the General Council, he avers, is nonfunctional: two of its members, in fact, cannot get out of Paris because of political unrest there. Moreover, Leonard does not like the rumor that Sorin wants to pull all Holy Cross members out of France and bring them to America: France, Leonard maintains, is the birthplace of the Congregation and needs its presence now more than ever.

Leonard may have overplayed his hand, and unfortunately the ax was soon to fall. In the minutes of the August 15, 1871, General Council meeting, drastic action was taken on the grand old man of Holy Cross:

> For many years Brother Leonard, scorning infractions of his vows, his oaths, his promises to repent, his repeated promises constantly broken, has worked to sow discord among his Brothers and has become the instrument of the devil, regarding the Constitutions, in order to trap them in a kind of coalition having for its purpose the separation of what God has united by the authority of his Vicar on earth. Nothing would correct him, neither multiple public humiliations nor threats from superiors, nor his protests to Rome during the Chapter, especially to Cardinal Barnabo; his vows today and his new protests not assuring the administration nor sufficiently repairing the scandal given, the General Council, after reading the last deliberation of the Provincial Chapter, decides:
> 1) that Brother Leonard, so often relapsed from amending, no longer merits the Congregation's confidence
> 2) that he will be deprived of all honor and any voice in the chapter

3) that he will be publicly stripped of his professed insignia, that is the statue of St. Joseph and the blessed cord

4) that he will always be placed after the last professed person

5) that he can correspond with no member of the Congregation, except his superiors, until he has given sufficient proof of conversion

6) that he will accept the obedience to be given to him, or better yet, if he wishes, he will receive permission to leave the Congregation.[30]

These are unbelievably harsh pronouncements on the head of one of the oldest members of Holy Cross. Leonard, after all, entered the Brothers of St. Joseph in 1825, just five years after its foundation, and he had risen to the highest positions possible for a Brother in Moreau's Community. But this was no longer Moreau's Community. It was Sorin's, and the harsh hand of Sorin is evident in Leonard's public fall from grace.

What had happened to the cordial sentiments that had been proffered by Leonard to Sorin since 1868? Were they all a façade under which hid a snake ready to strike? The facts do not support such a conclusion. Leonard was no doubt as shocked by the Council's decrees as we are today. Moreau himself commiserated in January, 1872, that Leonard had not been afforded due process.[31] What seems to emerge from the Council minutes is a picture of a hasty trial and judgment meted under the hand of Sorin, who was present at the meeting. Sorin, divided between his first love (Indiana) and his job as Superior General, had adopted a new homeland and had even, according to rumor, thought about closing down all Holy Cross operations in France. Leonard represented to him the strongest of the old, entrenched French guard. To get him out of the way would afford Sorin greater leverage for his autocratic methods, which worked handily in the Indiana frontier on his fiefdom but would not wash without draconian displays of power in France. Who would confront Sorin when so many considered him the only man capable of saving the Community during its crisis? There is no paper trail of any machinations sown by Leonard to pull the Brothers away from the priests. Sorin and his puppet council were probably acting on paranoia and rumors. Their actions were unjust and, quite probably, uncanonical (for lack of due process). In the words of Father Moreau: "Poor Leonard submitted when on retreat to treatment he did not merit, and which he ought to report to Bishop Simeoni: he [Leonard] is professed and has the right to a canonical trial before being so humiliated and degraded. Even the servants at the Précigné seminary spoke about it—that he was going to appeal to Bishop Fillion as a Superior and separation from the Salvatorists."[32] Moreau, of course, was a veteran pastor, and Sorin was an offshore administrator divided between continents. It did not help Leonard, of course, that at this time his confidential communications to Bishop Fillion were being betrayed to Sorin. Bishops, for one reason or another, feel it their prerogative to toss religious and their confidential correspondence back to major superiors whether as a way of lessening their own episcopal burden or as a way of letting religious communities handle their own affairs. Sometimes the very correspondence from the religious is sent to major superiors. Fillion, either out of a wish not to get involved or out of respect for Sorin's authority, tossed Leonard into the Frenchman-turned-American's claws. The result was calamitous for Leonard who, at age seventy and with fifty years of service to the Community, deserved better treatment than he got from Sorin.

Sorin, of course, was not new to public humiliation of subjects. His cavalier treatment of old Brother Vincent Pieau is narrated in Costin: Sorin told Vincent to drink wine in front of a visitor knowing that wine made Vincent ill, then stopped the old man just short of sipping and told him to leave the room. Sorin wanted to prove the old man's absolute sense of obedience.[33] It was a cruel gesture. Sorin's ways were imperious and contrast totally with Moreau's concern for his subjects' dignity, but Costin has written more kindly of Sorin that "like God, Father Sorin seems to have made a point of testing his favorites occasionally."[34] At St. Mary's Sorin publicly humiliated

Sister Heart of Jesus for traveling to Detroit to visit a doctor without permission—at a time when he himself was hobnobbing hither and yon at will:

> When we were all assembled … Father Superior present … Mother Superior brought Sister Mary [of the Heart of Jesus] into the chapel dressed in secular dress. She knelt on the floor, made her accusation, and asked pardon of us all. Reverend Father Superior said she deserved to be sent away, but as she begged to be kept, they would excuse her. The novices present, who love her, cried aloud to see her dressed like a Lady.[35]

Sorin the aristocrat tried to establish himself as an icon whereas Moreau the founder never tried to further himself at the expense of others. How many places did Moreau name after himself or his patron saint? How many did Sorin?

There is no evidence that Leonard attempted to defend himself after the 1871 summer retreat where he was demoted and disgraced. Unlike Moreau, who fought vigorously after the 1864 and 1866 chapters to salvage his good name, Leonard did nothing but accept his punishments. Does this indicate he was guilty? Not necessarily. Having seen the slanders leveled at the Father Founder year after year not only by Sorin, Champeau, and Drouelle, but also by the rank and file men of Holy Cross who deserted Moreau, Leonard may have been traumatized enough by Sorin to simply give up and try to live with whatever simple dignity he could muster for the remaining years of his life. He would still have sixteen years in Holy Cross before his death. Sorin, of course, was not content to leave Leonard anywhere near the center of the French community where the Brother could refresh his stained reputation. Sorin not only took away Leonard's religious insignia, he also took away his career. After decades of teaching, Leonard was sent as a cook to the boondocks where he was to prepare meals for a single Brother (a young one at that)[36] under, let us remember, the injunction to correspond with no one besides his superiors. Was Sorin so threatened by a Brother that he had to have the man isolated? Apparently so, and yet there is no evidence that Leonard ever intended to work to separate the Brothers from the priests—his goal was to make sure only that the Brothers would endure as a unit if the Congregation folded. His fault, if any, was a lack of concern for the fate of those priests who had joined Holy Cross in good faith and zeal.

Leonard's next extant letter is dated October 12, 1875. It is feast day greetings to Sorin sent from the Brothers at Soligny and the "penitential group" at La Grande Trappe: "May your august patron St. Edward, who undoubtedly enjoys heavenly rewards in proportion to earthly merit, be your powerful protector to fortify you in the virtues you practice and obtain for you grace to succeed in important works and in the good governance of your numerous children in Jesus Christ."[37] The letter is signed by Leonard and four others. Two of the signatures are illegible and one signature is followed by "J.S.C." (Josephite of Holy Cross). Leonard is living out his days in peace and without rancor. By 1876 the interdiction on correspondence has apparently been lifted as Leonard sends a short letter to Vincent Pieau thanking his American confrere for a recent letter. Leonard is quite sick. He praises the day of his baptism (July 14, 1802) and expresses happiness at recent events in the Congregation. He then turns to his own troubled past:

> I sincerely desire that whatever had been attributed to me as oppositional to the submission which I expressed at the 1868 Rome chapter may be forgotten. I forget and pardon the wrongs done by those who brought me the precious crosses that ensued. I wholeheartedly pardon and ask the same pardon for whatever, promising and assuring that no one will get either a spoken word or a written word from me about the past, every trace of which is erased according to the wish of the Superior General.[38]

These words of reconciliation and resignation come from a man on a sick bed, a man who has accepted his fate and does not nourish resentment. It takes an extraordinary character to step aside from positions of power and let others work as best they know how. And why was Leonard ordered to expunge any trace of his side of the story? But Leonard evidently found peace in his solitude and isolation with the Trappists in Normandy at the very monastery where Moreau, at the grotto across the lake, first conceived a plan for his new Congregation and where Moreau brought his little band of Salvatorists by foot for their first retreat.

A year and a half later Leonard writes to Brother Gregory (Henry) Leroy, in response to a request for remembrances of Jacques Dujarié. Leonard replies that he has but one handwritten letter by Dujarié, a circular from 1834, with lines intercalated by Brother André Mottais: Leonard cherishes it as a souvenir of the two deceased founders. Leonard's handwriting, for a man of seventy-five years is steady and quite beautiful. Was Leonard forgotten by his Community? No. In an anonymous history of the Brothers of St. Joseph, dated 1877 and filed with Leonard's papers in the Holy Cross General Archives, note is taken that Leonard was publicly humiliated for supposedly advocating in 1868 a separation of the Brothers and priests, but when Salvatorists advocated such a separation at the 1872 General Chapter in America, no one considered their actions criminal. The anonymous author adds that Cardinal Barnabo himself had said to a Brother capitulant in 1868: "This union is not wise—if the plan of the first founder had been followed, you would today have expanded all over the place." Priest-less communities of Brothers, the author notes, have thrived: the La Mennais Brothers have grown from 1200 to 1500, the St. Lawrence Brothers from 900 to 1000, the Marist Brothers from 2000 to 3000, while the Brothers of St. Joseph have only 150 men in France. Although one would be tempted to attribute this document to Leonard, enough evidence points to another hand.[39] What we must recognize is that a half dozen years after Leonard's demotion received opinion was still that Leonard did work to separate the Brothers from the priests. The archival material, of course, does not support that conclusion, but he apparently remained a hero to separatist Brothers.

The truth is we have precious little from Brother Leonard after his downfall: four letters in sixteen years. He lived a quiet life until his death on June 9, 1887, which was announced to Sorin in a letter dated four days later and written by the French provincial Father Hippolyte Lecointe, who writes from Angers but a short paragraph on the passing of the long-lived Leonard:

> The last news you receive from France tells you of the death of the good Brother Leonard. Almost at the moment when God called him to account for the 85 years given him, he warned me that soon I would have to answer for my own life and administration.[40]

We are given no details of his death at Meslay, the single consolation being that the provincial afforded him the sobriquet "good Brother," which is often more formulaic than thoughtful when applied to a Brother. We do not know what Sorin's response was to the news. We can only hope he repented the shameful treatment he had accorded one of the most important of the early Brothers of St. Joseph.

We are left with the question: was Leonard a prophet or a fool? Did his warnings about the growing inequalities of the two Holy Cross societies of men presage the griefs of 1945? Or was he simply a disgruntled reactionary? The answer, I think, is that he was a prophetic fool—for the sake of Christ. St. Paul could ask for no more.

CHAPTER FOUR

Vincent Pieau: Patriarch in America

Brother Vincent was born Jean Pieau on February 15, 1797, in Courbeveille, France. The town, located ten miles southwest of Laval in the district of Mayenne, is one of a number of small towns that contributed its young men to a resurgence of religious life after the atrocities of the French Revolution and its rampant anti-clericalism had died down. Though volatile sentiments against church workers had never been as strong in the Laval area as they were in Paris, there was enough hostility in the outlying districts forcing clergy to hide during the notorious Reign of Terror. One such clergyman, James Dujarié, had to take much of his seminary training on the sly and be ordained to his ministry in secret, hiding out on farms in the area around the town of Ruillé-sur-Loir, where he would eventually be named pastor and enjoy a long and fulfilling career. The river on which Ruillé sits is not the great Loire, notable for its grand chateaux, but rather the more humble Loir, which runs parallel to the famous river forty miles south. Ruillé itself would figure importantly in the life of Brother Vincent.

How the French Revolution affected the young boy named Jean Pieau we have no way of knowing. He was born near the waning of its worst violence so his own schooling was not nearly as troubled as that of Father Dujarié. He was orphaned early, and in 1822, at the age of 26, he traveled to Ruillé to join Dujarié's young band of Brothers, organized a little over two years earlier. The group, known as the Brothers of St. Joseph, was loosely organized, Dujarié himself having insufficient knowledge of formal religious life. The Brothers' acceptance of a religious garb has been captured in a painting by Brother Harold Ruplinger: three young men stand on a road adjacent to a wheat field with Dujarié's parish church in the distance, Dujarié handing a black soutane to one of the candidates, the other two already vesting. No church service, no vows—simplicity itself. The investiture took place on November 25, 1821. After the event, the young men went into Ruillé with Dujarié and settled into a modified monastic existence.[1]

Ruillé, thirty miles southwest of Le Mans is a gentle town, its most prominent structure today being the chapel of the Grand Providence, the motherhouse of the Sisters of Providence. In the 1820's the town contained the "Grand Saint-Joseph," a large home used for Dujarié's Brothers of Saint Joseph. Today this building is an apartment house. The only buildings left original from the Brothers' first years are the church and Dujarié's rectory, the latter incorporated into one of the side buildings now sitting on the front road thirty yards from Dujarié's church.

Jean Pieau, when he arrived in Ruillé, would not have lived at the Grand Saint-Joseph because it was not purchased until 1824. He would have lived in the rectory, sleeping in either the rat-infested attic with other Brothers, or in the laundry room, barn, or stable where young men had to bunk because of the numbers arriving to join the group. Dujarié housed twenty-five to thirty recruits in the early years. How spacious the Grand Saint-Joseph must eventually have seemed to the men—it had classrooms, a large refectory, and ample sleeping quarters. The property also had a garden, a pond, and a small brook.

There is something exciting about a new venture that cannot be repeated in later years, no matter how successful an institution becomes. Father Dujarié started his Brothers with one young man named Pierre Hureau, who responded to Dujarié's call in July of 1820. Pierre was twenty-five years old. One other young man, Louis Duchene, joined Pierre that summer in August. Louis was nineteen and a member of Dujarié's parish in Ruillé. He was, in fact, Dujarié's godson. Neither of these two men persevered in their religious vocation. Pierre left a year after he arrived and therefore would not have been at Ruillé when Jean Pieau arrived there in 1822. Louis did not leave the Brothers until 1825 and would thus have known Jean Pieau. Two other men came to Ruillé in the fall of 1820: André Mottais (aged twenty) and Etienne Gauffre (aged twenty-eight). Both persevered, the former destined to become extremely important in both the history of the Brothers of St. Joseph and its metamorphosis, the Brothers of Holy Cross.

The formation of the religious recruits in Ruillé was often cut short by the pressing calls from pastors for Brothers to come and run their little parish schools. Father Dujarié, kind to a fault, responded as quickly as he could to the pleas, and unfortunately many vocations were short-lived because the young Brothers so sent out, one by one or in pairs, were inadequately trained in academics and woefully unprepared for the challenges they would meet both professionally and spiritually in the schools.

When Jean Pieau joined the Brothers on October 9, 1822, the group numbered sixteen, including himself. Three of the four who joined in 1820 persevered, as did all six who joined in 1821 and six who joined in 1822 before Jean Pieau arrived. Few of them, of course, would have been on hand in the fall when Jean Pieau arrived since the school year would have begun already at the beginning of October. We do not know either when Vincent would have gone out on his first teaching assignment. He began his novitiate training on August 17, 1823, and he was awarded his teaching diploma on November 2 of the same year, so he may very well have begun teaching while he was still a novice. Religious rules were fluid at the time, and a young man was often called upon to fill a need. The Brothers of Saint Joseph took no vows of poverty, celibacy, and obedience. They made only a yearly "promise" of obedience to Jacques Dujarié. Thus without the canonical force of the evangelical counsels, it is a wonder that any members of the early group endured. During the next seven years, Vincent rose to a position of respect and authority among the Brothers. During the tumultuous days of the 1830 Revolution, he weathered with André and Dujarié the rocky economic times that threatened the existence of the frail community.

On September 1, 1831, the remarkable document that came to be known as "The Pact of Fidelity" was drawn up by the Ruillé Brothers, with the help of a young priest from Le Mans, Basil Moreau, to whom Dujarié was turning to more and more for assistance and advice. The "Pact of Fidelity" was an attempt to boost morale among the Brothers by emphasizing their need to remain faithful to their ideals. Vincent, as one of the four Brother-Directors, would have been instrumental in creating the document, which was signed by thirteen Brothers and one aspirant. The most poignant of the points in the "Pact" is number four, which stipulates the men would remain loyal to each other even if the group were disbanded.

During these years, after a decade of struggling for legal recognition of his little group of Brothers, Dujarié faced harassment from local officials over his ability to hold religious property in his own name. By careful maneuvering in October 1834, he ceded ownership of the Ruillé motherhouse to Brother Vincent and Brother Baptiste (Jean Verger). It is significant of the great faith that Dujarié had in Vincent that Vincent was chosen for this ruse, he and Baptiste being styled on the document "two men of confidence … who agreed to dedicate themselves to the teaching of youth," as if Vincent had not already been so dedicated for a dozen years and as if Dujarié himself were not devoted to the same apostolate. Significant of the regard in which he was held in those early years, the following was afforded Vincent in a letter to him from André Mottais: "I know only you are capable of giving authentic testimony of what has been done since our origin."[2]

In 1833 Dujarié considered having his Brothers pronounce two perpetual vows: obedience and stability. Neither vow would blanket poverty and chastity, disciplines which Dujarié felt his men were not yet strong enough to pledge. Those who wished to take the vows of obedience and stability could so petition only if they had worked already ten years in his Community. Thus Dujarié in his failing years was already considering vows as a way to keep his flock together. He was not alone in his worries. Brother André Mottais suggested in the late summer of 1834 that a meeting was needed in which Dujarié and three Brothers could discuss in detail with the bishop the financial and spiritual crises of the Brothers of St. Joseph. Brother Vincent was one of the three Brothers chosen for the task. At the time he was resident in Ruillé, in charge of the boarding school there. After this meeting, André wrote to the bishop again, suggesting that the Brothers be amalgamated into a society composed of three branches: Brothers, priests, and ordinary teachers. Vincent, as close as he was to André, was undoubtedly privy to André's vision.

André's concern for the wellbeing of the Community flowered into a letter tri-authored with Brother Vincent and Brother Leonard to Bishop Bouvier in April of 1835. They suggested that a set of rules they had drawn up (without Dujarié's help) be reviewed by the bishop. Brother Leonard himself wrote another letter to Basil Moreau (in June) apprizing him of continued problems and asking him to assume direction of the Brothers. Brother Vincent was probably privy to this letter. At the August retreat in 1835, held in Ruillé for the Brothers as usual, André, Vincent, Leonard, and Dujarié discussed with Moreau the details for the transferral of superiority. On the final day of the retreat (August 31), all the Brothers gathered in the chapel at the Grand Saint-Joseph and waited. Dujarié struggled to reach the altar to address the bishop, formally asking Bouvier to entrust the Brothers to Moreau's care. Brother Vincent must have been swept up in the emotion of the moment as he witnessed the man he had worked alongside for over a dozen years give up his role to a younger, more energetic priest. Within weeks the novitiate moved to Le Mans, but Vincent was left behind in Ruillé to continue running the boarding school at the Grand Saint-Joseph. The school dwindled to half a dozen students so by August 1836 the property was sold, and Vincent moved to Le Mans where he assumed direction of the new boarding school to be opened in November.

Vincent's position among the Brothers of Saint Joseph should be recognized for what it was: he is repeatedly named as one of the four "Brother Directors" resident at Ruillé, guiding the Community as Dujarié's health worsened. His living at Ruillé, while most of the Brothers were farmed out to pastors in small towns, indicated just how much Dujarié relied on his local presence. It was an earned respect that Vincent enjoyed throughout his religious life.

Of the fifteen men who entered the Brothers previous to Vincent, only five were professed when the group came under the care of Basil Moreau, a young Le Mans seminary professor. Moreau was bright and knew the right people. He was unfailingly honest and vitally interested in church work. Previous to Dujarié's request, Moreau had gathered a few young priests to join him in a small association that could supply priests for retreat work in the diocese of Le Mans. To these half dozen priests, Moreau linked the Brothers entrusted to him by Dujarié. Setting his headquarters in the Le Mans neighborhood known as Holy Cross (Sainte Croix), he thus created a religious organization that soon became known as the Brothers and priests from (of) Holy Cross. The Brothers continued to be styled "Josephites" and the priests "Salvatorists," but to the outside world they were the religious from Holy Cross. On March 1, 1837, the Brothers and priests accepted a document called the "Fundamental Pact," which prepared them for their eventual union as two societies in one Community. Papal approval came two years later—on March 12, 1838. Although the Brothers had been taking vows for years, none of Moreau's priests took religious vows until 1841. Thus the first five years of the new Community consisted of vowed religious Brothers and secular priests. Moreau himself took religious vows in 1840, but no other priest took religious vows until 1841.

Moreau brought to the Brothers a canonical regimentation that they had not had before. Himself familiar with monastic life, he was able to forge a Community that, like the Christian Brothers, blended monastic ideals of discipline with non-monastic apostolates, primarily teaching in French elementary and secondary schools. One of the first requests he made of the remnants of Dujarié's Brothers was that they profess religious vows, which Moreau felt were needed to give the group a stability and cohesiveness which they had lacked in Ruillé. The first man to profess in Le Mans was Brother André

Mottais. His commitment was made on August 25, 1836, with vows of poverty, celibacy, obedience, and stability. Bother Vincent made his (temporary) profession of vows one year later, on August 30, 1837. His final vow document (August 22, 1838) reads as follows:

> I, John Pieau, Brother Vincent, in the presence of Him who must judge the living and the dead, under the protection of Mary ever Virgin, of Saint Joseph and of my guardian angel, vow to God and promise to keep to death, poverty, obedience, and chastity, according to the rules of the Society of the Brothers of Saint Joseph and under the authority of our Reverend Father Rector [Moreau], requiring me, by vow, to persevere in my vocation and to fulfill all the tasks that it will please my legitimate superiors to assign me.[3]

There is no vow of stability in this formula. Some men took longer to profess: Etienne Gauffre (the fourth man to answer Dujarié's call, did not profess any vows until 1842, some twenty-two years after he had joined the Brothers.

From 1823 until 1841, Brother Vincent taught in Ruillé and in Le Mans, steadily building a reputation for being a highly effective educator, a reputation that stayed with him throughout his almost seventy years as a religious Brother. We can surmise that he was content with the move of headquarters from Ruillé to Le Mans and that he was elated at the Community's growth under the firm direction of Basil Moreau. Since the two men were almost the same age, Vincent two years older than Moreau, we can understand the warmth and respect the two shared for each other, evidenced on every page of the letters extant from Vincent to Moreau. Unfortunately we have no letters remaining from Moreau to Vincent.

One sad duty that Vincent was called upon to share was to watch at the bedside of the dying Dujarié, who had been brought from Ruillé to Le Mans by Moreau so that the old priest could live out his final years among the Brothers. As Dujarié lay dying on February 17, 1838, Moreau kept only three Brothers in the room: Vincent, André, and Antonin. They whispered encouragement to the dying man and witnessed his final breaths a little past noon. For Vincent the death would have meant the loss of his first superior, the man who saw in Vincent promising virtue and the talents of a valuable educator.

Because of his excellence as a teacher and his long, faithful relationship with the Brothers, Vincent was chosen by Moreau in 1841 to be one of seven missionaries sent to America. Touched by a plea from Celestine de la Hailandière, bishop of the Indiana Territory, for Brothers to serve in that diocese, Moreau assembled a group in the summer of 1841 and sent them off in the fall by steamship to begin Holy Cross work in the New World. The oldest of the group was Vincent, who, at forty-four, was the only one certified as a teacher. He was chosen because he could train the two novices sent with the group, and he could train new recruits in Indiana. Brother Joachim (age thirty-two) was a tailor, Edward Sorin (age twenty-eight) the chaplain-superior, Brother Lawrence (age twenty-six) a farmer, Brother Francis Xavier (age twenty-one) a carpenter, Brother Anselm (age sixteen) a novice, and Brother Gatian (age fifteen) also a novice. The two youngest were chosen for the mission because they showed promise of learning English quickly. Indeed both did learn the language within two years, and Gatian developed an especially fine sense of English vocabulary and style. With a lottery and private donations, Moreau was able to raise the money needed for the trip.

Although Brother Vincent was almost a generation older than Sorin, Vincent was not entrusted by Moreau with the primary leadership position for the group. That job was given to the chaplain. The young priest was talented, but his preeminence in the group of seven can today only be understood in the light of Moreau's concept of authority for the new Holy Cross Community. When Moreau was considering the offer from the Le Mans bishop to assume direction of the Brothers of St. Joseph, one of Moreau's stipulations was that his new group of auxiliary priests would be given the major superior roles. Thus Brother Vincent, with twenty years of religious communal living behind him, was entrusted to the care of a man with some three years experience living in religious life. That Vincent accepted such an arrangement is testament to his supreme sense of humility and Moreau's perception of leadership qualities in Sorin. Throughout his life Vincent never sought promotion or positions of authority, content to serve where he was needed, in whatever capacity he was asked to work. A master teacher, he was not above menial kitchen tasks. At St. Peter's in Indiana he did laundry and baked bread, which he pronounced "not bad" with his customary understatement in matters relating to his own talents. In the notes for the Notre Dame Council of Administration, an entry for 1844 shows that Brother Vincent is to "attend to sugar making." What he used as a base for sugar is not indicated.

Vincent's duties over the years were multiple. Another council entry for 1844 indicates he was to care for the sick "in the new infirmary." In other entries he is to teach writing and catechism. In 1846 he is both steward and cook. In 1847 he is to go by train with Brother Stephen to solicit money for Notre Dame. In the same year he is Master of Studies and "overseer" (probably a prefect over the students), Assistant Superior, and "Singer." His role as a singer is not outlined. He clearly was a factotum who could be used to fill any vacancy that arose at Notre Dame.

From Le Havre the seven set out on August 8 aboard the *Iowa*, along with five Sisters of the Sacred Heart, who were delighted to have the ministry of a chaplain available. All traveled steerage, even Sorin who declined a cabin offered to him. The sea in the English Channel proved rough, requiring eight days to maneuver through it. Everyone got seasick quickly, except Vincent, who took care of the others until he too fell ill. Once on the open sea, they all recovered and enjoyed a privilege given them by the Episcopalian captain: they were allowed to go above their steerage quarters to a little room on the cabin deck where they assembled for religious exercises. The room was also used for the baptism of a two-year old girl who was deathly ill. Her Protestant father gave in to the pleas of the Sisters to have the girl christened, an odd take on theology since the child was probably already baptized. She died two days later, and Sorin presided over her burial at sea, an event he narrates in his *Chronicles*.

On September 13 the *Iowa* pulled into New York harbor where Sorin kissed the ground. After staying in the city for three days with a family named Byerly, Brother Vincent and the others began their trek west with three hundred dollars Hailandière had left for them. The trip would take twenty-five days—almost as long as the Atlantic passage. From Albany to Buffalo they traveled via the Erie Canal, and in Buffalo Brother Vincent went with Sorin to see Niagara Falls, which they reached by train. From Buffalo to Toledo they traveled by steamboat. Eventually they reached Fort Wayne and, two days later, Logansport. Unfortunately as they passed by Terre Haute they were unable to stop to visit Mother Theodore Guerin and the Sisters of Providence from Ruillé. Finally on October 8 they arrived at Vincennes where the bishop offered them a choice of two locations for their headquarters. They opted for a one hundred and sixty acre farm called St. Peter's, twenty-seven miles due east of Vincennes. The property had a little church, two log cabins (one a kitchen, the other a school), and probably a single cabin for the six Brothers and a candidate (Charles Rother) they found waiting to join them. Sorin lived in a room off the church. The living quarters for the Brothers must have been poor indeed as Mother Guerin later wrote of Sisters she had once seen there, "Had I been there I should not have had the courage to allow them to pass the winter in such a house. I cannot conceive how the good Brothers could have lived there for a year."[4] Although the buildings have long since been destroyed, the bell from the little church remains in the keeping of the Midwest Province Brothers.

Immediately the bishop wanted Brother Vincent to stay in Vincennes to run the cathedral's elementary school. Vincent had been sent to America by Moreau for the express purpose of training recruits, and thus he was needed at St. Peter's, but Hailandière insisted so Vincent obeyed. His separation from the community at St. Peter's accounts, however, for one blessing: the rich trove of letters he wrote from Vincennes are our primary resource for understanding the character of this gracious and generous man in his early days on the frontier.

The first letter that remains from his early correspondence was sent to Mother Guerin a few months after the Holy Cross missionaries had arrived on their new continent. He thanks Mother Guerin for her gift of a carriage and two oxen, noting that the beasts are "very good natured:"

> We have to thank you, my dear Sister, for your carriage and the two fine oxen. They have worked well recently, and the Brother farmer [Brother Lawrence] has looked for a board carriage at Washington [Indiana] with which he can test their strength. What is better yet, they are very good-natured. For all of that we thank you and offer you our wishes for a New Year and a big share of our prayers, as feeble as they are, on condition that you give us a share of yours and those in your house.[5]

He points out that he had brought a package from Sister St. Bernard d'Arbentre for the Terre Haute Sisters and has already sent it on to Terre Haute.

With Brother Vincent in Vincennes was Brother Anselm, the second youngest of the group. They lived in the bishop's "palace." Vincent's bedroom was next to the chapel, an arrangement much to his liking. Since Brother Vincent was the only experienced teacher among the Holy Cross missionaries, St. Peter's School was, in his absence, run by Sorin and Brother Gatian, the fifteen year old boy who, though incredibly bright, was to be a thorn in Sorin's side over the coming years.

In Vincennes at the cathedral school, Brother Vincent would have been in daily contact with the bishop, a transplanted French aristocrat ill suited for life in the American wilderness. Imperious by nature and arrogant, Hailandière antagonized even his own diocesan priests (what few he had) to the point that they complained so effectively about the bishop's ways that Halandière was eventually removed and lived out long years on the family estate back in France where he continued to veto throughout his life every request made to Rome by the Sisters of Providence in Terre Haute for ecclesiastical approval of their constitutions. Although Brother Vincent never once complained about the bishop, we have plenty of evidence from the diligent young Brother Anselm that the bishop was less than gracious.

The little school at St. Peter's got underway, but soon the bishop was concerned that the school was too close to Vincennes where the Eudists already had a school. He therefore offered the Holy Cross men a large tract of land in the north of Indiana near South Bend, and the men jumped at the chance to get away from proximity to the bishop. When some of the missionaries from St. Peter's left in November 1842 to head north, Brother Vincent was left behind in Vincennes with Brother Anselm. Then in February 1843, when Brother Vincent was summoned to Notre Dame, seventeen year old Brother Anselm was left alone in Vincennes to run the bishop's school. The boy's health eventually degenerated under the tension, and after a brief period of recuperation at Notre Dame (where his heart remained), he was assigned by Sorin to run a school alone in Madison, Indiana, far from Notre Dame.

On the other hand we can imagine that Brother Vincent's ease with the bishop had something to do with both his patience and his maturity: at forty-four Vincent had seen enough of the world to know that some situations are best weathered by quiet acceptance of reality. The bishop too, no doubt, had more respect for a man near his own age than he had for a teenager like Anselm. We can imagine in hindsight what fireworks would have exploded if it had been Brother Gatian rather than Brother Anselm left behind in Vincennes. The volatile Gatian would never have suffered the harassment that Anselm endured. Calamitous sparks would have flown between Gatian and Hailandière, a scenario that may very well have helped Sorin decide to take the impetuous Gatian along with him on the first wave north to Notre Dame.

But before the venture to Notre Dame, while the Community still remained at St. Peter's, Brother Vincent wrote many letters that give us a good idea of his life on the frontier. In early March of 1842 he tells Sorin that he is happy at the prospect of traveling to St. Peter's to celebrate the feast of St. Joseph (March 19) with the Community there. It is a major feast for the Josephites and Vincent's happiness is appreciable. He has suggested to the bishop that he travel by carriage "like a priest" and the bishop has agreed, evidence of the amity that must have existed between the prelate and the teacher. But a week later in another letter to Sorin he announces sadly that the carriage plan has unraveled. He gives no reason why. We can guess the carriage was either broken (doubtful) or commandeered by the bishop (more likely), so Vincent writes, "God be praised I still have the legs of a fifteen year old."[6] He plans to walk the twenty-seven miles, leaving Vincennes at 7 AM on the day before the feast. (Brother Anselm would probably have walked with him.) Vincent adds that he has never before had so many children in one classroom: if they all showed up, he would have eighty, and every day there are new faces.

A month later Vincent writes a letter to Moreau in France, the first letter we have from Vincent to Moreau. It is a long letter written, of course, in French—Brother Vincent never learned English. He reports to Moreau that the novitiate at St. Peter's does not lack for recruits. His own school in Vincennes is a model of decorum: the townspeople are amazed that the children process two by two to school and to church, never fighting or swearing as they had before the two Brothers assumed control of the school. We learn in this letter of the stock that the early missionaries put in rewards for the children: mention is often made of little medals and crosses given to the students for proper recitation of their lessons. The children, of course, are not perfect yet, and Vincent regrets their lack of silence during class. They could also be rambunctious. When one boy throws a rock at another and the latter takes revenge on the following day, Vincent expels them both from school, over the protests of both the bishop and the assistant vicar Michael Shawe.

At this time Vincennes was a town of about three thousand, half of the citizens being Catholic. Since quite a few of the townspeople were French, Vincent did not lack for company or conversation. He relied on one of the bishop's seminarians to instruct the children in reading and arithmetic. Vincennes was fortunate to have a Catholic secondary school run by the Eudists. It enrolled twenty boarding students, a typical number for religious schools on the frontier. It was this school that eventually prompted the Holy Cross Community to decamp from St. Peter's where they had hoped to establish their own secondary school alongside the grade school they were already running.

Today we smile at Brother Vincent's zeal for converts and his overt disdain for Protestants. For example, he notes in May 1842 that "twelve unfortunate blacks were made Methodists"[7] by triple immersion in the Wabash River. But he was a product of his times when each church guarded its own turf and rejoiced at defections from other churches. Success was often counted in numbers, and any soul converted was another jewel in the crown of a missionary. Anxious to speed the work of the Holy Spirit, Vincent was a model of such zeal. His interest in recruiting, however, never took a nasty turn. We have the distinct impression that his intentions were sincere and his methods gentle, and we value his letters for information on pioneer life:

> We all eat at Monsignor's [the bishop's] table and as well as he does. There are ten students [seminarians] in all, of which only three are in theology, and the others in different courses. The high school of the Eudists is bigger. They have just under twenty boarders. Our cathedral is rather nice. It's the most beautiful I've seen in the United States. Only the Wabash River separates us from Illinois, formerly very barbarous and wild. Our house is situated in a vast plain. One-quarter hour by road finds marshes on almost every side shaded by woods. Snakes, turtles of all kinds, abound there. There's especially a kind of small beast they call wood ticks (resembling our bed bugs) which pierce the skin in such a way that if you pull them out, they sooner leave their head than let go, and after having pulled them out, there remains a swelling and itching which lasts three to four weeks. Mosquitoes are also beginning to

buzz loudly in our ears. They're enemies of another kind, more bothersome than the first.[8]

His capacity for hard work and selfdiscipline would have endeared him to frontiersmen who appreciated these qualities in a person.

The summer of 1842 found Brother Vincent back at St. Peter's. He describes the celebration of Trinity Sunday with great care to Father Moreau in France. Forty men from the church cut a path through the forest (with the permission of a "pagan" who owns the land) and build an altar of repose in a clearing. The path is decorated with arches of tree branches and white cloth. The procession itself is segregated by gender and age: little boys first, followed by little girls, then the women of the parish, and finally the men, including Protestants and "pagans." The Brothers form a rear guard and provide some of the music. The rest of the music is supplied by two choirs of ladies. It is an ecumenical procession with non-Catholics apparently happy to be involved. The ceremony in the clearing begins with a sermon two hours long, delivered by a neighboring missionary. The subject matter? All the possible proofs for the Real Presence, a topic that Vincent notes "would have bored our Catholics in Europe."[9] One has to wonder what the Protestants in the crowd thought of the topic. Eight days later the group celebrates again with a ceremony much like that of Trinity Sunday. The sermon, however, is only an hour long. Today we do not appreciate how rocky the relations between Protestants and Catholics were in frontier days, but collaboration between religions was often necessitated for the sake of children who needed a good school to attend, and the Brothers educated all children who showed up at their classrooms.

By early October Brother Vincent and Brother Anselm returned to Vincennes for the opening of the school year. Their trip was undertaken in bad weather and the pair arrived at the bishop's palace wet and exhausted. His Excellency was less than gracious and told the missionaries their vacation had been too long. The Brothers may have lengthened their stay at St. Peter's knowing that in the following month the Holy Cross Community would be starting its move north. The group was going to be split up for many months. Brother Gatian and Brother Francis Xavier would leave with Sorin and five novices for northern Indiana in November 1842. Brother Lawrence and Brother Joachim would remain at St. Peter's with eight novices and a postulant. Brother Vincent and Brother Anselm would remain in Vincennes. Then in February all remaining in the south would travel to Notre Dame, except for Anselm who would be left hostage to teach in Vincennes.

We have excellent details of Brother Vincent's move that following February to Notre Dame, a journey of almost 250 miles, because a letter from Brother John (Frederick Steber) to Basil Moreau chronicles the trip undertaken by the group of eleven. Vincent traveled with two of his fellow Frenchmen (Lawrence and Joachim), six novices (including the letter writer John), and two postulants. John writes that a "boarder" accompanied them: this student (Lawrence Kirwin) was at one time a novice named Brother Celestine and may have been in the process of rethinking his religious vocation when the group left St. Peter's. The primary vehicle was a large wagon that Brother Lawrence had made. Drawn by four horses, it contained beds, trunks, and kitchen supplies, all to a weight of nearly three thousand pounds. Most of the men walked, along with eight head of cattle (oxen), because the cart could accommodate only three or four men at a time. They left St. Peter's on a sheet of ice since the rain of the previous day had frozen. Why they would undertake such a journey in midwinter is incomprehensible to us today, but their wish to reunite with the group at Notre Dame probably explains their venture as well as any other explanation, except perhaps Sorin's call for them to come and Hailandière's wish to see them gone. The immediate cause for their leaving was the loss of their diocesan chaplain Father Chartier, who had a fight with the bishop and left the diocese. Brother Vincent may have seen this as an opportunity to get out of St. Peter's so the group quickly assembled their belongings and made a hasty exit.

The horses could barely maneuver the ice, and the oxen slid "from one side of the road to the other."[10] Heading west to pick up the Wabash River at Vincennes, near Washington they encountered a hill that posed a real problem. Getting to the top, the horses and cart slipped back down to the bottom. It was only with the help of local people that the hill was conquered. The fingers of the missionaries were numb with the cold, frostbite a real possibility. In Washington, the horses were reshod to ready them for future ice. Staying at the home of a man named Gallagher, the group was told that no one in the vicinity would consider such a move in the dead of winter.

Undaunted, the men left the next morning. After seven miles they came to the west fork of the White River. Being ferried across on a flat boat, the oxen became restless, jumped into the frigid water and swam back to shore through the narrow channel which had been cut into the ice to accommodate the boat. Then eventually getting their cattle to the west bank, the missionaries moved on, the snow becoming deeper as they traveled, sometimes to a depth of five feet. We can only guess what must have been going through the minds of the three Frenchmen who only two years before had known only the mild winters of France. No doubt their American novices and postulants would have been better acquainted with Indiana winters and must have given the Frenchmen good advice for surviving the ordeal.

Every day in the late afternoon, Brother John would take one of the horses and ride ahead to find lodging for the night, generally with pioneers unfamiliar with Catholic missionaries. The Brothers and their young recruits would sleep on the floor in front of the fireplace, sharing blankets, until 5:30 AM when they would get up, cook their own breakfast, and go on their way. During the daily trek, when one traveler would feel hungry, he would ask Brother Vincent for some bread. Since everything was frozen with the cold, Vincent would take a loaf, put it on a tree trunk, hit it several times with an ax until chunks broke off. This was their only food while on the road. No one complained.

One of the simple joys that buoyed their spirits was their dog Azore who never flagged. When John would go ahead of the group to find a place for the night, Azore would go along, then run back to the other missionaries. After supper, he would go outside and sleep in the cart. John opines, "Many a time have I envied him his bed."[11] The wish was probably as much a desire for Azore's good-natured vitality as it was a desire for warmth or privacy.

Part of the journey would have been undertaken on the Wabash River, navigable as far north as Terre Haute for large boats and as far northeast as Logansport for small boats. We do not know how much of the trip was facilitated by riverboat, probably no more than half. As they neared South Bend, one of the wagon wheels broke beyond repair. Buying a large sled, the men put the wagon on it and moved forward, covering distance more easily than before because of the ice and snow carpeting the ground. They probably should have tried a sled days before they were forced to try it. The entire trip took two weeks. Sorin's trip north the previous November had taken only eight days. Most of the men were in good shape, but Lawrence had frostbitten toes, novices Joseph and Paul frostbitten faces. Notre Dame to them was worth the suffering. In addition to being reunited with their St. Peter's companions, they were overwhelmed by the beauty of the place. Brother Vincent walked into five hundred and twenty-four acres that Halandière had purchased from the old missionary Theodore Badin, who had acquired it in 1833 to start an orphanage.

At Notre Dame Brother Vincent settled into an active routine. He was in charge of the novices, and he was, as the only certified teacher, in charge of teacher training. In addition, he probably taught courses in French to the students who were beginning to show up at the new secondary school. There were, of course, breaks in his routine. In April of 1844 he watched at the deathbed of Brother Joachim, the first of the French missionaries to die in America.[12]

One month later, in May 1844, Brother Vincent set out for France in order to escort a third colony of missionaries to Indiana. (A second had arrived by themselves in June 1843, consisting of two priests, a seminarian, and five Marianite Sisters.) Vincent traveled to New York by way of Detroit and Buffalo, using a steamboat on Lake Erie. The steamboat trip for Vincent and his companion Brother Augustine (Jeremy O'Leary), who was heading to Le Mans in order to teach

English at Sainte-Croix, cost five dollars for the pair, semi-private cabin and food included. The boat ride took them three hundred miles to Buffalo in two days. From Buffalo to Albany they traveled by canal, a three and a half day trip. Finally on June 6, after a two-day stay in a town where Augustine had relatives, they arrived in New York City. They were booked on the *Duchess of Orleans* bound for France.

One month later, Vincent writes from France to Sorin telling him that he has paid a visit to Sorin's elderly father:

> Your father, who was in bed, jumped up when he saw me. We chatted, but he stopped so that he'd get to morning Mass. Following that, we had lunch together at his place. I stayed there until 10 o'clock, and before leaving I received 20 francs from your brother (he's generous). Your father gave me 10 also, and the Curé of La Brulcatte 5.[13]

Not on a pleasure junket, Vincent was under orders from Sorin to solicit money for Notre Dame, so he canvassed in Laval and various towns, including Ruillé. Apparently the trip was a success, and Vincent was able to meet scores of old friends. He had hopes to bring Moreau back to America for a visit, but the founder decided that a visit to a planned foundation in North Africa should come first. For new personnel, Vincent received for Notre Dame one priest (Alexis Granger who would prove to be very important to the colony), Brother Augustus (Arsene Poignant), Brother Justin (Louis Gautier), and three Marianite Sisters. Vincent left Augustine in Le Mans where he had decided to study medicine.[14] The colony of seven were booked on the same boat Vincent had come on. They arrived at Notre Dame a month later, on September 10.

Back at Notre Dame, Vincent was entrusted with his former duties, still very much needed as trainer of future teachers, and just as he had been used by Dujarié years before in France to visit schools administered by young Brothers, so too was he sent to supervise the work of Brothers in their little schools on the American frontier. The death of one of these young men must have touched him profoundly—the drowning of Anselm in Madison, Indiana, on July 12, 1845, at the age of twenty. Vincent does not document his own grief for the young man, but he had visited Madison in the previous October on one of his supervisory trips, and he must have felt the loss as if it were the loss of a son. He had known Anselm in Le Mans when the sixteen-year old boy was a novice under Brother André Mottais' care at la Charbonnière. Vincent had traveled the Atlantic with him, lived with him in the episcopal residence in Vincennes when Gatian, Francis Xavier, and Sorin had moved to Notre Dame. Vincent taught next to the young man in the cathedral school and guided him in the first years of his profession.

The teaching duties of Vincent and Gatian at Notre Dame in the early years were confined to Notre Dame. These two men were the only Brothers on the Indiana frontier trained for the classroom. The first mention of "Holy Cross" in the national *Catholic Almanac* occurs in the 1842 edition under "Brothers of St. Joseph:" "The Brothers of St. Joseph, lately arrived from Europe, intend to open a school in Davies county, where the novitiate of the institution will be kept. The Rev. L. [sic] Sorin is Superior."[15] It is noteworthy that the original intention was for a school to be run by the Brothers, but Brother Vincent is not named. The entry in the *Almanac* for the following year (1843) reads as follows: "The Brothers of St. Joseph. At St. Peter's, near Washington, Indiana. The members of this community are 12 in number. A school will be opened for the reception of young men on the first Monday in September. Young men of any religious profession will be received, without preference or distinction."[16] Again, Brother Vincent is not named.

The *Almanac* entry for 1844 and the entry for 1845 relocate the school to Southbend [sic] but place it "near Washington, Ind." The entry notes thirty-two Brothers and three priests are at the school. In 1846 the *Almanac* lists the school as "under the direction of the Priests of the [sic] Holy Cross." The Brothers are disappearing from official view. The *Almanac* does note, "One of the Brothers is a physician, but for greater security, the services of the most experienced of the faculty will be procured in cases of serious diseases."[17] Moreover, "the faculty is formed of the priests of the [sic] Holy Cross and the most competent Brothers, one of whom is annually sent to Europe to complete [sic]." There were in 1846 eight priests, thirty-two Brothers, five postulants, and forty boarders at Notre Dame.[18] The phrase "most competent" for the Brothers is particularly galling. The *Almanac* must have been compiled by an inveterately clerical compositor, with information misfed from either South Bend or elsewhere. The 1846 *Almanac* at least gives the location of the school correctly: one mile from South Bend.

In the 1847 *Almanac*, the description reads: "Conducted by the Brothers of St. Joseph, who have an extensive farm connected with the University of Notre-Dame-du-Lac. This circumstance enables the institute to receive among the Brothers of St. Joseph, not only those young men who are qualified to keep school or to teach a useful trade, but even such as can but work on the farm."[19] The Brothers are slowly devolving into non-teaching status at Notre Dame.

In the 1848 *Almanac*, five priests are named (Sorin, Cointet, Gouesse, Shawe, Delisle) but no Brothers are named. And by 1849 the Almanac crows that the priests are devoted to mission and to education while the Brothers are "chiefly instituted to teach the poor and the destitute; they take charge of orphan asylums, and teach useful trades, and they also discharge the manual offices connected with a college, and a farm."[20] Clearly Notre Dame is becoming a clerical bailiwick, the Brothers simply adjuncts to the university. None of them apparently teach at Notre Dame, not even Vincent. Their schools (for the "poor and the destitute") are presumably elsewhere.

However, in the 1856 *Almanac*, two Brothers are listed at the end of the faculty: priests first, professors second, Brothers last! Brother Basil teaches German and instrumental music, and Brother Amadeus teaches penmanship. Brother Basil is the only Brother on the Notre Dame faculty in 1861 and 1863. In 1865 he was joined in the Music Department by Brother Leopold. These disciplines (music and penmanship) are, of course, traditionally academic only marginally, the Brothers apparently not prepared to teach the classics or the hard sciences. But the compartmentalization of apostolates at Notre Dame can only in part be attributed to Edward Sorin. When the Brothers of St. Joseph began in 1820 under the guidance of Jacques Dujarié, they were teachers, all of them, although some of them were used to help build the Grand Providence of the Sisters in Ruillé.[21] Under Moreau, who assumed direction of the group in 1835, the practice of accepting non-teacher candidates for the Brothers gradually changed. Moreau privileged his priests above his Brothers from the outset and accepted Brothers for "manual" labor, a practice consistent with the practice of most religious orders in the Church. In America, therefore, Sorin simply continued the trend, and its sad conclusion for Notre Dame is that within ten years of their arrival in Indiana, the Brother-teachers were teaching in grammar schools, the priests teaching at the university.[22] This is most obvious in the 1848 *Almanac* description.

During the years 1845 to 1849, Bother Vincent remained at Notre Dame absorbed in his duties both to the Community recruits and to the secondary school students. One of his tasks was not much to his liking, but he undertook it with his customary obedience. Sorin appointed him Sorin's spiritual monitor, requiring Vincent to evaluate the priest from time to time. How much of what Vincent said to Sorin about Sorin's faults we have no way of knowing, but it was to Sorin's credit that he even asked for the frank exposition of the state of his character as perceived by another person. Vincent, of course, was a safe bet to be an honest and confidential monitor. In a remarkable document written by Vincent to Sorin in 1847, Vincent itemizes half a dozen shortcomings he sees in his priest-superior:

> It was indeed necessary to make me speak up through obedience because it is so difficult and even dangerous to examine the actions of a superior who can have special motives which make him act, motives which can be known only to himself. I'll tell you then very simply things such as

I see them for you to meditate on with the good God during your retreat.[23]

The faults? Sorin does not confide in his assistant (Alexis Granger). He does not obey his nurses in times of sickness. He makes promises he does not keep, e.g., saying he will dine every Friday at the novitiate. Sorin overrides the authority of the secondary school administrators. He keeps the local chapter in the dark about important matters. He does not give enough Sunday talks on the vows to the Brothers. That Sorin kept the document is testament to his good will. That he followed any of Vincent's advice is doubtful: Sorin was a law unto himself, basically zealous for the success of his fiefdom. An introspective man given to prayer and contemplation, Sorin remained to his death absolute master of his domain, willing to listen but inclined to follow his own counsel. Yet he and Brother Vincent had a deep and genuine respect for each other that bolstered each other's fortitude during the sixty years they worked together mostly side by side in Holy Cross.

In spring of 1849 at the age of fifty-two, Vincent was presented with a challenge: he was sent to New Orleans with four Brothers and three Sisters to assume direction of St. Mary's Orphanage, an institution founded in 1835 by a young diocesan priest who died in 1837 of typhoid incurred from his heroic efforts to save his orphans during a hurricane. St. Mary's had languished for a decade under inadequate supervision, and the prelate of New Orleans (Anthony Blanc) was very anxious to have a religious community take the children under its wing. The orphanage sat on Chartres Street right on the Mississippi River levee, down river from the heart of the city.[24] When Vincent arrived on May 1, 1949, he found ninety-eight boys in pitiable condition. The miserable blankets they had were quickly burned by the Sisters. Thanks to the generosity of the Ursuline Sisters and the Sisters of Charity, Vincent and his staff were able to turn things around for the good.

Spring flooding in New Orleans was an annual problem, and two weeks after Vincent's arrival, a dike broke in the city and water in the downtown area stood at four feet:

> The Mississippi broke its dike, which we here call a levee. Water rushed in and is still rushing like a torrent in a large part of the city, from there into the sugar and cotton plantations. The inhabitants have to save themselves. The loss is immense. It is thought that the water won't reach us. It's still half a league away. Two or three thousand workers are employed to fix the levee, but in the evening they aren't any more ahead than in the morning. They made the water run into ditches. Although these ditches were reinforced with stones and bricks, they haven't been any less carried away by the current. God sometimes shows men His power before which all ingenuity and knowledge can do nothing.[25]

Fortunately the orphanage, five miles from downtown, was spared. Cholera, however, plagued the city and sixteen orphan boys had died in the two months before the Brothers and Sisters arrived. Water was unhealthy to drink so they drank only the water collected from downspouts.

Gradually Vincent had to deal with problems among his staff. Brother Theodulus, the cook, came down with a fever, and Brother Louis developed an open sore on his hand. The cook proved to be a particular problem. Theodulus was a man who could complain at length, and he did so in several letters to Sorin. Vincent went out of his way to accommodate the man, but Theodulus' whining was chronic. At the same time, young Brother Basil started to be a problem. Having recently gone through the trauma of teaching in Brooklyn, New York, under terrible circumstances, he seems to have brought his unhappiness to New Orleans. He threatened to return to Notre Dame if Vincent did not procure a priest to live in the orphanage and help with the ministry.

As if the problems among the Brothers were not enough, two of the three Sisters came to be at odds: Sister Mary of Calvary and Sister Mary of the Five Wounds, the latter described by Vincent as "a little busy-body or at least too moody."[26] The Sisters may have resented taking orders from a Brother when they had been answerable only to a priest before. Within two months of his arrival, Vincent was busy reshuffling his staff to make up for their weaknesses. Ever the kind man, he was not well suited to be a superior since he lacked the knack of making people do what they did not especially want to do. Although he could maneuver students admirably in a classroom and guide novices through their formative years, he was never able to command his peers with the steely resilience that men like Moreau and Sorin could muster to rein in their subjects. His heart must have been excessively kind. He was certainly sensitive to a fault and absolutely devoted to his vow of obedience.

By July Basil was beginning to show promise as a prefect. Theodulus' health had improved, but he wanted to return to Notre Dame anyway. Vincent himself took charge of doing the steward's job. He rose every day at 4:30 and hitched a horse to a little cart, which he drove through the hotel area of the city to collect leftover food for the orphanage. Sometimes he had to pick old cigar butts out of the food he was given. By 7 AM he was back at the orphanage. During the day he gave relief to Louis, Basil, and Francis, who supervised the boys seven days a week all day long and needed occasional breaks:

> The Bothers in charge of the children get up at 5 AM, and the children at 5:30. As you see, no prayer for them, no more than for me. Then one hundred children on their backs all day long. They can't leave them alone for a minute. No particular examen for the Brothers, who teach class, and very often none for me either, because with Brother Theodulus being incapable of doing his job, I have to replace him as much as I can. The two Brothers are very glad that I take part of the recreation supervision because they're tired of always

being with the children and have their studies and classes to prepare.[27]

Vincent thus supervised the boys' recreation periods, and he took responsibility for one of the dormitories.

By August Francis was starting to chafe. Vincent agonized over the situation, and soon he himself was begging Sorin to be replaced. He sent Brother Louis back to Notre Dame in order to save Brother Basil. The two had irreconcilable differences. Then Sister Five Wounds started to make demands on Vincent. It seems he could satisfy no one. The subjects saw a power vacuum and rushed to fill it. Had Vincent been stronger, he may have calmed down some of these people, but he suffered instead of guiding firmly. His subjects smelled weakness. The New Orleans atmosphere was, of course, no help: these Yankees and Frenchmen were unused to the horrible heat and humidity, and they were susceptible to the recurring plagues of cholera and yellow fever that threatened the city.

Theodulus did little work. Sister Five Wounds was flexing her muscles. Basil and Francis worked like slaves, as did Mary of Calvary and Mary of the Nativity. Theodulus complained to Sorin that Vincent chose Francis as a spiritual monitor and that Francis thus took it unto himself to tell Vincent how to run the orphanage. Thedodulus thus gets orders from two people, and he bristles, faulting Vincent for weakness and Francis for arrogance. It was, of course, a smoke screen for his own indolence. Vincent, at the end of August, was still asking to be replaced.

By October 5 Theodulus had settled into doing some work as sacristan, and Vincent was pleased. Basil continued to be successful in his work but neglected his spiritual exercises so Vincent worried about the young man's long-term effectiveness. Francis, on the other hand, seemed to be doing fine. The need for a permanent chaplain had become so acute, however, that Basil and Theodulus threatened to leave if a priest did not arrive soon from Notre Dame.

Eventually Vincent got his wish to leave. The Minor Chapter Book at Notre Dame contains a note for May 24, 1850, that Brother

Vincent "shall be called back if possible, and Brother Ignatius sent in his place, that is, to take the employment of Brother Theodulus who shall succeed Brother Vincent in his charge of Director of the asylum."[28] But Vincent remained in New Orleans for at least another half of the year as an entry in the Chapter book for November 15, 1851, documents once again a resolve that Brother Vincent will be recalled from New Orleans. Finally an entry for September 27, 1852, indicates that Vincent "will replace Br. Eleazar and Alexander on Saturday morning, to give them time to go to confession." Thus Vincent was back at Notre Dame when a terrible crisis occurred.

On September 13, 1852, Sorin was appointed by Moreau to become superior of the Holy Cross mission in Bengal. Under the pretense that he was unworthy of episcopacy, an honor that would follow the move to Bengal, Sorin refused the obedience. One month later Moreau wrote again to Sorin commanding him to take the position in Bengal. Moreau also responded to a letter from the Minor Chapter at Notre Dame which had protested Sorin's transfer. Brother Vincent, of course, would have been part of the Minor Chapter during this entire affair. In January 1853, the Minor Chapter decided that Father Cointet "should go to the motherhouse as the legal deputy of this establishment [Notre Dame] for this year, and should try to settle there the difficulties actually existing between both houses."[29] The language of the resolution is brash, pretending to a kind of equality with the motherhouse, an equality which it canonically did not have.

A month later Sorin delivered to the Minor Chapter a decree to separate from Le Mans, had them sign it, and mailed the document to France. Curiously there is no entry in the minutes for the Minor Chapter concerning this event. An entry for two days later treats of small matters, e.g., the purchase of some cows. The rebellion by Sorin was, in fact, a secret kept to himself and the few members of the Minor Chapter, including Brother Vincent, who apparently could be browbeat. Sorin had the encouragement of two American bishops who felt that European missionaries should break their ties to their motherhouses, but Sorin lacked the backing of his own Indiana bishop and a canon lawyer whom he consulted on the matter. Within a year Sorin went to France and was reconciled to Moreau. He got, of course, his own way and stayed at Notre Dame.

Brother Vincent must have been ripped apart during the year of this unfolding drama. He was born in France a few miles from Sorin's hometown. He had worked side by side with the man for a dozen years as Sorin's trusted mentor, through the hardships of St. Peter's and the early years at Notre Dame. He had guided Notre Dame people to New Orleans and worked to save that apostolate for Sorin through trying times. At the same time he was trusted beyond a doubt by Moreau who had worked with him as far back as 1834 to transfer the Brothers of Saint Joseph out of Ruillé as Father Dujarié's health failed. Moreau selected Vincent for the foundation in Indiana and relied on Vincent's religious values to shepherd novices in America. When the Sorin crisis peaked, Moreau sent word that Brother Vincent was to submit to Le Mans a quarterly report on the state of affairs at Notre Dame, indicative of the lack of trust Moreau held in Sorin. Thus Vincent was torn between two allegiances. That he signed the decree of separation in 1853 merely reflects the influence Sorin exercised over his local subjects. Anything to keep local peace, Vincent signed the document, a document written entirely in Sorin's handwriting, created before Chapter discussion. Vincent was not a man who confronted crises well. He was a man of prayer who sought refuge with God and let others fight over worldly particulars. Sorin and Moreau both needed the good will of such a man in their respective camps. That Vincent survived the power struggle is testament to his conviction that such a matter was something he was not supposed to arbitrate. He chose the line of least resistance. Moreau, fortunately, knew the cause of the rebellion and never faulted Vincent, as demonstrated by his appointment of Vincent as quarterly auditor.

A few years later, Brother Vincent was on hand at Notre Dame to welcome Moreau on the only visit Moreau made to America. On August 27, 1857, the founder arrived for a three-week visit to Holy Cross institutions in Indiana, Chicago, and Philadelphia. Returning to France with him on the *Arago* was Brother Vincent, just as a financial crisis hit the United States and threatened the property at

Notre Dame. Holy Cross in America survived, but Vincent, who was always at the heart of Notre Dame, must have been missed. Later, back in America, Brother Vincent fell ill in February of 1859 and was extremely sick for a month and a half. In charge of the Notre Dame budget and statistics at the time, Vincent was sorely needed as the local chapter scurried to ready the annual report for Le Mans. Throughout his life he was a valuable contributor to his Community, and people were able to sense in him a special significance. Late in his life, Vincent made a trip to Rome with Sorin. At their papal audience as Vincent started to kneel in front of the pontiff (Pius IX), the pope raised him up proclaiming him a "patriarch" too worthy to kneel in front of a pope.

As Vincent aged, so did Sorin. As part of the 1866 cabal that forced Moreau out of office, Sorin no longer feigned a love for the founder, but Sorin recanted on his deathbed and proclaimed himself a fool for distrusting and disgracing Moreau. That death, however, came in 1893, twenty-two years after Moreau's own sad death. As Moreau's fortunes fell, Moreau was hounded from office and the motherhouse sold in France, along with the boarding school that Brother Vincent worked in as its first director. Could the secondary school in Le Mans have developed into a great university like the secondary school in Indiana? We will never know. Fate, ever ironic, saw Sorin elected in 1868 as Superior General of Holy Cross, a post he held until his death in 1893.

Tradition tells us that Vincent once visited Texas. He would have been in his late seventies or in his eighties at the time since the Doyle property saw its first Brother farmer in the autumn of 1874 and St. Edward's Academy did not have its first students until 1878. There would have been no reason for Vincent to visit the farm. He would, of course, have been very much interested in a visit once the apostolate had developed an educational angle. If he visited in 1878, he would have found six students under the supervision of Father Shea and Father Spillard. An actual school building was not erected until 1879 (on Doyle land that today no longer belongs to the university). A second building was put up in 1881. The school moved to the present site of St. Edward's University in 1889. It is pleasant to think of Brother Vincent sitting under the great umbrella oak at the new site, but we are able only to conjecture about his visit to Texas or his activities once there.

Of the seven Holy Cross men who came to America in 1841, Vincent, eldest of the missionary colony, outlived most of them. Joachim died in 1844. Anselm drowned in 1845. Gatian left the community in 1850 and died on his family's farm in France in 1860. Lawrence died in 1873, much lauded for his contributions to the success of Notre Dame. Only Sorin and Francis Xavier outlived the patriarch Vincent. Francis Xavier was the last to die (1896), his grave dug by a novice named Bernard Gervais, whom many members of Holy Cross remember today. How very different were the fortunes of these seven men: Joachim the cook, Anselm the energetic young teacher, Gatian the rebel, Lawrence the businessman-farmer, Francis Xavier the carpenter-mortician, Sorin the potentate, and Vincent the patriarch.

On Sorin's orders in late spring of 1861 a double burial valut was dug in the chapel of the novitate at Notre Dame. He intended it to be the final resting place for himself and Brother Vincent with, as lugubrious as it may sound, Moreau's right hand in a reliquary positioned above the two graves.[30] Brother Vincent was never buried in the novitiate chapel, nor was Sorin. They both rest in the quiet Community cemetery on St. Mary's Lake at Notre Dame, Vincent with the Brothers, Sorin with the Indiana provincials. Death came to the patriarch Vincent on July 23, 1890, at the age of 93. His most striking portrait is now displayed at the Moreau Province retirement facility named after him: the Brother Vincent Pieau Residence in Austin, Texas. Bother Vincent in the painting matches what we know of him through letters and tradition: calm, wise, and kind, an elderly man with a full gray beard. He sports a pillbox hat under which his eyes burrow into the viewer, the gentlest of smiles completing his face.

Fortunate those who knew him, who lived with Vincent Pieau, who cared for him in his final days. If he ever longed for his homeland, he never said so in his letters. Content to follow the Spirit to America, he gave a total gift of himself to his Church and his Community, never looking back. The joy he knew endures in those who revere his memory.

CHAPTER FIVE

Lawrence Ménage: Pioneer Businessman-Farmer

A dozen years after Napoleon's Concordat brought peace at last to France and calmed the rabid fires of the French Revolution, Jean Ménage was born on March 12, 1815, at Brécé, in the district of Mayenne.[1] We do not know the names of his parents, but we can presume they were probably farmers in the area.[2] Brécé is located in northwestern France about 36 miles from Mont-St.-Michel and 150 miles from Paris. Its region is the lovely Pays de la Loire, and its department, Mayenne, is the area from which many of the early Brothers of St. Joseph came. Visitors today are attracted by the historic village Sainte-Suzanne (29 miles away) and the botanical gardens at Clivoy (just north of Laval), Pellerine, and Haute-Bretagne. The closest city (3 miles west) is Rennes, the capital of Brittany and home to one of the last apostolic ministries of Holy Cross Brothers in France, a boarding institution for young men attending a local technical-training school. Fifty miles to the east of Brécé is Laval, known for being a military stronghold in the Middle Ages, and fifty miles east of Laval is Le Mans. Within three miles of Brécé are the towns of Gorron, Columbiers-du-Plessis, Lesbois, and Hercé. Today Brécé has a population of 800, not much bigger than it was in the nineteenth-century.

At the age of 25, Jean Ménage made the hundred-mile journey to Le Mans where on July 7, 1840, he entered Basil Moreau's fledgling religious community at Sainte-Croix. If we can believe Edward Sorin, it was Sorin who induced Jean to come into Holy Cross.[3] This may well be a fact. After all, Sorin's hometown (Ahuillé) was not far from Brécé, and Sorin, from gentlemen-farmer stock, could have known the Ménage family, probably also farmers. At any rate, a month and a half after Jean's arrival at Le Mans, on August 23, he was accepted as a novice and professed as Brother Lawrence less than a year later on July 25, 1841. Obviously impressed with Lawrence's abilities and promise, Moreau selected him to be among the seven missionaries sent from Le Mans to the Indiana territory in America. In fact, within two weeks of his first profession, Lawrence was on board the *Iowa* steamship bound for America, setting off from Le Havre on August 8, 1841, with his companion Brothers Vincent Pieau, Joachim André, Marie (later named Francis Xavier) Patois, Anselm Caillot, and Gatian Monsimer. The group was headed by the twenty-eight-year old Father Edward Sorin. With them traveled a Sister of Providence bound for St.-Mary-of-the-Woods near Terre Haute, Indiana. Sister Francis Xavier (Irma le Fer de la Motte) wrote a vivid letter recounting the passage over on the *Iowa*:

> Our packet is one hundred and fifty feet long … The doors of our rooms are of citron and mahogany, the locks of silver … On board are some beautiful birds that the passengers are taking with them, also a large cow, some sheep, pigs, ducks, chickens, and rabbits, which serve us for food.[4]

All the Holy Cross men fell seasick and were nursed by Brother Vincent until he too fell sick.

The *Iowa* docked in New York on September 18. After resting in the city for three days, the group set off for Indiana, a trip that took almost a month. On October 10 they arrived at Vincennes, stayed for four days with the bishop, Celestine de la Hailandière, and then settled in at Black Oak Ridge just east of Vincennes. The property, known as St. Peter's, was 160 arpents big with 60 of those arpents under cultivation, a fact probably dear to the heart of Brother

Lawrence, who was destined to make his mark in Holy Cross as a very successful businessman-farmer. The small buildings were less than suitable for habitation, but the men moved in nonetheless, happy at last to have a home. The little church on the property was the fourth church constructed on that site. The location was eventually abandoned as a mission by the diocese in favor of a place closer to Montgomery, where a church built in 1847 still stands today.

Soon it became obvious that the St. Peter's location was not a good place for what Holy Cross wanted to do in America, i.e., found a boarding school for boys. Although the group attracted four Brother candidates and five students by early winter, it was determined that a school would not thrive there because the Eudists already had such a school with twenty students in Vincennes and the bishop did not believe another school would succeed in the area. Thus he offered the Holy Cross community a large parcel of land (524 acres) in northern Indiana. Sorin jumped at the opportunity to get as far away as possible from the bishop. Unfortunately, the bishop wanted two Brother teachers to remain behind for the Vincennes cathedral grade school. So when Sorin, Marie (Francis Xavier), and Gatian headed north in November 1842 for the new property at Notre Dame, Vincent and Anselm were left behind in Vincennes. Lawrence and Joachim were left behind at St. Peter's with eight novices and a postulant. The group remaining at St. Peter's was put under the direction of Etienne Chalier, a diocesan priest who had been a postulant for only a few weeks. Why Sorin would leave the group in the hands of a new arrival when Vincent and even Lawrence were both capable religious, especially Vincent who had been in religious life for over twenty years, is anybody's guess, but it probably had much to do with the quaint notion that religious foundations best thrived with a priest in charge. Leaving Lawrence behind at St. Peter's would, of course, have allowed him time to wind up the fall harvest before the snows set in. Three months later, on a Monday morning in February 1843, all remaining Holy Cross members (except young Anselm and a novice named Celestine, who were left hostage at the bishop's school in Vincennes) set out for Notre Dame. That the group would not wait until the spring thaw is testament to their desire both to reunite with Sorin and to escape from Hailandière. On February 27 Lawrence and the group reached Notre Dame.

We have very few items remaining in Brother Lawrence's hand: eight letters, a memo, a receipt, and two copies of his last will. Thus to reconstruct most of his life is impossible. For example, his activities in his first years at Notre Dame can only be guessed at. He probably assisted in the erection of the first brick building in 1843 (today called Old College), possibly even helping make the bricks from marl dug from the banks of the St. Joseph River. He may also have helped put up the second brick building (1844), today part of Columba Hall. Undoubtedly he was entrusted with the farm enterprise, a most necessary part of the early community's survival, drawing on the skills he probably learned as a young man in France. The first real chronicle of his activities, however, dates from 1850, the year he set out for California with six companions to look for gold in the heady days of the Gold Rush.

Edward Sorin's own account of the California venture[5] is terse but helpful in understanding the motives for the expedition: the prevention of an imminent scandal and the need for money to pay bills. It is impossible to determine which motive was uppermost in Sorin's mind: "1. that of preventing a terrible scandal which might ruin the work; 2. that of trying a means of paying arrears of indebtedness."[6] The first motive is questionable since in Sorin's own words, he noted that Brother Gatian, his bête noire, "was going to leave the Society to marry and to settle down near the college."[7] This explanation is suspect because Gatian was not involved with a woman at the time. He, in fact, was very up front in both his journal and his letters to Sorin from Brooklyn that he was infatuated with a Notre Dame student named John Hays.[8] In short, Gatian was gay. What is sure is that Sorin wanted Gatian away from Notre Dame so badly, with an earlier Brooklyn assignment only temporarily successful at his removal, that Sorin was willing to lose the services of Brother Lawrence, who was chosen to go to California with Gatian, Bother Justin (Louis Gautier), Brother Placidus (Urban Allard), and three locals (George Woodworth, Gregory Campeau, Michael Dowling). They formed the "St. Joseph Company" and left Notre Dame for California on February 28, 1850. Lawrence was not selected to act as leader, an honor that went to George Woodworth, but Lawrence would, of course, have been the spiritual leader of the religious Brothers.

The first letter we have from Lawrence on this trip is dated March 5, 1850, from Mount Joliet in Illinois:

> After travelling 5 ½ days we arrived 3 ½ miles on the other side of Joliet. Everyone seems happy and in good spirits. We've already had some mishaps in crossing some streams. We broke a wagon part, but Mr. Campeau made a new one in the evening and we'll be fine. Brother Gatian almost had a bad accident in crossing a stream. He fell under the horses, but I stopped the wagon in time.[9]

Lawrence writes as if he is responsible for the other Brothers and even tells Sorin that Placidus wants Sorin to be told that Placidus is sorry for any trouble he may have been to Sorin. Sorin had, in fact, included Placidus on the trip because he thought it would be helpful in curing Placidus of a bad temper. Sorin little knew that this expedition would work in this regard more than he could imagine: Placidus was the only one of the seven adventurers to die in California.[10]

Lawrence's next letter is posted ten days later (March 15, 1850). It is a brief letter complaining of Woodworth's laxity in protecting their provisions from theft. Moreover Woodworth makes them work on Sunday, as if the day were like any other day. To Lawrence's letter Gatian adds a curious postscript with a tone that indicates how brash the young man could be with Sorin:

> When the horses broke loose without a driver, Brother Lawrence promised a thousand Aves. We do not have the time to say them. Would you have them said for us? It is a

small miracle that the horses with our large wagon galloped 3 miles alone without any accident.[11]

We owe all the rest of the details of travelling to Gatian, who proved to be an energetic and precise chronicler. Lawrence emerges only here and there in the Gatian letters: on May 26 he had a toothache, and on July 31 he informed the group how their destination, Placerville, got its name: the city, east of Sacramento, was known as "Hangtown" because of the lynching of three men "on a tree still standing in town."[12]

Their search for gold began on August 1, 1850, and the work was not easy, nor would it prove very profitable. In a letter by Lawrence to Sorin dated November 1, 1850, from Placerville, we learn they have finally received a letter from Sorin and have built a little house for the winter. Brother Justin has been sick, and they may have to sell the house to pay doctor bills. But one bright ray of sunshine is Lawrence's dream of keeping cows for milk to sell in Sacramento. The business would yield a profit of fifty dollars per day. However, the setup cost would be $20,000. This was not, obviously, very practical thinking. The only successful moneymaker has been Justin, who had set up as a cobbler.

Nine days later Lawrence pens a short, sad letter to Sorin:

> Several days ago I wrote to you about our sick man. Today it pains me to tell you Bother Placidus died on November 6. You can appreciate how sad it was for us to see him die without a priest; but there's no use thinking about it because the nearest one was in San Francisco. He had a fever; he didn't speak for 2 or 3 days before he died; he was sick for a week and had a very edifying death, going out like a candle.[13]

Placidus was buried on-site, but the grave has been lost, quite possibly to the south fork of the American River when it was diverted years after Lawrence and the other men left the area. One can imagine the devastating effect this death had on the St. Joseph

Company half a continent away from their Community base, living in semi-squalor, deprived of sacraments. It is a wonder they did not decamp immediately. The rest of the winter went by without a letter from Lawrence. His next letter is posted on March 26, 1851, from Sacramento. He has just received Sorin's January 5 letter. Lawrence tells Sorin that Captain Woodworth wants to go home but continues to look for gold with Bother Justin. Lawrence and Michael Dowling, however, have taken up the transporting of merchandise between Sacramento and Placerville. They sometimes make a hundred dollars a week, but the future does not look bright for the group.

As the group carried on, there were but four remaining of the original seven. Gatian had left the St. Joseph Company and Holy Cross at the beginning of the winter. He stayed on his own in California before returning to France in 1860 to die on his father's farm at age thirty-four. Then Woodworth, Campeau, and Dowling left the Company. The venture was pretty much dead. Finally Sorin called Lawrence and Justin back to Notre Dame. Any money they had was used for living expenses[14] so Sorin achieved only one of his original goals: getting rid of Gatian.

Once back at Notre Dame, Lawrence returned to the things he did best: farming and managing money for the university. A letter from him dated June 1, 1858, posted from Kalamazoo (indicating he traveled for his work), contains only details of business transactions and sheds no light on the man himself except that he evidently was good at what he did. In June 1867, he was appointed by the Notre Dame Council to set up a farm at Ames, Iowa, but the task never came into being because no record exists of its creation. He continued to oversee the finances of the Manual Training School at Notre Dame as is attested by a tuition receipt dated December 5, 1864. In 1868 he chaired an interesting committee as witnesses a document dated June 19:

> The committee appointed by Very Reverend Provincial to inquire into the expediency of replacing the hired women by Sisters beg to submit the following.

1. They find there are about 30 women engaged in the kitchen, washhouse clothes rooms and drying rooms who receive $12.00 per month each for ten months in the year at a cost of $3600.00.

2. The committe [sic] are of opinion that they should be replaced by Sisters (except in the washhouse) at a salary of $100.00 per year each.

3. The committee [sic] are also of opinion that the Brothers should received from St. Mary's one dollar per day or $300.00 per year and Board or in fair exchange one Bother for 3 Sisters.[15]

The document is signed by Brothers Lawrence, Paulinus, and Edward. One wonders how the Sisters of the Holy Cross accepted their trade value as three to one. Certainly today women would never agree to such an appraisal of their labor rate.

That Lawrence was a trusted member of the Notre Dame councils is attested to by an incident in 1864. That year Schuyler Colfax was running for public office and wanted the votes of the Notre Dame Brothers. Sorin, under pressure from Colfax, had the matter discussed at length in council. The Council apparently delegated Lawrence to canvass the Brothers on Colfax's behalf. Whether Lawrence did so or not is not clear: he may have asked Brother Francis Xavier to do the canvassing. At any rate, Colfax lost the precinct.[16]

A Lawrence letter dated November 15, 1869, is curious from an archival point of view: the letter, written in English, is not in Lawrence's handwriting but is signed by him in French. The hand is a beautiful cursive and the text has some elegant phrasing, quite unlike any of the letters Lawrence wrote from California decades earlier. The letter is posted from Notre Dame to Sorin who was away possibly on one of his many trips to France after he became Superior General in 1868:

Enclosed please find duplicate of Rev. Fr. Toohey's draft for 2000 francs as requested. I am sure you will be very sorry to hear that your favorite horse Black Hawk died yesterday; he had not been working for some time, so I presume he died of old age. The times are getting very hard. Money is very scarce and business dull. I was informed that Judge Egbert took sixty Judgments in one day at Plymouth Marshall County. The prospect for wheat is poor, the price in South Bend is only 95 cents per bushel. You will perceive by the enclosed clip that the financial prospect in New York is gloomy. Bro. Francis de Sales has just returned from a collecting tour for the University; he reports money very hard and fears that many of the parents will withdraw their children at the end of the session. It was lately reported in the papers that the secratary [sic] of the Treasury in Washington stated that Specia payment might be resumed next July. The College is doing very well. We have a good number of students. Rev. Father Ruthmann left for New Orleans on Thursday last.

votre tout devoué
Frère Laurent[17]

The English is quite good. Could it be that by this time in his life the businessman-farmer had been afforded the luxury of a secretary? By this date Lawrence may have needed help in what he had helped blossom as a thriving farm at Notre Dame. But the signature is clearly that of Brother Lawrence.

The last letter we have remaining from Brother Lawrence is also written in good English, but not in his hand. Only the signature was penned by him. The letter, dated January 24, 1870, is addressed to Very Reverend Father General, i.e., Sorin:

I have been for some time thinking of writing to you but postponed it in hope that I would have something more pleasing to communicate.

About the 16th of December one of the students died of dyphtheria and as there were many in the infirmary with sore throat, the effects of colds; it created quite an excitement soon after another died which caused almost a panic among them.

Nearly all the boys from Kentucky went home and will not return. Brother Thomas went there to induce them to return and did not succeed. The impression among the parents is that the climate is too severe for them and no doubt it will militate very much against the college in that section for some time to come. Besides there has been much trouble caused by some of the prefects. Father Superior has much to suffer. In fact more than most men could endure. They will sometimes demand the expulsion of boys or threaten to leave. To all appearances there is a poor prospect for the coming session. I do not think we shall average more than 200 students. I am informed that 118 boys may have either been dismissed [,] left or ran away since the commencement of the session. The discipline appears loose and much injury caused by the letters going out. The novitiate is in a poor condition [.] no candidate has been received for a long time [.] There is but one postulant [,] a boy at present in the house. It is badly in need of a good Master of Novices. No doubt the unsettled state of the finances of the country and the stagnation in business is another cause of the falling off in students. Also drawing on them when not prepared to pay sometimes leads to the withdrawal of the boys. With the falling off students we have still the heavy amount to pay professors [,] an evil which should certainly be remedied as soon as possible.

John Harper's has failed in 260,000 dollars [.] many of our large business men in this county are heavy losers. A.B. Judson loses $60,000.

Wishing you Very Reverend Father a very happy new year replete with every blessing, I remain your obedient son in J.M.J.

Frere Laurent[18]

It seems a little disingenuous to wish Sorin a Happy New Year when the letter is filled with bad news, but the letter does speak to Lawrence's open and honest personality, almost childlike in its faithful reportage and consequent sentiments. How much of the phrasing is Lawrence's and how much is to be attributed to a "secretary" is beyond our knowing, but phrases like "stagnation in business" and "replete with" seem miles beyond the pedestrian language Lawrence used in the California letters. On the other hand, a phrase like "dying out like a candle" which he used of Brother Placidus in 1851 may very well indicate in the man the educated soul of a poet even if his mind were not the educated mind of a classicist. Diamonds are often found in the rough.

Lawrence undoubtedly received many letters himself as director of the Notre Dame farm. One letter, dated March 1, 1858, and posted from Baltimore, speaks to his business acumen:

I have duly received your favor of the 24th inst. requesting me to take and negotiate one of four judgment rates of O.G. Howard of Lancaster, Ohio, dated January 1, 1858 bearing 10 per cent per annum interest after maturity at

1 year due, January 1859	2163.11
2 years due, January 1860	2284.94
3 years due, January 1861	2406.83
4 years due, January 1862	2528.69

This to be done to enable Mr. Sorin to pay his notes to me. This paper can not be negotiated here unless at a very unusual heavy rate, say 2.1 or 3 per cent per month, if at all, as our market is well supplied with paper that is known here—city paper at high rates. I know by no means the ability to discount the paper myself and I cannot take it in lieu of the notes I hold of Mr. Sorin. I have passed into other hands the notes of Mr. Sorin with my assurance that they would certainly be paid at maturity and have no controul [sic] over them. I was obliged to do this to meet my own liabilities which were pressing. The notes will have to be paid. It was a very hard settlement made with Mr. Bower of the account as I had to pay 1 to 2 per cent per month for money in the absence of payments from your institution and besides lost about $250 on the notes having 4 to 5 years to run, which I negotiated with the Bishop in St. Louis. I can do nothing whatever now to serve you in regard to the paper or would with pleasure. It just occurs to me that as the Bishop of St. Louis cashed the long notes received from your Institution (4 and 5 years) he might possibly be willing to cash one or two of those notes also and if you would prefer this negotiation to be made through me I will make the effort with pleasure. If done at all I suppose the rate will [be] about 12 per cent.

    If I can serve you in this way it will afford me pleasure.

    Yours truly,

    A. Richardson[19]

The technical nature of the contents and the business language used both indicate that mid-point in his career at Notre Dame, Lawrence not only had the respect and confidence of both local and distant businessmen, but he obviously dealt with very important money matters for Sorin. The letter proves what many have said over the years of Brother Lawrence: he was good in his work and enjoyed the respect of colleagues in and out of Notre Dame. Already by 1848, in fact, Lawrence was representing Notre Dame in court: "Brother Lawrence will go to the court house as the representative of the Institution in the lawsuit concerning the height at which the water of the lake is to be kept."[20] Sorin, as we might expect, had a high regard for Lawrence, but Sorin being Sorin, the priest could also make strong remarks as he did in 1848 of Lawrence: "Brother Lawrence 30, professed and a good religious but an enemy of everybody by reason of his excessive zeal and want of tact."[21] It may have been these very traits, however, that induced Sorin in 1852 to have Lawrence replace Vincent Pieau as Sorin's monitor, a position that required the monitor to meet with Sorin every month and point out Sorin's strengths and weaknesses. The practice no longer continues in Holy Cross.

Eventually the good businessman-farmer came to the end. He died on April 4, 1873, at the age of 57 after being sick for a few weeks. The next day Sorin circulated a beautiful obituary on the man:

> Last night, at the close of the Feast of Our Lady of the Seven Dolors, as the College clock struck nine, he gave up his soul to his Creator, fortified by all the helps of our Holy Church, and surrounded by a number of his fellow-Religious Priests and Brothers, who continued to pray around his bed until he had breathed his last ...
>
> Brother Laurence was one of the six companions I first brought with me from France, in 1841. Three of this little band have long since gone to their reward; but of the other three still remaining none had inspired me with more confidence than the subject of this notice that he was likely to survive us all; for, more than any of the rest, he possessed a robust constitution, which had naturally given us the hope that after we should have disappeared he might be spared yet awhile to keep his watchful eyes upon the field we had so long cultivated together. God, in His inscrutable designs, has ordered it differently; we resignedly submit to his infinite wisdom ...
>
> Bro. Laurence carries with him the deep and unfeigned sentiments of esteem and respect, not alone of his entire Congregation, but all with whom he came in contact, either as a Religious, or as Agent or Steward of the Institution. For more than thirty years spent here he was always, as everyone knows, foremost among those who sought honestly and earnestly to promote the interests of the Community; and if any one is to be named as having contributed more than others by earnest and persevering efforts of mind and body, to the development and prosperity of Notre Dame, if I did not do it here, the public voice would declare it, and name Bro. Laurence. No Religious in our family ever possessed and retained more constantly the confidence of his Superiors and of the Community at large.

Uneducated and unpolished, and with all the appearance of a common man, he was undoubtedly possessed of an uncommon mind, of which he frequently gave evidence in the weekly Councils of Administration, and even in the General Chapters of the Congregation to which he was three times deputed, and where his voice was always listened to with marked attention ...

In the death of Bother Laurence we sustain a serious loss which none can realize better than myself, however much his memory may be held in gratitude and love among those who knew him best, or whom he assisted most by advice and example, or in pecuniary transactions. It was myself who brought him to the Community, thirty-three years ago; and although I have seen, more than many other men of my age, Religious of undoubted fidelity, of great zeal and devotedness, I can remember none whom I would place above our dear departed one on these various points ...

The Community loses in Bro. Laurence one of its first pillars; but his spirit will not die with him, or disappear: his virtues and examples shall live forever on the spot where his name is identified with every acre now cleared, every building erected with his personal assistance. The neighborhood itself loses one of the hardiest pioneers, and one of its efficient and honest citizens. [22]

Folklore would accept by this time that Sorin brought six Brothers with him to America, and not the other way around, and it seems a bit snobbish for Sorin to proclaim Lawrence "uneducated and unpolished" in the same letter in which he praises Lawrence for hard work and solid contributions to the strength of Notre Dame. Lawrence was buried at 3 PM on April 6, 1873, in the Community cemetery on St. Mary's Road, Notre Dame.[23]

In the local South Bend press, Lawrence was fondly remembered:

One of the original six Brothers who came with Father Sorin. He had for many years been superintendent of farm and general outside financier and business manager for Notre Dame ... He had a wide acquaintance and was possessor of a very sociable personality. Many distant friends at funeral.[24]

On campus his death served, at least in one instance, for a good old-fashioned guilt trip laid on the students:

Brother Lawrence, one of the pioneers of the community, was buried this morning [sic]. He was a familiar figure on the campus. He was especially in evidence during these past months, making two or three trips a day inspecting the new buildings—and thanking God meanwhile for the blessings he had bestowed on the University. He used to drop into the Sorin Chapel now and then during the morning, to make a visit or an hour of adoration, and watch the boys at their devotions ... You are in debt to him because every day he said the beads at least once that you would be good boys. He was intensely interested in the development of daily Communion at Notre Dame, and much of the growth of the devotion is probably, in God's eyes, laid at the feet of this good man of prayer. Pay off a bit of that debt by your prayers for the repose of his soul now. And say a prayer now and then for some more of the venerable members of the Community who pray for you just as Brother Lawrence did.[25]

As disingenuous as some of this tribute may seem, subservient as it is to a more spiritually informed purpose, Brother Lawrence's death really did have a deep impact on the students:

We rarely mention in *The Scholastic* the virtues of the inmates, even when they have fulfilled their allotted share of labor on earth and have gone to receive the reward they aspired to; for during the days of their probation they lived a hidden life—and we, who know that nothing would have so much grieved them in life as to have their good deeds paraded before the world, respect their wishes even after they have departed ...

But in the death of Brother Laurence we feel that we would be doing violence to the feelings not so much of his associates in the religious life as of the host of friends outside whom he attached to himself during his intercourse of thirty-two years, if we were to pass it over in silence, or with a mere announcement without any comment ...

Brother Laurence held almost without interruption for the third part of a century the responsible position of steward or business agent of the Community of Notre Dame, and during that time he made many staunch friends among the farmers of the county and among business and professional men of South Bend and Chicago ...

This was shown at his funeral—at which, in spite of the inclemency of the weather, many of the most prominent men of South Bend were present. As we glanced over the church, crowded with his friends who had come to pay this last tribute of respect to him, we saw the faces of many whom we did not know, and who certainly did not know us, but who all had known and respected Brother Laurence these many years. Among those whose features were familiar to us, we saw those staunch old friends of Brother Laurence, Messrs. Zahnle and Sam. Jennings, among the farmers; Judge Stanfield, Judge Veasey and Judge Turner; Messrs. Koehler, A. Coquillard, Wills and Treamor, among the businessmen of the city. Beholding the church so crowded, by men whom we did not know, we remembered that within the last two weeks, when Brother Laurence was lying very ill, we were accosted on the road or on the streets by perfect strangers to us, who first, to make sure of us, asked if we "were from the College," and on our answering affirmatively, demanded news of Brother Laurence, and expressed their regrets for his dangerous illness and their hopes for his recovery.

We would fain give here our own sentiments concerning Brother Laurence, whom we knew and respected even when we were a boy, and with whom our intercourse has always been pleasant and cordial. But to say we admired his sterling worth, his sound judgment on matters that came within his sphere of action, his unaffected piety and his goodness of heart—which we experienced particularly when he was our *compagnon-de-voyage* from Paris to New York—would add nothing to the universal sentiment of esteem in which his memory is held.[26]

The sweetest part of this tribute is not the list of worthy locals who crowded into the funeral, but rather the closing anecdote about the student's trans-Atlantic travel with Brother Lawrence. The student's trip probably dovetailed with one of the voyages Brother Lawrence made to attend a General Chapter in France. At Brother Lawrence's death, Father Timothy Maher, CSC, succeeded him as Steward and General Business Agent.[27]

With the passing of Brother Lawrence, only Brother Vincent and Brother Francis Xavier remained with Sorin of the original pioneer Holy Cross religious. Joachim had died first (1844), Anselm second (1845), and Gatian left the Community (1850). Vincent remained alive until 1890, Sorin until 1893, and Francis Xavier until 1896, all three bringing the pioneer legacy almost up into the twentieth-century. We like to believe, however, that the legacy rode, as so many legacies do, on a solid financial base. Both Sorin and Lawrence were wise moneymen. One can see it especially in the photograph we have of Lawrence: he is corpulent, dressed like a successful businessman, and his face bears the unmistakable traces of a man sure of himself and his work.[28] This is the man who kept Notre Dame fiscally credible to parents and investors for the first thirty years of the institution. Visitors to the campus today should never forget what Lawrence, the pioneer businessman-farmer, did to assure that Holy Cross got off to a good start in America.

CHAPTER SIX

Francis Xavier Patois:
Carpenter-Mortician

Brother Francis Xavier was born René Patois at Clermont (Sarthe) in France on July 27, 1820, the year that Father Jacques Dujarié founded the Brothers of Saint Joseph in Ruillé-sur-Loir.[1] We do not know who his parents were or what they did for a living or how many children they had. He may have been an orphan like his long-time confrere Brother Vincent Pieau. He came to Sainte-Croix, Le Mans, in the autumn of 1840 on September 6 when he was twenty years old, perhaps arriving as a skilled carpenter, the craft at which he would labor in America for over half a century. On the other hand, he may have come to Holy Cross as a poor farmer who would learn his craft from the Brothers in Le Mans. The latter case is doubtful since he was there less than a year before he was professed on July 25, 1841, and shipped out for America ten days later with Brother Vincent, Father Sorin, and four other Brothers: it would be difficult to learn the carpentry craft in the short time René Patois enjoyed at Le Mans. We know that he was apparently an impressive and promising religious man, being the most recent of the America-bound émigrés to enter the Community, arriving at Le Mans even later than the adolescents Anselm (aged 16) and Gatian (aged 15) who rounded out the group chosen by Father Moreau for the Indiana mission.

René Patois left for America under the religious name Brother Marie, the sixth man in Holy Cross to be given that name. In the first century of the men's Congregation of Holy Cross, it was customary to recycle religious Brothers' names as men died off or left the Community. In assembling the General Matricule for Holy Cross, Brother Bernard Gervais carefully noted with Roman numerals the place each Josephite assumed in the line-up of each name. Thus René Patrois, on assuming the religious name Marie, became the sixth Josephite to be given this name, his predecessor with the name (fifth in the line-up) having left the Community October 21, 1840, three months before René Patrois became Brother Marie on February 2, 1841, when he began his novitiate training. Thereafter, the name "Marie" drops out of the Holy Cross matricule, except when used in combination: Marie-Joseph, Marie-Constantien, Marie-Julien, Marie-Augustin. There is a further Holy Cross Marie (#247), but he was received in Canada. Religious names could be duplicated if the religious involved lived in different countries. Thus when Brother Marie Patois changed his name to Brother Francis Xavier (August 21, 1848), there was already a Brother Francis Xavier in France, who was born Joseph Ménand in 1824, came to Holy Cross in 1838 (two years before René Patois), and died at Neuilly in 1888 (eight years before René Patois).[2] Once Marie changed his own name to Francis Xavier in 1848, there thus would have been two Francis Xaviers at the same time in Holy Cross, but since they lived on distant continents the matter was not considered a nuisance that would lead to confusion. He is sometimes confused in histories and archives with his contemporary Francis Xavier (at Le Mans) and even with the Sister of Providence Francis Xavier.[3] René Patois may not have been born René at all: four matricules give his name as "Renault," two give it as "René." And His family name is variably spelled as "Patois," "Pattois," "Patoy," and "Pattoy."[4]

As a novice in Le Mans, Brother Marie would have come under the direction of Basil Moreau, the founder of the Holy Cross Community, but he would not have had any contact with the great Brother André Mottais, who had shipped out for Algeria on the Community's first foreign mission in May 1840, months before René Patois arrived at Saint-Croix. Moreau was a very astute judge of character and knew his men well. He undoubtedly sensed in Brother Marie a stability of character that would serve the young man well in rough missionary circumstances and whose carpentry skills would be valuable in the pioneer Indiana territory.

We know nothing from Marie himself about his experience on the Atlantic crossing in 1841, but details of the voyage have survived in an important letter by Sister Francis Xavier who accompanied the group, arriving at Le Havre for embarkation less than a month after her first vows.[5] All eight missionaries (one priest, one Sister, six Brothers) left France aboard the *Iowa* on August 8, 1841. All was not bleak on the voyage:

> Our packet is one hundred and fifty feet long ... The doors of our rooms are of citron and mahogany, the locks of silver ... You would see on board some beautiful birds that the passengers are taking with them; also a large cow, some sheep, pigs, ducks, chickens and rabbits, which serve us for food. You would enjoy yourself climbing up the masts, but you would also see some little boys of your own age in the steerage, carrying water, cooking, and obeying their parents promptly.[6]

Sister Francis Xavier was obviously writing to one of her younger siblings, given the charming details of climbing the masts.

The *Iowa* docked in New York harbor on September 13, 1841. Then Sister Francis Xavier parted from the Holy Cross men, and the men spent three days with a family named Byerly before pushing on for Indiana, a trek that would take almost a month, almost as long as their sea voyage.

When the group arrived at Vincennes on October 10, Sorin chose one of two settlements offered by the local bishop, Celestine de la Halandière. The place had a small church and three cabins. Not exactly a paradise, it was deemed by saintly Mother Theodore Guerin unsuitable for human habitation, and she was aghast when she heard that the men would spend the winter there,[7] but it was, of course, just the sort of fixer-upper that would have challenged the creative instincts of a carpenter like René Patois. In fact, he soon made a bed for each Brother so they would not have to sleep on the floor.[8]

The first letter written by a Brother in Indiana was written by Brother Francis Xavier and posted to Basil Moreau on October 1, 1841. As one might expect of a carpenter, his first thoughts concerned wood:

> I am happy at having made the sacrifice of leaving and am very well adapted to the atmosphere of the woods. It's rather natural because I am in my element: we don't lack lumber, and we don't even have to leave the woods to return home. I'm sure that not one of the three Brother carpenters would want to return to Sainte Croix. We've measured oaks 20 feet around, straight as candles, and as high in proportion. These poor oaks die standing. You can't take a step without encountering a rotting tree. If they fall in the road, instead of removing them, people make a new road.
>
> I'm working at things for the house. I have a carpenter with whom I wouldn't know how to chat because we don't understand each other, and all I can say is, "Yes, very well."[9]

The sweetness of this letter to Moreau is evident in the simple, almost childish delight Francis Xavier finds in his new surroundings. He is becoming "adapted to the woods," as he puts it so charmingly, and he does not lack for basic materials living, as he does, in the middle of an old-growth forest. His reference to "three Brother carpenters" is curious in that he was supposedly the only Brother carpenter to arrive from France: Vincent, Anselm, and Gatian were teachers, Lawrence was a farmer, and Joachim was a tailor (pressed into service as a cook). There were, however, many young men who joined the fledgling group in Indiana, so they might have included a carpenter or two. But Francis Xavier would not have been referring to any of them because although his letter is dated October 1, 1841, from St. Peter's in Montgomery, Indiana, in the chronology of events the band of seven from Le Mans did not arrive at St. Peter's until October 14, and they would not have had any novices on that date other than Charles Rother who was waiting there for them when they arrived.[10] On October 1, 1840, Francis Xavier should have been in Fort Wayne, en route to Vincennes. Thus the reference to "three Brother carpenters" is enigmatic. He may have, however, included Lawrence the farmer and Joachim the tailor as possible carpenters. After all, Lawrence was a man of many talents and Joachim seemed fluid in his trade. Francis Xavier's reference to "working at things for the house" suggests that the letter was indeed written from Montgomery as the locale of the letter ("St. Peter's") indicates.

A year later, however, the local bishop had proved himself more than obnoxious, and Edward Sorin jumped at the chance to escape north to a larger piece of property the bishop offered him. The trip was made in two contingents three months apart, Brother Francis Xavier being included in the first contingent on November 16, 1842. Francis Xavier, Gatian, and Sorin, along with three novices, took eleven days to cover the 270 miles at the outset of one of the worst winters on record for Indiana. The trip has been most wonderfully related by Brother John Steber, with delightful details concerning their dog Azore,[11] and their first impressions of Notre Dame were captured rapturously by Sorin in his now famous letter to Basil Moreau:

> Everything was frozen over. Yet it all seemed so beautiful. The lake, especially, with its broad carpet of dazzling white snow, quite naturally reminded us of the spotless purity of our august Lady whose name it bears, and also of the purity of soul that should mark the new inhabitants of this chosen spot. Our dwelling struck us as being just about the same as St. Peter's. We just glanced at it, though, because we were in a hurry to enjoy all the scenery along the lakeshore of which we had heard so much. Though it was quite cold, we went to the very end of the lake, and like children, came back fascinated with the marvelous beauties of our new home. May this new

Eden be always the refuge of innocence and virtue! Here I could willingly exclaim with the Prophet: "The Lord ruleth me ... He hath brought me up on the water of refreshment."[12]

Needless to add, Brother Francis Xavier at age twenty-two would have shared in this exuberant reaction to the new home for Holy Cross in America.

Late in his life, a year before his death, Francis Xavier himself recalled part of this journey from St. Peter's to South Bend for the *South Bend Times*:

> We came through from Vincennes in an old stage coach, which the Bishop [de la Halandière] who sent us here picked up somewhere. It was too small a conveyance to hold us all and our baggage, so we took turns at walking. When we arrived at South Bend we stopped for several days at the home of the first Alexis Coquillard as there were no accommodations for our party at the mission. We did not ford the river, ferry it, or go over it in row boats, but crossed it on the old bridge north of the brickyard. Alexis Coquillard, Jr., might have gone with us, but he was a small boy then.
>
> There was nothing at Notre Dame but the old log house seen in the drawing. Additions were soon made to it for the accommodation of our party and in a short time the brick house now standing beside the lake was built by Benjamin Coquillard. The picture made under my direction will be found in the Golden Jubilee book.[13]

The elder Alexis Coquillard mentioned here was not only an important figure in early South Bend history, he was also instrumental in helping the Holy Cross pioneers adjust to the Indiana territory. When Francis Xavier arrived with Sorin and four others from Vincennes in November 1842 and stayed their first nights in the area at the home of Alexis Coquillard, they were enjoying his hospitality just thirteen years before the kindly fur-trader died while inspecting the ruins of his burned out flour mill: the beam on which he was walking collapsed and he fell sixteen feet to his death. He is buried in the north wall of the little chapel on the grounds of Cedar Grove Cemetery more than likely in a coffin made by Brother Francis Xavier.[14]

As the Brother-carpenter settled into life at Notre Dame, he found his talents well used not only in construction projects but also in instruction. The Manual Labor School was chartered in 1844,[15] and Francis Xavier's work in it is documented several times in the student newspaper: "The Manual Labor School is a great charity, which is sustained by the Brothers of St. Joseph unaided by anyone else. Under the solicitous care of Mr. Sheerer, CSC, Bros. Constantine, John, Xavier, Francis Joseph, Charles, Alfred, and others, the students receive that instruction which will fit them for those stations in life they will hereafter fill."[16] Although there is a touch of condescension on the part of the student-writer (himself undoubtedly not from the Manual Labor School), it is evident that industrial arts were thriving at Notre Dame alongside the classical and commercial curricula that catered to sons of the upper crust. Sadly, the industrial arts buildings burned to the ground in 1849, but Sorin resolved to rebuild them immediately, and with his customary bravado oversaw a resolution in the Minor Chapter that "no lightning rod shall be placed over the college at least for the present, by a reason of confidence in God's Providence."[17] One wonders if it were really a mortal shaking his fist at the divine in this instance or simply a lack of funds to pay for lightning rods, which can be a huge expense for rare usage.

In 1850 Brother Francis Xavier received an obedience to work in Rome at an orphanage that Sainte-Croix had opened at the invitation of Pius IX,[18] but the obedience was revoked, probably much to the relief of both Francis Xavier and Sorin. As a skilled wood worker, Francis Xavier would have been an asset to the orphanage, but his craftsmanship was much needed in Indiana. In 1847, for example, he enhanced the chapel of the Holy Cross Sisters in Bertrand (Michigan) by carving for them an altar and making frames for their Way of the Cross.[19] In 1851 he made steeples for the St. Joseph Church in South Bend.[20]

We have precious few letters by Francis Xavier, but the 1863 crisis between Notre Dame in America and Sainte-Croix in France affords us a very beautiful letter from the carpenter to Basil Moreau. The letter is dated January 27, 1863, and is posted from Notre Dame:

> Please excuse me for not writing since our difficulties began. You perhaps interpreted my silence as a mark of respect for the Congregation. But let me say first of all that nothing would be less true than to believe me lacking love for her! She is my mother, and I'm attached to her from the bottom of my heart. Everything that concerns her concerns me, and my happiness here couldn't be greater.
>
> If therefore I have not told you sooner the pain caused me by our sad divisiveness, and if I had not asked for advice from the Motherhouse, as a member of the Administrative Council, it's because I always believed that our misfortunes would end and we would end up working through them. But seeing the letter Brother Lawrence [Menage] just received, I urge you to consider the profound regret I feel over the state of things and my wish to see our union flourish again. Without this union our days are incomplete. We would not prosper, scandal would result, Religion would be dishonored. Notre Dame du Lac would collapse undoubtedly succumbing to the first, but a House of this importance couldn't fall without a shock to other parts. The Motherhouse, the Congregation, would receive, I believe, a fatal blow. But if you tell me, very reverend Father, "All this comes from you, from your Council; it's you who caused this state of affairs; it's the administration of Notre Dame [du Lac] who is totally at fault; it's she who refused to obey my orders," may it please God, my good Father, that we could complain to you and put an end to dissension, which we are suffering from, and bring about order and peace. Now, the administration of Notre Dame du Lac, not knowing what will happen nor how to act, throws itself into your arms—do with us what you will.

God alone knows how much I love the Congregation and its superiors and also how much I am attached to the Motherhouse, but I can't think without crying about the possibility that Notre Dame du Lac could fall into ruin.

The thing which most surprised and pained the Brothers (and undoubtedly also the Priests) is to see the Rev. Father Visitor [Charles Moreau] begin the Visit and leave without finishing it. What are we to do about the Sisters? Is it necessary to accept the consequences because of the difficulties? Thus we remain upset. Brother Vincent just fell sick, and I think our difficulties caused his sickness. May they not worsen! Heavens, let them end. If we have acted imprudently, pardon us, we will make honorable amends, but let us have peace and goodness!!

I beg God to have pity on our unhappy Congregation, that things will work out safe and sound, that the darkness will dissipate, and that we'll enjoy happiness, security, and peace before eternal happiness.

I also beg the Lord, with all the fervor I'm capable of, that He will deign to give us, very reverend Father, long and peaceful days, in the bosom of our large family—henceforth united—all children, united in heart and soul, with no other desires or aspirations than to do God's will as shown in that of the Superior General.

I am with the deepest respect and affection, my very reverend Father, your very obedient son in JMJ,

Brother Francis Xavier, formerly Mary[21]

The squabble between France and Indiana during the American Civil War precipitated from many problems fomenting over many years and included machinations of a treasurer sent from Le Mans (Brother Amédeé Dayres) and failed foundations in New York City.[22] Moreau decided an official Visit was warranted, but his choice of official Visitor could not have been more infelicitous: his own thirty-nine year old nephew Charles, an honest but brusque priest. Sorin, by the summer of 1862, had threatened to resign from both Notre Dame and the Congregation. It was in this context that Brother Francis Xavier sent his letter to Basil Moreau pleading for understanding. He was not afraid to finger the exact areas of conflict between Notre Dame and the Motherhouse.

Very late in his life, Francis Xavier sat down with a Professor Edwards at Notre Dame to talk about earlier days. The interview notes are dated October 26, 1897, according to Brother Bernard (Gervais?) in marginalia dated April 1943. Edwards must have written them down the year after Francis Xavier's death. Edwards asked Francis Xavier about the 1863 fight with Le Mans. Francis Xavier replied that France kept asking for money, and when Francis Xavier told the Visitor, Charles Moreau, that the Lake could not continue to send money ("We would have to sell out"), Charles Moreau said, "Who cares if you do?" Francis Xavier pointed out that they had many old Irish religious who had brought money with them to Notre Dame: "We can't sell out and let them starve." He also noted that Charles Moreau wanted some of the money Propaganda Fidei had given to the Lake, but Francis Xavier replied that if they did give Le Mans some of that money Propaganda Fidei would drop them from their list.[23]

We should not be surprised that Brother Francis Xavier was secure enough in his position at Notre Dame to presume a direct appeal to the eminent founder in France, but one item attributed to his incompetence during that turbulent time has proven false. In the 1864 Congressional elections the Republican candidate Schuyler Colfax leaned on Edward Sorin to have the Notre Dame religious vote for him since it was his party that let Notre Dame keep its post office and it was his party that continued to exempt the Brothers from military service. At the local council, Sorin raised the issue and the matter was discussed for one or two hours, according to Hope, who writes that Brother Francis Xavier was chosen to warm up the religious to vote Republican, but he "either forgot or neglected this most important matter"[24] and the Irish vote swung against Colfax. Infuriated, Colfax did nothing to prevent immediate draft proceedings against five members of the Notre Dame community. Happily General Philip

Sherman's wife intervened in Washington[7] so the draft motion was suppressed.[25] Hope's citation[26] on this matter is not helpful since it points out that Sorin in his *Chronicles* imputed inactivity or worse to Francis Xavier, actions that turn out to be untrue: nowhere in his *Chronicles* does Sorin write that Francis Xavier forgot his duties or neglected them. Sorin wrote: "it [the mandate] was badly carried out, or rather was not carried out at all, the member to whom it had been entrusted foolishly relying on a third party who did not understand the consequences and took no steps in this matter."[27] What Hope failed to conclude is that the unnamed third party was culpable and not Francis Xavier, whose only fault may have been the poor selection of a person to spread the word about voting for Colfax or to convince members to do so.

However, there is more. The actual Notre Dame Council of Administration minutes for this election episode are quite interesting. The Council met four times that month (October 5, 11, 17, 24) and the Colfax matter was brought up in two of these meetings. The minutes for October 17 note that the minutes for October 11 made no mention of "actions which the Council had taken on the 5th inst. respective of the elections that were to take place here a few days later" (in the week of October 5). Thus the October 17 minutes fill in the lacunae:

> On the 5th day of October the members of the Council assembled determined that owing to the many works of friendship and good will we had received from Mr. Colfax of South Bend and other officers of the Government, the Community, that is, all such members of it who can vote, should vote for Hon. Colfax as a representative in Congress and for other Nominees of the said ticket. And Bro. Lawrence was specially directed by the president of the Council to carry out this resolution which (as it was afterwards discovered) he failed to do.[28]

There is no mention of Francis Xavier at all in the document, and the culprit, Brother Lawrence Menage, is named as simply having failed to do his commission, not that he delegated it to a third party. Thus, Arthur Hope spun a citation out of context, substituting Francis Xavier for Lawrence. Of course it may be that Sorin knew that Lawrence had elicited Francis Xavier as that unnamed "third party" to do his dirty work for him, but such a scenario makes little sense. Lawrence was an outgoing and popular figure in the Notre Dame community so deputing him to sway voters makes some sense, but gentle little Francis Xavier was hardly the kind of person who would chat up voters: he was too honest a man to compromise his principles for any political reason, so acting as a political barker was hardly in character for him. Could it have been that the assignment was so distasteful to Lawrence that he passed it along to the gentle Francis Xavier knowing that it would die the death it deserved? Sorin does not say, and we can only guess, but one thing we must do is clear up the facts: Francis Xavier was not chosen by the Council to spread to his colleagues the good word on Colfax.

By the 1870's Francis Xavier had expanded his work at Notre Dame with the opening of a store on campus where he sold "pious pictures."[29] The student newspaper notes that "all persons desiring pictures of the late Rev. Fathers Gillespie and Lemmonier can be accommodated by him."[30] According to a later issue of *The Notre Dame Scholastic*, the "picture-store" was located "in the Franciscan building, opposite the College" and was open every Wednesday afternoon at one o'clock.[31] In June of 1876, Francis Xavier was also selling sacred vases and church candlesticks so his clientele must have reached beyond the campus, college students having little need for such items. *The Scholastic*, however, hawked the merchandise: "Such articles can scarcely be found in the country at the prices at which they are to be sold by him,"[32] and six years later Francis Xavier's inventory had expanded to "religious articles of every description." The store was by then located across from the post-office, "and those who require anything in his line can be supplied with the best and the cheapest."[33] The Notre Dame Bookstore is born! As if the man did not already have enough to do working in the Manual Labor School and burying people who died in the South Bend vicinity.

We do not know how Francis Xavier came to be the designated undertaker at Notre Dame, but as the master-carpenter of the pioneer group, he would have been the obvious choice to make coffins. His first client may very well have been Brother Joachim, who died within two years of the group's arrival at Notre Dame. From coffins to undertaking, it was just a matter of getting a hearse and a reputation. He acquired both soon enough, and by the time of his death he was an accepted part of the South Bend burial scene. We do not know how many dead he buried a year. The nineteenth-century records for Cedar Grove Cemetery name no undertakers. But we know he buried non-Community people because Cedar Grove was his bailiwick (in addition to the Community cemetery, located first near the present day Columba Hall and later moved up St. Mary's Road to its present location). He built the beautiful little chapel in the Cedar Grove Cemetery, and he even gave the place its name, according to Bishop Alerding—Francis Xavier's favorite trees in the cemetery were the cedar trees.[34] Francis Xavier expanded the cemetery in the spring of 1878.[35] We do have extant two sheets of his accounts book for Cedar Grove, and they give evidence that he was successful: the sheets are printed with his name prominent. Since these two sheets chronicle a return customer (Mrs. Dignan buried two daughters and a husband with Francis Xavier's services), we can presume he was effective in his mortal ministry.[36] In 1882 Francis Xavier's coffins cost ten or twenty dollars, and use of his hearse cost five dollars. Grave digging was two dollars.

On Memorial Day in June 1882 Francis Xavier attended a special ceremony at Cedar Grove: "In the morning, a delegation visited the cemetery at Notre Dame, where a number of departed braves await the last trump. Prof. Howard, who was a soldier during the late war, led the procession. B. Francis Xavier, the amiable guardian of God's acre, was in attendance, and expressed himself much pleased that his silent braves had not been forgotten."[37] Not only is this notice touching for its proof that early on Notre Dame was cognizant of the poor Miami and Potawatomi who had been forced off their land, it also shows that Francis Xavier took a personal interest in "his silent braves."

It is this kind of personal note that would impress young *Scholastic* journalists before they would leave their idealistic academic world and head out to live in the cold reality of an industrial America on the move.[38] Folklore has, however, colored some of Francis Xavier's dealings with Native Americans. On March 14, 1891, he buried a Miami Native American named Chippa, reputed to be one hundred and fifty years old.[39]

Eventually death caught up with Francis Xavier, death's main adjutant at Notre Dame. According to Bartholomew Crowley, on November 12, 1896, Francis Xavier "dropped dead on the steps of his office this morning at seven o'clock. He had just eaten a hearty breakfast and was on his way from the dining room when stricken with apoplexy."[40] Apoplexy was the nineteenth-century term for what today we would call a stroke. The *South Bend Tribune* noted wryly that an anonymous writer who had written earlier that Francis Xavier "has made coffins for all who have died at Notre Dame and most likely will do the same kind office for many more yet before he drives the last nail in his own" was actually himself buried by Francis Xavier in November 1874.[41] When he died, Francis Xavier was but 76 years old, yet he had outlasted all the other six Holy Cross pioneers: Sorin by 3 years, Vincent by 6, Lawrence by 23, Gatian by 36, Anselm by 51, and Joachim by 52. The United States Provincial at the time of Francis Xavier's death, William Corby, remembered the old carpenter-mortician in a circular letter dated one day after the man's death:

> Brother Francis was a model religious, regular at all the exercises, industrious to the very last, devoted to the Community, and who led a life of great self-denial. He was a cabinet-maker by trade. From the very earliest history of his life in America, in 1841, he was employed as an undertaker, and he was frequently called up at night, and had to go eight or even twelve miles to attend the dead. Hundreds of times he was exposed in rains or snow-storms; perched upon an uncovered hearse, slowly making his way to the church or

cemetery. The most remarkable fact in his history is that he came with Very Rev. E. Sorin in company with five other Brothers in 1841. He survived every one of that devoted band who founded Notre Dame. It would be hard to find in history a more devoted band of missionaries than the band of which Brother Francis Xavier was the last survivor.[42]

Of course it would be difficult to write an obituary for Francis Xavier without mentioning the pioneer band that arrived in Indiana in 1841, and Corby touches nicely on that part of Francis Xavier's history.

The student newspaper, *The Scholastic*, also had its say on the Brother's death. Two days after his death, a full page with a centered picture appeared in the middle of the November 14, 1896, issue:

Another link between the present and past of our Alma Mater has been broken; the last of the silken strings that bound the Notre Dame of '42 to the Notre Dame of '96 has been snapped in twain. Brother Francis Xavier is dead! and with him passes away the last survivor of that little band of heroes who changed the bleak forest into a bright fairy-land, and reared on stones cemented with their blood the domes and turrets of our noble college home.

They were hard and painful, the days when Notre Dame was founded. That winter when they broke their way through the fallen trees and the drifted snow is set down in history as one of the coldest since 1607. Even the Indians, accustomed as they were to the rigors of winter, were almost exterminated. Many of them were frozen to death. It was impossible to carry needful provisions with them, and the pain of hunger was added to the pain of cold. South Bend was hardly a small village, and when a pound of coffee was wanted a messenger was dispatched—ah! the irony of that word!—all the long journey to Detroit.

The work of the religious at Notre Dame in those hard, early days was a continuous crucifixion. Health they had and eager appetites, but the merest comforts—even the merest necessities sometimes—were absent. But Providence fitted the back to the burden. The founders of Notre Dame were stalwart and rugged as the Norsemen. Like giants they exulted in their strength, and the continuous struggle with primeval nature inspired and strengthened them. Trials they knew, wrestlings within and without; and sometimes it seemed that the favor of Heaven itself was withdrawn from them, and the labor of months and years destroyed. But they toiled on undiscouraged and undismayed, and at last they hewed their way to the light.

Brother Francis Xavier was one of these brave pioneers. The days of his stewardship were longer than those of his early companions, but not till the hour of his death did he relax his tremendous energy and zeal. He was the local undertaker from the very beginning—he buried all who have died at Notre Dame. Many times in a week he was roused from his sleep at night, often to ride far into the country in the rain and the cold, but a word of complaint was never on his lips. "As cheerful as an undertaker" is not, we believe, a proverb; but it would soon become one if all the craft had as much sunshine in their hearts as he. His life was full of labor, done in a spirit of duty and with no eye to earthly reward, and in the consciousness that he was doing God's work he found his solace and his recompense. From his fellow religious he won a peculiar veneration, and from the poor, whom his ministrations assisted, a very special love.

Since Father Sorin died, Brother Francis has been the Patriarch of Notre Dame; but no stranger who saw the silent, unobtrusive Brother, as he moved actively about his work, would have guessed it. He wore his honors gracefully, and to the end he remained the prayerful, laborious, amiable, humble religious that he was in youth. Such men never die. They live again in every life which their example has helped to sanctify. The days of the founding will seem ancient now that Brother Francis has passed away, but the memory of his good, long life, and the fragrance of his Christian virtues, will never depart from those who knew him. God grant his noble spirit rest![43]

And so Brother Francis was laid to rest at a ripe old age for the times—seventy-six. And who dug his grave? Two days before Francis Xavier died, there arrived at Notre Dame a young man to join the Brothers of Holy Cross. His name in the Community would be Brother Bernard Gervais. He was told by his novice master on November 12, 1896, to go to the cemetery and help dig the grave for Francis Xavier. Bernard lived a long life and was for many years the only touchstone at Notre Dame to the early pioneer men of Holy Cross.

But an indignity remains for Francis Xavier: his tombstone at Notre Dame uses the name "Reynault Patois" for this pioneer Brother, thus continuing even after his death the matter of multiple names. Was his first name "René" or "Reynault"? Was his family name "Patois" or "Patoy"? For the pioneer Brother who changed his name from "Marie" to "Francis Xavier" early in his career at Notre Dame, perhaps he is today finding playfulness endemic in what historians would make of his chameleon name changes.

CHAPTER SEVEN

Anselm Caillot: Ready to Serve in Indiana

At the end of the eighteenth century, the Department of La Mayenne in France saw a radical transformation of its economic base: the linen industry, ruined by war and political turmoil, gradually gave way to agriculture.[1] Farming as an occupation grew by leaps and bounds. In 1815, only 48,000 hectares in La Mayenne had been devoted to grain crops, but by 1862, 100,000 hectares were so used. Wheat was exported even to England. Livestock too began to develop as a commodity, and cattle production grew rapidly in the northwest corner of the department.[2] In this idyllic part of the country is the city of Angers, and fifteen miles southeast of Angers nestles Gennes, a quiet town on the Loire River, fifty miles south of Le Mans. Here, the fourth of four children,[3] Pierre Caillot was born in 1825 on the feast of St. Joseph, March 19, and from this village of Gennes he left at the age of fourteen to follow a new life as a Brother of St. Joseph.[4] Previously under the care of Jacques Dujarié, the Brothers were transferred to the guardianship of Basil Moreau in 1835. Thus Pierre Caillot would have been among the earliest religious to be shepherded by the founder of Holy Cross.

We can only guess at Pierre's gradual transformation into Brother Anselm, the second man to bear that name at Ste. Croix, but we know that he impressed Moreau enough to be chosen as one of the seven men for the first colony to be sent to America. Why would a sixteen-year old novice, too young even for vows, be shipped to a foreign land? He and an even younger man named Urban Monsimer (Brother Gatian) had impressed Moreau with their aptitude for language. We must presume also that Moreau was impressed with the energy of both of these young men. Indeed, their subsequent letters demonstrate an exuberance that would be cut short by early death for Anselm but would develop into brash epistolary attacks on Edward Sorin by Gatian. Life in the New World would never be dull for either of the teenage boys.

Of the twenty letters we have written by Brother Anselm, only six and a half are in English. The others are in French. All the letters are written to Edward Sorin at Notre Dame, except number 14 (addressed to Father Moreau in France) and number 19 (addressed to Brother Vincent). Two of the English letters (numbers 2 and 3) are dated as early as July 1843, when the young man was but eighteen years old and had been in America fewer than two years. The English is remarkably good. Anselm never became the polished writer that Gatian became, but he penned letters smoothly in two languages. Anselm's twenty letters that remain represent almost fifty percent of the correspondence sent by Brothers to Sorin between June of 1843 and July of 1845. It is not that Anselm was a particularly prolific letter-writer, but rather that he was one of the few men not stationed at Notre Dame. Letters to Sorin came in those two years mostly from Anselm and Brother Mary Joseph (Samuel O'Connell).[5] Anselm wrote first from Vincennes and then from Madison, Indiana, Mary Joseph first from Madison and then from Vincennes. The two men switched jobs sometime between August of 1844 (Anselm's last letter from Vincennes) and December (Mary Joseph's first letter from Vincennes).

Anselm's first letter is dated June 18, 1843, four months after Brothers Vincent, Lawrence, and Joachim had abandoned the foundation at St. Peter's (Montgomery, Indiana) and had travelled north with six novices and two postulants to join Sorin and the rest of the Community at Notre Dame. Their chaplain at St. Peter's had left the diocese after an argument with the bishop.[6] Anselm, at age 18, was left alone in Vincennes as teacher and principal of the cathedral's grade school. He alludes to some troubles he has had in administering the school, particularly some matter involving Brother Celestine, who had been left with him when Brother Vincent's group headed north in February. We do not know exactly what the problem with Celestine was, but that this Brother had a reputation as a trouble-maker is evident in the Notre Dame chapter books: there he is mentioned in the entry for the Particular Council of August 14, 1843: "After invoking the H.G. [Holy Ghost] the Particular Council took into consideration Bro. Celestine's dismissal and resolved that sufficient money should be given him to defray his expenses to Logansport, unless he could be prudently induced to stay until the reception of his aunt's money." Celestine left the young Community, or rather was forced out, three months after Anselm's first letter to Sorin. This first letter by Anselm is short and already tinged with the poignancy that colors most of his correspondence, a poignancy to be expected of a young man separated from all members of his Community, far from headquarters, longing for support and camaraderie.

Anselm's second letter follows the first by one month and begins with anxious assurances that he has been faithful to his religious exercises:

> I was surprized [sic] by the bell and though I have had always a multitude of distractions in my exercises, I have never omitted any one, ex[cept] the particular examination, and that for punishing some boys after school and once the spiritual reading, knowing not w[hat] time it was.[7]

He is overworked: four or five new students have enrolled since Brother Vincent was reassigned to Notre Dame, and now Anselm also has responsibility for eight seminarians. He does not specify the nature of his duties to the seminarians, but it may have included prefecting in addition to after-hours tutoring. The vicar general of the diocese, Father August Martin,[8] is instructing him in natural history, and Anselm, perhaps counting on Sorin's interest in the subject (Sorin did eventually spend money to build a museum at Notre Dame much to the chagrin of Brother Gatian), uses the moment to force Sorin to a decision about Anselm's vacation at Notre Dame: "I have six different kinds of tortoises and snakes and some insects, which I will bring to South Bend if you juge [sic] it proper ... If you want the tortoises I will be obliged to buy some poison to stuff them up." These ingenuous suggestions follow in the same rambling paragraph in which the young man asks his superior when he should take his vacation and if he has to travel north alone. He also writes that he has to know if he will be returning to Vincennes or not for the next school year so he can pack accordingly. School assignments were made late, of course, oftentimes a kind of surprise saved for the end of the annual retreat in late August.

For a first letter in English by this teenager, the style is good but occasionally Frenchified. For example, an expression like "4 or 5 new scholars have come since the Brother's departure," as Anselm refers to Brother Vincent, makes use of the definite article where English would not. There are also several misspelled words (but nowhere near the number found in letters by his contemporary Brother Francis). Anselm writes another short letter in English to Sorin a week later; then he corresponds only in French until his final five letters to Sorin in 1845. The short letter written on July 16, 1843, also contains odd expressions ("I have changed of room") and misspellings. It may have been that Anselm tested his wings in writing English letters early on but abandoned the practice for the next year until he felt more comfortable with his new language. Sorin, I suspect, preferred getting letters in French, and Brother Vincent never mastered English, as he admits in one of his own letters.

Within the third letter, there are hints that Anselm is dissatisfied with his living arrangements: he has been shuffled to a new bedroom so his old one could be converted into a sacristy, and the new bedroom is so damp that every four or five days his shoes become moldy if he does not brush them. His books suffer the same fate. His new room had belonged to the bishop's valet, and although bigger than Anselm's previous room, it is clearly not to his liking. This room matter will continue to be an issue in Vincennes.

By July 26, Anselm has still received no word from Sorin about the starting date for the annual retreat. The matter leads to a nasty exchange with the bishop, Celestine de la Hailandière. Apparently the bishop was irked by Sorin's suggestion in a letter to Anselm that Father Martin would preach the retreat. Hailandière snaps at Anselm, "The pastor of the parish could not leave his flock to go preach a retreat to Brothers 300 miles away."[9] The previous Monday Hailandière had told Anselm to make his retreat in Vincennes, an eventuality Anselm wanted no part of: "I replied in a slightly angry tone that that didn't matter as long as I had a Brother to help me next year and that I certainly wouldn't be able to do everything all alone. To that he said that Sister did the free school well by herself but unfortunately I forgot to tell him that she didn't have to teach French." Anselm leaves the bishop and goes to Father Martin's house on the pretense of bringing him an insect. He tells Martin what the bishop had just said, and Martin tells Anselm to complain to Sorin. Bishop de la Hailandière apparently did not enjoy the loyalty of even his own clergy. Several days later the bishop tells Anselm he may go to the retreat at Notre Dame provided he can find a horse to borrow. Anselm breaks down in writing to Sorin:

> My Father, I can't fool you that in learning all this news, I had some resentment against you as well as the Community, because after wearing myself out teaching for a year and having the Community's interests in everything I did, it seemed to me that you'd not hold back six or seven dollars to let me enjoy the benefit of the retreat with my confreres.

Anselm is quite lost in Vincennes. Antagonized by the bishop (as almost everyone was), he had some support from Father Martin, but nothing near what he needed as a fledgling in the Holy Cross family.

The problems with Hailandière continue. In letter number 5 (October 26, 1843), Anselm writes that the bishop has accused him of stealing a kitchen brush, not teaching properly, and giving too much vacation time to the students. Anselm runs all three accusations into one sentence, and the effect on the reader is bewilderment: why would a bishop bedevil his own cheap labor force in such a way? Anselm was confused in the situation and said nothing to the bishop. One suspects the lad was traumatized by the tongue-lashing. He has other complaints he dare not raise to the bishop, e.g., the coldness of his stoveless bedroom and the fact that the room is so dark he cannot see to draw. He is exasperated: "I'm telling you definitely that if I don't have another room or at least a stove in my room, I will not stay here, because the vow of obedience that I made does not oblige me to kill myself, or to make myself sick to obey the bishop who has at least more than ten rooms standing empty."[10] Anselm mentions the Sisters, and it is obvious he is jealous of their living quarters afforded them by the bishop and their adequately furnished classrooms. His own classroom has been stripped clean of furniture, and all the books were mildewed when he arrived. Toads and caterpillars had taken over the classroom, and someone had turned the room into a temporary dormitory for girls. Moreover, most of the furniture from his bedroom was missing along with his mirror and brushes. The grievances grow: he has to chop his own wood, mend his own clothes, and "do all sorts of things that have nothing to do with my contract." In short, Anselm feels exploited, probably no worse than other religious throughout the nineteenth century in America, but nonetheless the situation rankles this young man. He rages: "I beg you in the name of Mary to get me out of here soon." Then he relents, "But meanwhile your will be done." It is easy to admire Anselm even in the outbursts of anger we find in the letters. Sorin was his safety valve: by writing about his anger, Anselm defuses himself. The above letter ends with a note that school has started: twenty students have shown up for his class. It is late October.

In letter #6, we learn that the lost mirror and brushes have turned up, but the bedroom is still cold. In this letter we have another indication that Anselm is an artist: he boasts that he is adept at oriental painting and hints that with a few lessons he could be perfect.

This talent Anselm will use to try to finagle his way out of hated Vincennes:

> As a good teacher of this kind of painting can't be found in America, I'm going to propose to Father Rector [Moreau] to return to spend a year in France to learn all of it, which is hard because it includes landscape and portraiture. I would learn at the same time linear and academic drawing, etc.[11]

Today we would call this process the method of discernment, but given the times and situation, it seems opportunism. Anselm continues:

> Don't believe, Father, that I wish to defrock. No, truthfully, but as Father Rector promised I could return sometime to France, I prefer to go there now while I am yet young because I would have much more facility in learning drawing, and I'd be more able to give service to the Community. Otherwise I'd prefer to go only after a long stay in this country—or not to go at all. I won't nag. (But you know the usefulness of drawing and painting in a college [secondary school]).

He is, of course, using the threat of leaving the Congregation to force Sorin's hand for a move out of Vincennes. He appeals to authority (Moreau) above Sorin's head and suggests long-term benefits to the Community for his leaving Vincennes. He demurs and insists he will not "nag," but then he attaches a coda: a trained art teacher would be very valuable at Notre Dame. Anselm is desperate and understandably duplicitous. We can imagine Sorin's reaction to this ruse, a young fox writing to an old fox, the master of ruse.

Meanwhile at Notre Dame, where Anselm longs to be, the Holy Cross community thrives. Brother Lawrence uses his business and farming skills to help Sorin establish a firm economic base for the new school. Brother Gatian, a bright and brash boy who emigrated with the group at age fifteen, is fast becoming the intellectual divining-rod of Notre Dame: he keeps minutes for all meetings, teaches math and French, and harasses Sorin into keeping local community rules strict. Brother Joachim cooks for the men, and Brother Francis Xavier is chief carpenter and mortician. The patriarch Brother Vincent, a generation older than the others, trains novices and edifies all who know him. At age forty-four he is the oldest of the missionaries and the one most deeply steeped in the spiritual charism of Holy Cross.

Letter #7 is upbeat in spite of troubles: the bishop has given Anselm a quilt and offered to move him to a new room (colder and darker!). Father Martin has given up on the bishop, or so he tells Anselm, and Brother John is causing scandal at St. Peter's and Washington by passing himself off as a philosopher and a former Brother. Although he lives in the bishop's house, Anselm has to walk to the seminary for his meals. Only the bishop and his priests are allowed to eat at the bishop's table, and Anselm notes he would rather eat in the kitchen than walk to the seminary. Anselm's class is up to forty students including two black boys whom Anselm would like to dismiss. He gives no reason. As he mentions that the black students were placed in the school specifically by the bishop, it may be another show of the bishop's authority that bothers Anselm, or it could be that Anselm is simply prejudiced. He ends the letter to Sorin asking if Moreau has said anything about Anselm's returning to France to study drawing for two years. In a letter we no longer have, Anselm himself apparently wrote to Moreau requesting the change. The complaints in the extant letter are obviously mitigated by the hope Anselm has for a brighter future.

Two months later, in letter #8, Anselm is in despair: Father Martin, his trusted support, has turned against him. Anselm calls him "my greatest enemy" and outlines his grievances against the priest:

1. No longer coming to visit my class.
2. No longer speaking to me.
3. Refusing to ask for anything from the bishop for me …
4. Depriving me sometimes of my meals, etc., etc., etc.
because, as I told you in my last letter, he told me that when

I'd arrive at the dining room after the others, I'd have nothing to eat, and that I could go eat wherever I wanted, that I'd have no privilege here. On that point, having told him that I had rules to follow, he replied that that meant nothing to him, but that it was necessary to follow the rule he gave me, and if I weren't happy, I could go elsewhere.[12]

It is no wonder that Anselm is being given the silent treatment if we remember how he had used Martin as a go-between previously as Anselm jockeyed with the bishop for a position in the house pecking order. He is an outsider and now feels the total devastation of isolation and degradation for bucking authority. Either Martin tired of the complaints Anselm brought to him, or Martin saw his own bread was buttered by the bishop, possibly a little of both. In any case, Martin could fall back on a local clerical support system that Anselm was denied. Having been told in a letter from Sorin that Martin still likes Anselm, the young Brother is unable to accept the fact and doubts he will be able to approach Martin. The friendship has soured that badly. Anselm uses the situation to beg a new assignment:

> Reverend Father, once more, please call me away from here for my own good, because I'll perhaps lose my vocation here. I don't doubt but that Mr. Martin seeks to prejudice you against me, but, if you still have confidence in me, be assured that I will do all in my power to remove the bad opinion they have about the Brothers.[13]

He does not specify at this point in the letter what bad opinion "they" have against the Brothers: he will save that salvo for the finale of the letter. But first he has one further atrocity to report: Martin is starving him. Apparently there is a rule about being late for meals that may or may not have applied to all members at the seminary. On several occasions, Anselm has no food all day long because, he insists, he could not hear the meal bell and his clock is irregular: "How can you expect me to like Mr. Martin who is the cause of all that?" Earlier

EARLY MEN OF HOLY CROSS

in the letter Anselm complains that Martin publicly humiliates him when he shows up late for a meal by demanding to know why he is late. Martin has apparently labeled Anselm "proud" in a letter to Sorin that Anselm here mentions. In closing his letter, Anselm remarks that a rumor is circulating that the Sisters and Brothers sleep in the same dormitory. He does not name the clergyman who repeated it to him, but it was probably Martin since the letter circles around Martin from beginning to end. The Sisters and Brothers in question are undoubtedly those at Notre Dame, not in Vincennes, because Anselm lives in the bishop's house (Martin would have known this). If there was such a rumor, it is nasty gossip, but whether there was such a rumor or not, Anselm uses the very idea of a rumor as another wedge in his argument to leave the den of lions he lives among. In a state of persecution, the mind grasps at anything for relief.

Two months later, Anselm is subdued. He seems formal to Sorin as he writes in letter #9 that he will attempt being kind to Father Martin. There is no allusion to the meal problem, but now it appears that he has been barred from recreating with the seminarians. Although he notes he was previously apt to join the seminarians only rarely, sometimes weeks passing between visits, he is now forbidden their company entirely. The noose tightens.

From the next letter (May 10, 1844) we learn that Anselm had been sick in April with an unsettling cough, which lingered because, he notes, the meals at the seminary have not been very nourishing since Martin became superior. Anselm looks forward to the summer retreat at Notre Dame and goes over his options for travelling north with Brother Mary Joseph, via either horse or cart. He makes no mention of a new assignment. As if a letter of remonstrance from Sorin, which we presume Anselm had received, were not enough, we learn in letter #11 that Moreau had written Anselm a letter (received May 23), which pained the young religious. Sorin no doubt had told Moreau of Anselm's difficulties with the Vincennes clergy, and although Moreau is in favor of Anselm's return to France (Anselm quotes him to that effect), Moreau defers to Sorin's judgement in the matter. Would that Anselm had saved the letter! His own February letter to Moreau does not remain either, but if his sentiments to Moreau were as desperate as those we have seen to Sorin, it is not difficult to imagine Moreau's being touched by the situation, more than Sorin apparently was. Sorin, of course, knew Anselm better than Moreau as the boy had been under Moreau's care at Le Mans for only one year before the emigration of the first colony to America. Anselm speaks of his bargaining with Moreau to teach English at Ste. Croix for a few years in exchange for the chance to study art under Brother Hilarion. He again suggests to Sorin that Sorin needs an art teacher at Notre Dame, and he is just the man for the job:

> Since I've been here, I've sold almost all the flowers that I did, and the men and women who bought them have framed them as masterpieces. Although I've had only a single painting lesson, which Brother Vincent gave me, I have gained a reputation as a painter here.[14]

In this letter we have the first mention of Anselm's new friend Tourneux who is helping Anselm find a horse to ride up to the retreat at Notre Dame.

In letter #12 Anselm returns to the horse matter. Then he chides Sorin for not letting him know of Brother Vincent's trip to France as Anselm wanted to send letters along. He tells Sorin to get art supplies for him from France as his are depleted. He continues to speak highly of his own artistic talents. Finally he is happy the year is almost over, and his one regret is that he may be sent back to Vincennes after the retreat.

Letter #13 is dark. It is August 4, and Anselm has been sick with a debilitating fever since the previous Wednesday. He had left the classroom at 10:30 in the morning, unable to continue teaching, instructing the boys that school would resume the following day. It did not. No one in the house bothers to look in on him as the days pass. Only Tourneux visits him:

Father, I can no longer continue the subject. I'm too weak to
tell you more. What I can tell you in truth is that they don't
take as much care of me here as a human being would of a
sick dog. I can't stop crying in telling you this, my well-loved
Father, but it's the truth. I take God as witness: during the
two and a half days I was so sick, no one came to ask "Do
you want anything" except Tourneux who came three times
after work, etc.[15]

It is strange that none of the bishop's staff take an interest in the
young man, especially as Anselm is running the boys' school
singlehandedly, but we must believe Anselm. It is interesting that he
makes no case for a new assignment, the sickness apparently clearing
his head of any manipulative thoughts.

We have a gap of five months in the Anselm correspondence
as the next letter is not written until January 14, 1845, and it is sent
from Madison, Indiana, to Father Moreau in France. In the letter
we learn Anselm had been dangerously ill for two months, during
which time Sorin came to hear the young man's confession. We
presume Sorin travelled to Vincennes although the letter is not clear
on this point. Anselm's previous illness may have abated enough
for him to make the trip north to Notre Dame for the annual retreat
at summer's end. At any rate, Anselm was in a coma or near-coma:
he could not "hear or speak or see." When Sorin asks Anselm if he
knew that he had made his confession the night before, Anselm says
no. Sorin tells him he must make a deathbed confession, and Anselm
does so that evening. The exercise revives him. On November 17 he
leaves Notre Dame for his new assignment in Madison, changing
places with Brother Mary Joseph who is sent to Vincennes. It seems
unconscionable that Sorin would send Anselm off on his own again
to run a school hundreds of miles from the Community when the
young Brother had recently been deathly ill. For Sorin, obligations
to mission superseded concern for individuals, at least in this case.

Fortunately the situation in Madison was salubrious for Anselm:
the pastor, Father Delaune, was kind, and Anselm was far across the

State of Indiana from Hailandière.[16] The work, of course, was heavy. Anselm was the only teacher for sixty boys who were at all levels of education. But he thrived. His schoolroom still exists, the basement of St. Michael's Church. It is long and well lit by windows running the length of the west wall. He had a small room off the east wall that served as his bedroom, but he probably took his meals with Father Delaune across the street in the rectory (now a private home). He loved the children. He took up painting pictures of flowers, which he sold to local people. With six thousand inhabitants, Madison was not a small town, boasting eight elementary schools and two secondary schools. Two of the elementary schools were Catholic. St. Michael's was the only Catholic Church, but there were twelve Protestant churches in town. Anselm did not lack for pupils, both Catholic and Protestant. In spite of the overwhelming work, Anselm makes no repetition of his desire to study in France. One can sense his relief to be away from Vincennes. Who would not be? Hailandière was the poorest excuse for a bishop and administrator the territory would ever see, and he terrorized the local church, including Mother Theodore Guerin whom he locked in the episcopal residence for several days in an attempt to get the deed to St. Mary-of-the-Woods. After his resignation in 1847, he returned to France, where he lived comfortably another thirty-five years, not dying until 1882.[17]

Anselm's fifteenth letter shows his impatience. He wants Sorin to direct Mary Joseph to ship to Madison all the things that Anselm had left in Vincennes. In Madison, Anselm finds that Mary Joseph had left him not so much as a prayer book, but in spite of the hardships of working without supplies, Anselm reports he is "delighted" to be where he is. The exuberance continues in letter #16. He comments on the town, remarks that he has been to Cincinnati on St. Joseph's Day to get the holy oils and meet the bishop there. He ends the letter by inquiring about reports he has received from Vincennes that Father Martin is spreading slander about him:

> He charged me, if I rightly understood you, to have had bad [sic] intercourse with a woman but that as falsely as 2 and

2 are 10. Indeed I don't know how a priest like Mr. Martin who pretends to be good can fabricate such stories. I would have justified myself sooner, but before, I wanted to know if it were true that some designing men had started stories or lies on me in that place.[18]

In letter seventeen, Anselm inquires about a trunk that he is still waiting for and notes that the fever that laid him low the previous year returns now and again. One wonders if Anselm's disease had been malaria.[19] This time the fever has lasted six days in spite of his daily medications. He already is making plans, however, to travel north for the summer retreat. Letter eighteen notes that his supplies have finally arrived, but his fever has returned and has lasted three weeks. He makes further plans for the retreat. On the same date he writes to Brother Vincent, rather curtly, chiding his mentor for items missing in the received package.

Anselm's final letter is dated July 10, two days before he drowned in the Ohio River. It is a letter full of excitement about the coming retreat at Notre Dame. Gone are the complaints about living conditions or local people. He is so totally happy in Madison that he wants to know what date he can tell the pastor Father Delaune to expect his return. He brags a bit about his successes:

I had a great dinner here on the 4th. More than 100 children were admitted to it and behaved very well. The most respectable ladies of Madison helped me to serve at table, and before the dinner sent me pies, cakes, and crackers of every kind. They appeared to take a great interest in it. I dare say, Dear Father, that you had not such a dinner at the Lake. After the dinner we marched 2 by 2 through different streets of the city. Three girls of about 16 or 17 years of age carried the banner which I had made the night before, and which though made in hurry, was, I have been told by several, finer than any of those the other schools had.[20]

The obvious affection he felt for the parents and students is reflected in their cooperation at the dinner. That affection would be repeated, sadly enough, a few days later when his body was recovered from the river. Protestants and Catholics alike took to this vibrant young man who died far from the Community he had joined only five years before. The details of his death we learn from a touching letter that Father Delaune sent to Father Moreau:

> I have sad news for you. Sudden death has taken Brother Anselm away from us. He came to see me Saturday afternoon, July 12, to tell me he was going swimming. After hesitating a bit, I agreed to accompany him. He went into the water about seven or eight hundred feet away from me, in a place which did not seem the least bit dangerous. He went out more than five hundred feet without finding water deep enough for swimming. I was in water about three or four feet deep, a little distance off the bank. All of a sudden, while he was swimming, I noticed an expression of suffering on his face. He went down, but I thought he was doing it on purpose. He came up, then went down again, while uttering a cry for help. What a moment for me! I was more than three hundred feet away from him and did not know how to swim. We were two miles from the city, with no houses nearby. He came up again and then sank. A moment later he lifted his arms and I saw him no more.
>
> All aghast, I hastened to give him absolution. He had probably received it that morning for, as usual, he had gone to confession, and he went to Communion at least every Sunday. I ran to a cabin. A child told me that there was an old man not far away. I ran to him and brought him with me and pointed out from afar the place where the Brother disappeared. "He is lost for good," he told me. "Right there is a drop-off at least twenty feet deep, and the current all around is very swift. Anything I could do would be useless." I went home, got some good swimmers together, and procured boats and nets.

All our efforts proved useless. It was ten o'clock in the evening before he was found, five hours after he had drowned. An inquest was held by the civil authorities, and then we brought him back to the church at one-thirty yesterday morning. He was laid out in the basement chapel. Some of the Irish settlers watched beside the coffin until daybreak. I clothed him in his religious habit and he remained exposed in the Chapel until yesterday afternoon at four. Everyone was dismayed by the event. Thank God for having borne me up throughout this trial and its accompanying fatigue. Sleepless, and almost without having tasted food, broken-hearted and yet forced to stifle my grief in order to look after all the details, I suffered more yesterday than I ever thought I could.

At four in the afternoon we brought him to the church. The coffin was uncovered, and the calmness of his features made him look as though he were only asleep. Protestants and Catholics alike gathered to the number of more than a thousand. The choir sang the Vespers of the Dead. With painful effort I preached on Chapter Four of the Book of Wisdom, beginning with verse seven. ["But the just man, if he be overtaken by death, shall be in rest. For venerable old age is not that of long time, nor counted by the number of years ... He was taken away lest wickedness should alter his understanding, or deceit beguile his soul."]

I had the thirteenth verse written in English on a black banner: "Being made perfect in a short space, he fulfilled a long time." After the Libera, the children from his school kissed his forehead; then the coffin was closed and covered with the funeral drape. The two schools led the funeral procession with the banner and the cross. The hearse followed, and then the people, two by two. I marched between the school children and the carriages. We crossed the city to the cemetery, which is a mile from here.[21]

There are curious points in this narrative. First of all, why were the two swimming so far from town? Sorin's *Chronicles* on the events do not use the word "swimming" but rather "bathing," indicating perhaps the pair's desire for some privacy. The *Chronicles*, of course, have been translated for publication, and we can never be sure why Sorin chose certain words to carry his meaning. Secondly, why would Delaune let Anselm swim out so far into the river? If Delaune, who had lived in Madison since August 1842, did not know the treachery of the river in this particular spot, the pair should have exercised more caution. Delaune is silent on this point.

Sorin mentions this death in his *Chronicles* under his consideration of deaths at Notre Dame for the year 1845. The sentence has an odd addendum: "It is true that the Society this year had to mourn the premature death of Br. Anselm, who drowned in the Ohio while bathing with Mr. Delaune; but no one thought of charging this death to the unhealthiness of Notre Dame du Lac, as was done the two following years."[22] This is indeed a cold assessment when one juxtaposes it with Delaune's tearful report to Moreau. Everything for Sorin, of course, was seen in the context of Notre Dame. Sorin is more concerned with the rash of deaths that plagued his foundation in the early years than he is with Anselm's loss, and although Sorin wrote his *Chronicles* years after the events themselves (the Anselm entry has to be dated beyond 1848 since Sorin uses that year in a subsequent paragraph), it is difficult to accept his unfeeling journalese as paternal.

In June of that fatal 1845 summer, Anselm had looked forward to the annual retreat when he could go to Notre Dame in August where he could spend time with his confreres in Holy Cross. Those his own age, like Gatian and the new recruits, would have given him a companionship he lacked in Madison. Who would have told the boy's parents back in Gennes, France? His father, a weaver, had already lost to fever his only other two children. Moreau himself may have made a trip to Gennes to inform the parents. Vincent does not document his own grief for the young man, but he had visited Madison in the previous October on one of his supervisory trips, and he must have felt the loss as if it were the loss of a son. He had known Anselm in Le Mans when the sixteen-year old boy was a novice at la Charbonnière. Vincent travelled the Atlantic with him, lived with him in the episcopal residence in Vincennes when Gatian, Francis Xavier, and Sorin moved to Notre Dame. Vincent taught next to the boy in the Vincennes cathedral school and guided him in the first years of his career. Vincent's grief must have been deep.

Today Anselm rests in Springdale Cemetery, Madison.[23] The same river that took his life may have inundated the cemetery in 1937 and buried his stone marker, but fortunately the grave was rediscovered in 2000. Before the discovery, the inscription on the stone was known only by way of a postcard in the archives of the Midwest Province, a postcard mailed from Brother Marius Bednarczyk to Brother Lambert Barbier at Sacred Heart College, Watertown, Wisconsin, and postmarked June 18, 1936. But today visitors to Springdale Cemetery can read the inscription on the stone itself: "BROTHER ANSELME / of the Society of St. Joseph / Born in France / 1826 / Died in Madison / July 12, 1845 / 'His soul pleased God: / therefore He hastened to bring him out.' / PRAY FOR HIM." The year of Anselm's birth is incorrect: he was born in 1825.

The grave is all we have left of Anselm besides his remarkable letters, but possibly in some farmhouse around Madison there is a painting hanging on a kitchen wall, a painting of flowers, a painting signed "Brother Anselm." That possibility, of course, lies only in the realm of speculation. He was proud of his ability to paint. It was one of his few joys in very difficult teaching situations. In a late letter, Brother Gatian does indict Sorin for Anselm's sufferings, and that is where judgment should remain. The quiet and swift waters of the Ohio River wash away much in Madison, but all the rough seas could not wash away the bad decisions of a neglectful superior. Anselm deserved better than he received, but at least he died knowing that he had finally succeeded in his teaching, won the love of his students, fulfilled the hopes of Madison townspeople, and established himself as a true son of Moreau's Holy Cross.

CHAPTER EIGHT

Gatian Monsimer: Rebel on the Frontier

Brother Gatian may seem a minor player in a long and complicated history of Holy Cross. Why should he of all people be examined for insight into the birth of Holy Cross? He was, of course, a product of his time and place: a farmer and a fine student. He became a successful teacher and a superb writer. He was entrusted with supervisory missions. His opinions were solicited. But his life ended in apparent failure, an itinerant outside of his chosen religious family, a sickly man dependent upon the generosity of his father and stepmother. There is tragedy in his life, cut off as he was at thirty-five, but there are moments of grandeur too in his life, and those reflect the energy of a man not afraid to confront authority and forge his own destiny. Urbain Monsimer (Brother Gatian) was a man who knew what he wanted and pursued his dreams doggedly. Had the boy been born fifty years earlier, he would have been at the heart of the French Revolution. Had he been in Paris then, he would have been an energetic participant, undoubtedly a member of a political debating club and close observer of the many assemblies that replaced and despoiled each other year after year. He had, after all, the intelligent tenacity of Mirabeau, the ascetic rigor of Maximilian Robespierre, and the fanatical rant of Jacques Roux. Of the three, he seems closest to Robespierre as Sagan characterized the revolutionary leader: virtuous, narcissistic, and paranoid.[1]

In the seventeenth-century Monsimers settled in Laval and St. Malo, and in the late eighteenth-century during the aftermath of the Revolution (1792), one Monsimer family left Chéméré-le-roi to settle at the Préau farm near Saulges. It was there that Urbain Jean Baptiste Monsimer (Brother Gatian) was born on April 3, 1826, at 7:35 AM, and it was there that he died in 1860.[2] His parents had five children including twins who died at birth in 1825. Urbain came next (1826), followed by Francis Constant (June 26, 1828) and August (August 12, 1833). In 1836 the family left Préau and moved to La Teillerie, a farm near Chéméré-le-roi where Francis died on July 26, 1841, at age 13, two weeks before his brother Urbain left for America as Brother Gatian. One can only imagine how poignant it must have been for the family to lose one teenager to death and another to a foreign country within so short a time span. The sole child thus remaining with the parents was August who was to live only to age twenty-two.[3]

The farm where Urbain was born and died at Préau is today owned outside of the Monsimer family, and although some of the buildings on the farm survive from Urbain's day (one barn has been converted into a kind of chapel), the house in which Urbain was born and died is gone. Only a slab of concrete remains to mark the spot. The Préau farm is quite remote from the access road. A long dusty road leads to the grassy driveway of the farm, which sits quite isolated among its fields. The nineteenth century buildings which remain are constructed of field stone meant to last, but none hold animals any longer. The Monsimer boys would have had a long hike from Préau to a school in Saulges, if there was one there—we know there was none run by the Brothers of St. Joseph. This may have been one reason why Urbain's father moved his family to La Teillerie.[4] For the two decades that the family worked the La Teillerie farm, they worshipped and schooled the boys in Chéméré-le-roi.

The Brothers of St. Joseph first established a school in Chéméré-le-roi in 1833 and would remain there until 1860. In the years that Urbain attended the school, he would have come under the tutelage of Brother Vital (August Lebreton) who was born in 1808 and entered the Brothers' Community in 1825 at age sixteen. He lived a long life in the Community, weathering the storms of 1830, the transfer of the novitiate in 1835, and the loss of the motherhouse property in 1869. He died at Angers in 1886 at age seventy-seven. Arriving at Chéméré-le-roi in 1836 from just having founded a school at Montourtier the previous year, he would have had under his wing the very bright, very energetic little Urbain Monsimer, who at age nine would have rapidly fallen under the academic spell of the capable Brother Vital. Those happy idyllic days at La Tellerie and in the school at Chéméré-le-roi would instill in little Urbain a thirst for religion slaked by his joining a religious group of men with whom he would find the challenge his young soul longed for and with whom he would be enriched by the spiritual maturity of men who would shape his destiny. He joined the Brothers of St. Joseph in the summer of 1840.

Gatian, in a letter dated ten years after his entrance at Ste. Croix, names Silvin-Auguste de Marseul as his first teacher in Le Mans. Gatian also took some classes from Brother Euloge (Antoine Boisard), a fellow novice who was thirty at the time and already a teacher. Gatian's math teacher was Brother Hilarion, who had come to Ste. Croix at age twenty, a few years before Gatian, and would die at age thirty-two in Algeria after teaching there for five years. Gatian does not mention having Brother André Mottais as a teacher, nor Brother Vincent, even though both of these religious veterans were living in Le Mans at the time. For his manual labor duties, the thirteen-year-old Gatian worked as a cook the first month of his arrival. He served as a subordinate prefect in the study hall under Brother Chrysostom and in the boarding students' dormitory under Brother Hilaire. He also prefected the grade school children's outdoor recreation and laid bricks for Brother John of the Cross.[6] Young Brother Gatian soon impressed the men who formed him in the religious life. His devotion to prayer, his bright, quick mind, and his attentive adherence to rules made him stand out as a natural for the Brothers of St. Joseph. Moreover, when Basil Moreau started to mull over candidates for an American foundation, Gatian would have been among his prized recruits.

Once Gatian had been selected for the American settlement, it was only a matter of waiting for the trip to materialize. He was undoubtedly the envy of many of his novitiate classmates who were passed over in the selection process. Once the names of the seven colonists had been made public, the group of men would have started the bonding needed to sustain them on the longest journey any of them had ever made and that, indeed, several of them would ever make. Moreau, despairing of money from Bishop Hailandière in Indiana to finance the voyage, turned to his local benefactors, his "associates" of St. Joseph: a lottery brought in enough money to get the travelers north to their seaport and across the ocean.

After staying in New York for three days with a family named Byerly, Brother Gatian and the others began their trek west, a trip that would take twenty-five days (almost as long as their Atlantic passage). They finally arrived at Vincennes on October 8, 1841, the second Sunday of the month, at sunrise. When Sorin saw Vincennes for the first time, he proclaimed it "another Jerusalem,"[7] but after twenty-four days of traveling from New York anything would have seemed a heavenly city, as long as it afforded the weary a place to settle down and settle in. At 9 AM they went into the cathedral in time for the bishop's High Mass. After the little band said the Te Deum antiphonally, they went with the bishop to the seminary (where the bishop lived) for a meal, and all stayed there overnight. The next day the bishop saddled his own horse for Sorin and took him ten miles away to see a piece of property on the Wabash River. Although the tract was large (160 arpents), Sorin did not like the place. By nightfall they were back in Vincennes. The next day Sorin rode east to see property at St. Peter's with the priest who was leaving the parish. The farm and church being proposed as a settlement for the Holy Cross Brothers was near the town of Washington and was also comprised of 160 arpents, 60 of them under cultivation. Sorin liked St. Peter's, in spite of the fact that the buildings were old and in disrepair. Having been constructed for the Sisters of Nazareth, they were used for only a year before the Sisters left. It was, it turns out, Hailandière's preferred choice for the Holy Cross settlement. What

Gatian's response was to the ramshackle accommodations we do not know, but we can suspect that his quick eye would have sized up the situation rapidly, and he may very well have offered some sharp opinions on the place. Sorin, at any rate, had no intention of fixing up the buildings to any great extent because he told Moreau that the group would probably be elsewhere by the following spring.

The group of seven colonists was enhanced by five young boys, former pupils of the St. Peter's pastor, and rounding out the settlement was a saintly old woman who was retained in order to teach Brother Joachim how to cook American dishes. Within two days a religious decorum was put in place with a local council formed and obediences assigned. Already waiting for the French Brothers was a colorful thirty-three year old candidate named Charles Rother, a German immigrant to whom the bishop had formerly entrusted the school at St. Peter's. Thus while the Frenchmen were acclimating themselves to their new surroundings and struggling to learn English, the little school could go forward under Rother's direction.[8] The little community at St. Peter's that fall and early winter numbered sixteen: six Brothers, one priest, four candidates, and five young students. Outside of the students, Gatian was the youngest, hardly much older than the boys he would soon be teaching, and he found himself in a multilingual environment: two novices spoke only German, one novice only English.

The foundation at St. Peter's lasted little more than a year. The relocation of the Holy Cross Community to northern Indiana was effected for several reasons, not the least of which was the desire to start a secondary school, a project not favored by the bishop because of the Eudists' school already being run in Vincennes. As could be expected, there was also growing tension between the bishop and Sorin. When the bishop, therefore, offered them a tract of over 500 acres at the far northern fringe of his diocese, they jumped at the chance to go, site unseen. Three of the original seven went north in November 1842: Gatian, Francis Xavier the carpenter, and Sorin. They took five novices with them: Peter, Francis, Patrick, William, and Basil. They left St. Peter's on November 16 at a terrible time of the year, the winter proving to be one of the coldest on record. Traveling by ox cart west to Vincennes, then north along the Wabash River, it took them two days just to reach Vincennes and another two days to reach Terre Haute. At Logansport they cut north, and on November 16, 1842, they reached South Bend. What awaited Gatian and the other seven was well worth the trip. In fact, it inspired Sorin to one of his rare moments of poetry:

> Everything was frozen over. Yet it all seemed so beautiful. The lake especially with its broad carpet of dazzling snow, quite naturally reminded us of the spotless purity of our august Lady whose name it bears ... Though it was quite cold, we went to the very end of the lake and, like children, came back fascinated with the marvelous beauties of our new home.[9]

What appeared as one lake under the snow was actually two lakes connected by a swamp, but the name Notre Dame du Lac ("Our Lady of the Lake") was already in place when Gatian and the group arrived so it stayed. The only building on the property was a log cabin too dilapidated to spend the first night in so the colony stayed in town. By early December the log cabin, forty feet by twenty-four feet, was fixed up well enough to accommodate the eight men.

The first letter we have by Gatian was written in February of 1846, a full four years after he arrived in America. The letter suggests that Gatian had been seeking counsel from his spiritual father in Le Mans, but whatever letters he received from Moreau are gone. Although he is the youngest of the expatriates, at the time he is not shy about his independence in spite of his being only nineteen years old. He seems to be a stickler for rules, with a blind adherence that does not bode well for a pioneer in a wilderness where crises and interruptions can challenge the rigorous dynamism of spiritual laws fashioned in gentler climates. The Indiana frontier was a lively and engaging area, even in the relative seclusion of the Notre Dame paradise where farming concerns and active little boy scholars tested the rigidity of prayer schedule and quiet time. But Gatian never showed much tolerance for those who did not buckle under to dictates, and if he were hard on others, he was also naturally hard on himself, incapable of appreciating the spirit behind the letter of any law.

Unusual also in this letter is the way in which Gatian writes of himself in the third person. After listing Brother Vincent's many jobs, he notes: "Brother Gatian is director of studies, prefect of discipline, head of the accounting office, secretary of four weekly councils, and in the boarding school, professor of the upper division course in which the students know as much as the teacher, supervisor of all recreations and of a dormitory, and professor of French to boot."[10] The job list, of course, is overblown. Since the college had but a dozen students, the job of "director of studies" would have been negligible. "Prefect of discipline" would have meant dealing occasionally with a boy who stepped out of line and could not be handled by one of the other Brothers. Still, we cannot begrudge Gatian the fact that his talents were stretched. Pioneer Brothers, especially talented one like Gatian, were expected to fill many shoes, and as a result the quality of their job performance was often less than satisfactory. He was, of course, a brilliant young man, and he knew it. Anyone today who reads his letters would marvel at their style and grace, the ease of his language skills.

During the winter of 1846 Gatian is silent, but at the end of spring in 1847 he writes again to Moreau. April at Notre Dame is usually a wonderful month, especially welcome after any of the harsh winters that choke the land east of Lake Michigan. With spring come daffodils and a lightening of spirits. Gatian, a man sensitive to change of any kind, writes to Moreau with renewed aplomb. Acknowledging reception of a letter from Moreau, Gatian specifies that he has delayed answering until he could see how Sorin would implement the reforms that Moreau had specified in a letter addressed to Gatian, Sorin, and Alexis Granger. Sorin obviously did not prevent this letter from getting into Gatian's hands, and we can imagine the delight that Gatian had in seeing some directives issued from the motherhouse in France. Gatian is not satisfied that Sorin is implementing the reforms specified by Le Mans because either "he [Sorin] is a consummate liar, or the explanations given to him at Ste. Croix weren't clear."[11] One can little doubt which reason Gatian believes. Years have passed since their immigration, but Gatian harkens back to their discontent on arrival when they found grave disparity between the way they had lived the Constitutions in France and the way they found the Constitutions followed in Indiana. This theme for Gatian is recurring, and it is a truism that many young people who are sticklers for rules do not survive very long in a religious community because they cannot reconcile rigid prescriptions with the reality of human frailty, especially their own. Rules thus become an unrealistic end in themselves that frustrate and eventually break a vocation into despair.

In one of Gatian's letters we are afforded a rare glimpse into Sorin's sense of humor. The bishop had proposed that a Brother be sent to sell Catholic books door to door and promised two mules for the apostolate. At Minor Chapter, Sorin painted the advantages of the scheme, no doubt all financial, and asked for responses. One councilor was absent from the meeting and Gatian remained silent taking everything as a joke as it really did seem a radical departure for a teaching community. Within two days Sorin had appointed Brother Joseph ("the buffoon") to the job and directed him to buy a cart, eventualities that Sorin revealed at the dining table. Gatian was furious and wrote a "nasty note" to Sorin saying that the councilors did not consider the previous Chapter meeting a consultation on the matter. Sorin reconvened the Chapter, proposed the venture, and listened to the debate. Gatian himself raised five objections, one claiming the venture would lose 700 or 800 francs because it was a stupid venture. Sorin replied, "You can only do good by taking risks." The vote was taken: Gatian and another councilor voted against it. The other councilors voted for it. Then Sorin pulled a fast move saying, "I vote against it and thus the responsibility rests on those who have voted for." One member objects: "Ah, Father ... If you believed the enterprise is useless, you shouldn't have proposed it, and if you believe it bad, you shouldn't undertake it." Sorin's response borders on dark comedy: "Too bad ... You've voted: it'll be carried out."[12]

In this same letter Gatian reveals that he has not written to his family in two years: "I don't like to write to them because I've lost the habit ... And because I've received no news from them since I've been in America." This is a sad remark from a young man so far from home. His mother being dead, he may not have been very close to his stepmother, but he speaks affectionately elsewhere of his younger Brother August and expresses hope that the boy is getting a good education. It is not unusual, however, for youth to be so caught up in adventure that they lose touch with a previous life, and Gatian was certainly in an environment extremely different from what he had known. The American frontier had little resemblance to the tame French countryside he had known, and the lure of quixotic adventure in exotic areas would be enough to dazzle any energetic young man.

In writing to Moreau, what Gatian does not realize is that his days in the Notre Dame Chapter are numbered: he is about to be excluded by Sorin with Moreau's approbation. Not knowing his fate, Gatian writes to Moreau as if he were running the Chapter and Notre Dame himself: he gives Moreau advice on the settlement of St. Mary's College in Kentucky, he thinks little of the Canadian superior Saulnier, and he deplores the fact that the Sisters have modified their habit. Once Gatian learns of his exclusion from the Chapter, the wind will be taken out of his sails, but if Sorin thought demotion would silence his most vocal critic, he was wrong. Moreover, Gatian's degradation may have escalated his descent into behavior that would, within two years, push Sorin to look for a way to get his fellow countryman away from Notre Dame. He was a time bomb ticking under Sorin's nose

One has to admire Gatian's honesty, even if it sometimes seems self-serving, an attempt to elicit from his superior some soothing words. In one matter, he needs counseling: he admits that his affections have come to be centered on a student named John Hays: "I can never and I'll never be able to stop myself from loving him, nor from wanting to be loved by him ... I've loved other children before him (but never as much as him)."[13] A student from Fort Wayne, John Hays was sixteen years old at the time and had been at Notre Dame since June 26, 1844. He was six years younger than Gatian and probably had taken several classes from Gatian because the Brother taught both mathematics and language courses.

During the four years they would have known each other, the two developed an emotional attachment that was probably more heartfelt by the tortured teacher than by his student. Gatian writes, "Nothing but the caresses of John Hayes can quiet me."[14] But Hays does not return the affection sufficiently, and Gatian blackens into despair. He then admits something very curious: he has written a letter to the Blessed Virgin "and I played the fool, and then repenting, I begged again and promised to act better, if I got that." The phrase "playing the fool" is used, and we are sure Gatian did something he regrets, but the specifics of the act are vague. He says he repented and promises to act better: "the child doesn't hate me now and acts very nicely to me." We do know, however, that Gatian was getting out of control. The final entry in his *Chronicles* narrates the following incident:

> Last Saturday, January 7th the Institution was greatly scandalized by Bro. Gatian who, pushed on by an irregular affection and his violent passions, began playing the fool during the Litany of the Blessed Virgin and continued at supper when Mr. G. Campeau, a boarder of muscular strength, by the orders of the Superior, endeavored to seize him, but it required six men to take him out of the room. He swore most horribly. Mr. Campeau came very near to breaking his (Bro. Gatian's) neck—however Bro Gatian calmed down and the next morning having obtained of the Superior what he desired, took the resolution of correcting himself. He also begged pardon of the Institution on the 9th Inst.

The entry, dated January 10, 1849, is narrated in third-person, even though it is Gatian himself who is writing it. The young man, if not unhinged, is certainly strange. Gatian's solution for his melancholy, he thinks, lies in being kept busy, and Sorin was probably of a like mind because the wily superior soon finds a way to keep Gatian occupied and away from temptation at Notre Dame: he sends Gatian off on a long trip to Brooklyn that he probably hopes will extend to months if not years.

As early as 1847 the bishop of New York had asked Sorin for Brothers to teach in his diocese. In the fall of 1848, Sorin and Victor Drouelle visited Bishop Hughes to explore the possibility, and one month later five Brothers went to New York. Because of difficulties securing actual employment in diocesan grade schools, three of the Brothers returned immediately to Notre Dame, leaving only Brother Basil (thirty-eight years old) and Brother Aloysius (eighteen years old) in Brooklyn. The two Brothers were to teach one hundred boys, but the situation was a financial disaster from the beginning since the pastor paid Basil and Aloysius nothing, letting them support themselves on whatever tuition they could get from their students. After Brother Vincent had failed to correct the situation, Gatian arrived to try his own hand in the winter of 1849. A sizable chunk of Gatian's extant correspondence was written from Brooklyn: fourteen letters to Sorin, two to Moreau, and one telegram. If anything, the young man took his supervisory duties seriously. The first letter is written in English and exhibits some rather grandiose pretention: "I have seen the great city at last, and I have pitched my tent on the seashore in the heights of Columbia Street No. 94 at the Baths of Brooklyn." This is poetic hyperbole.

His actual journey to New York had been harrowing. Riding in a sleigh from Notre Dame north to Bertrand, Michigan, where the Holy Cross Sisters had begun a girls' academy outside the domain of the Vincennes diocese, Gatian had to spend a cold, sleepless night before heading the next morning east to Niles where he caught the train to Detroit. He had another sleepless night because he missed his Notre Dame community intensely. He crossed into Canada and traveled sometimes by rail, sometimes by sleigh. Part of the way the sleigh glided over Lake Erie and occasionally the horses had to leap over two foot gaps in the ice. He passed through London (Ontario) and arrived at Buffalo, having gone 265 miles in two and a half days. He recounts several accidents, and the worst almost killed him.

The day after his arrival in New York, Gatian writes Sorin a long letter giving his first impressions of the situation in Brooklyn: it is quite hopeless. Gatian lays the blame on Sorin, Vincent, and Basil, each one culpable for a different reason. True to form, Sorin has opened an establishment without sufficient preparation of the personnel. Vincent was worthless when sent to Brooklyn. Basil, the elder of the two Brother teachers in Brooklyn, has alienated Mrs. Parmentier who runs the boarding house where the Brothers live. Gatian includes several lists of financial analysis, and the school seems salvageable, but a new teacher will be needed to replace Aloysius who has no training in algebra, geometry, or bookkeeping. Sorin's incompetence in assigning personnel is no idle insight from an irascible Gatian: Aloysius was sent out to teach at age eighteen, one year after he entered the community, and was terribly unprepared to teach the hordes of boys (between fifty and sixty) assigned to him in Brooklyn.

After three days, Gatian reports on the rambunctious students: they fight and yell "like so many wild Indians during Sunday school." These rowdies are not the lads who attend the school during the week (106 boys), but rather the one hundred lads who are dumped by their parents at the church on Sunday and expected to master their religious duties and decorum with an hour or two of pious tutelage. These were not docile boys, and to expect them to behave on Sunday was a little naive. The pastor, Father Bacon, has insisted that the Brothers accept both groups of boys and has threatened to blacklist the Holy Cross community in the diocese if the two Brothers refuse the combined duty. As far as Basil is concerned, although Gatian finds little fault in him, Gatian thinks Basil should be replaced as director in order to keep the peace. Basil will be gone within a month, shifted to New Orleans to help Brother Vincent run an orphanage. Meanwhile, Gatian pitches in and substitute-teaches for Aloysius who is often sick.

Gatian is, however, beginning to wear down. He is not only supervising the school and teaching almost full time, he has to run around Brooklyn to find a new boarding house. He also has to broker a deal with a printer to have rule books printed for Sorin. He advertises for a science teacher for Notre Dame and interviews a good prospect. He investigates a new organ for the church at Notre Dame. But the factotum is losing energy. His deafness is an actual problem and prevents him from having any kind of order in a classroom full of fifty-eight boys who have run roughshod over the teenager teacher Aloysius. Gatian tries, but as the boys talk constantly in class and he is unable to discriminate the source of the noise, he devises a pedagogical plan for Aloysius and leaves the classroom. He turns to prayer, promising to say a thousand Hail Marys if order comes back to Aloysius' classroom. The heavenly bribe does not work, and Gatian flails out again at the root cause of the disaster: Sorin, who simply sends people out on mission whether they are prepared or not.

As one might expect, when Gatian received no support from Sorin, he turned to Moreau, probably suspecting that his being sent to Brooklyn as a supervisor was only a ruse to get him away from Notre Dame and John Hays. A letter to Moreau at the end of March expresses his frustration. With a delicious sarcasm, Gatian remarks: 'Father Sorin and he [Drouelle] made the arrangements [for New York] so well and examined things so well that, having sent five Brothers in November, three had to go home immediately, and the two that Mr. Bacon wanted to keep preferred Purgatory to being at his place."[15] Gatian rehearses all the Brooklyn abominations: too many students to teach, unprepared Brothers, lack of adequate housing, an uncooperative pastor. Then he concludes for the first time that his loss of hearing can be attributed to frostbite suffered on the midwinter trip from Notre Dame: he has no hearing in the left ear at all and very little in the right ear. In early April Gatian tries again with a letter to get Sorin to make some decisions about Brooklyn: added to his loss of hearing and sight, now his sense of smell is weakening. He misses John Hays and wishes to be at Notre Dame. Finally, Gatian is recalled to Notre Dame, where his troubles will only be compounded.

Back at Notre Dame early in the summer of 1849, since Gatian had not changed in his attachment to John Hays, Sorin would have been looking for another way to remove Gatian from the area. Given Gatian's complaints about hearing loss, he would not have been useful in any of the schools like those in Vincennes or Madison. Sorin was stuck with Gatian. Then as the gold rush fever began to accelerate in America, Sorin saw a way to dispose of Gatian. In fact, he says as much in his *Chronicles* in which he specifies two reasons for his having sent Brothers to California: "1. That of preventing a terrible scandal which might ruin the work [Notre Dame]; 2. That of trying a means of paying arrears of indebtedness."[16] It is significant that Sorin puts the scandal ahead of financial needs, indicating his primary motivation was to get Gatian out of Indiana. He elaborates: "Br. Gatien was going to leave the Society to marry and to settle down near the college. He consented to depart for those distant regions." The matter of Gatian's threat to get married seems odd in view of his strong homoerotic attraction to John Hays. The Minor Chapter notes for September 28, 1849, do not indicate that a reason for the gold expedition was the Gatian scandal. In fact, Gatian is not even named as one of the three Brothers (Lawrence, John, Michael) for the expedition. The only reason given in the Minor Chapter notes is the need for money. Sorin, of course, may not have shared with the Minor Chapter his intention to use the expedition as a way to get rid of Gatian. In a letter written on August 15, 1851, to Sorin after the collapse of the gold expedition, Gatian apologizes to Sorin for forcing the priest to send Brothers on the expedition: "I am sorry that for my sake you have sent Bros. to California."

On February 28, 1850, Gatian set off for California with the "St. Joseph Company" (including four Brothers). It was winter, and the trip would take over four months, the group travelling about twenty-five miles per day. They used a large supply wagon pulled by six horses and a small wagon pulled by two. The adventure was ridiculous from beginning to end. Gatian kept the books, and of the $335.17 he lists as receipts, $259.55 had gone out as expenditures by the time the group reached Goose Neck, Missouri, on April 16, leaving them $75.62 for the remaining and greater part of the journey. Expenses included not only purchase of food but also repairs to the wagons and the shoeing of horses.

A long letter in Gatian's hand but written on behalf of and signed by all seven was posted from Goose Neck Creek, seven miles west of Independence, Missouri, on April 9, 1850. They cannot push on before the end of the month or the beginning of May because of the lack of grass for the horses so the men encamp on the frozen ground biding their time. They eat well each evening on pork, sausage, or codfish, but they sleep in a tent on whatever hay, straw, or leaves they can manage to scrape together. Gatian notes that the roads had been muddy, and on March 20 they had broken the master bolt on the small wagon. Some creeks have been problematic, and settlements have been sparse, some settlers being less than helpful. Finally by summer they reach California.

At the beginning of August, the St. Joseph Company begins their quest for gold with pan and shovel. It is difficult and generally unrewarding work in spite of Gatian's assertion that California is as rich as the imagination can represent it. Since previous miners have already worked the best areas, new miners, including the St. Joseph Company, find themselves in areas that have already been worked two or three times. Some men from South Bend have already gone home rich while others are broke. Gatian's prospects are bright, however, because he has made some valuable contacts: he says he may return to Hangtown with a speculator named Good, and he has found a former Notre Dame pupil of his named Garrett prospering on his own ranch. Obviously, Gatian is pulling away from the St. Joseph Company, and his days in Holy Cross are numbered. At this point in mid-September, the St. Joseph Company, Gatian writes, is doing moderately well and is worth a thousand dollars. This news must have warmed Sorin's heart, as well as the knowledge that Gatian was distracted enough to have made peace with his passions.

By the beginning of November, however, the fortunes of the Company begin to sour due to sickness, which afflicts all the Brothers. Brother Placidus dies, and Lawrence writes Sorin with the sad news, including the fact that there was no priest on hand for Placidus' passing. The effect of this death on Gatian must have been devastating. Whatever exuberance Gatian had entertained for California is now gone. He notes skirmishes between soldiers and Native Americans around the Placerville mines. He records the hanging of an eighteen-year old gambler. After working for a full week, he is able to pay board for only two days. Although there is no record of Gatian's request to break his religious vows and leave the Congregation of Holy Cross, it is apparent that the break is already finalized. He tells Sorin that he is leaving Placerville to head sixty-five miles north with a partner. He does not here identify his partner, but in a later letter he will allude to their less than happy relationship. His outgoing personality was never hidden under a basket so that to encounter him was to receive a strong impression either for good or for bad. He could make friends or enemies quickly.

In January 1851, Urbain (no longer calling himself Gatian) and an unnamed partner head north taking three days to reach Grass Valley where, carrying a sixty pound pack, Urbain suffers from vomiting and diarrhea. His partner runs off, leaving Urbain to convalesce with a Mexican man who speaks no English. After a week, Urbain heads back south for Dry Town, passing through Jacksonville. He arrives in Dry Town in Calaveras County without a penny but is soon making two dollars a day. A local blacksmith recognizes him and offers him fifty dollars a month to work as a smithy, a job Urbain accepts, giving up on mining because of his weak health. By the summer of 1851 Urbain, with Gregory Campeau from the original St. Joseph Company as his partner, has relocated in Shasta County (250 miles north of Placerville) where they live in One Horse Town on Clear Creek. We then hear nothing from Urbain for three years, and when he writes to Sorin again on June 20, 1854, he is back in Kelsey near Placerville where he started out. He writes about California politics and religion in general terms. Sounding more and more like a self-satisfied businessman, he gives Sorin advice on some trouble Sorin is having with a South Bend man.

After a two year hiatus, Urbain writes to Sorin in April, 1858, of his continued interest in courting a local girl, who, he claims, is head over heels in love with him, but in the following November, Urbain is a changed man, sick and embittered. He first blames his weakened constitution on his sedentary life at Notre Dame, implying that had he continued the outdoor life he knew as a young farmer in France, he would not be the broken man he has become. Unable to work for a month, he can stomach only bread and milk. Bronchitis has infiltrated one lung, and Urbain opines that a change of climate might help him. He thinks he will try either the Sandwich Islands (Hawaii) or Chile, a voyage to either of which would cure him or kill him, the latter outcome preferable, so he says, to a slow death by bronchitis and consumption (tuberculosis). Things are not looking good for Urbain.

The final letter from Urbain to Sorin was written from San Francisco on April 23, 1860. It is the most pitiful of all his letters, yet he begins it by giving Sorin advice on why Holy Cross should start a foundation in California. Reminiscent of the old Gatian writing from Brooklyn, Urbain neatly outlines five points why Sorin should send Brothers west. Urbain is dying. He weighs but one hundred and five pounds. He has the use of but one quarter of his lungs. Doctors have given up on him, and he says that he wishes to see his father in France one last time before he dies. He blames Holy Cross for his debilitation:

> I die, I think, the victim of the wretched system followed in your Institution and so many others. No attention is paid to health. Your subjects have not enough of exercise in the open air and they dress alike summer and winter, buttoning tightly across the breast as if the intention were to choke them as soon as possible. Why not dress according to the Rules of Science and common sense?

His logic is gone, and he does not acknowledge that hundreds have dressed as he dressed, including the robust Brother Lawrence and the aging Brother Vincent. The venom is fierce, but then he has suffered much, mostly at his own doing. With his closing thoughts, he invokes the Virgin Mary.

In his dying grief, Urbain turns against the one object that was the shining lure of his soul at age thirteen: the joy of being a Brother of St. Joseph. Inspired by his Brother teacher at Chéméné-le-roi, nurtured by the Brother teachers at Le Mans, encouraged by his confreres in America, he still ends up bitter and pathetic. But in the heart of this sad finale, there still beat an energy to complete a task, and with the same determination he had to master the English language, with the same sense of purpose he had in trying to save Brooklyn, and with the same drive he had heading west to California, he now, heavy hearted, travels east, first to New York and then to France.

The paper trail for Urbain ends here, except for the notice of his death in the parish records in Saulges, France. He did indeed return to die on his father's farm, in the same house of his birth. Nothing remains today of that house but a cement slab. On the outskirts of town, in a little cemetery surrounded by a stone wall, nestled amid wheat fields, Urbain lies buried with the Monsimers, but the exact location of his grave is unknown because the marker has disappeared. One can imagine the moment of his passing, in the quiet of the summer on the farm he had not seen in over twenty years, attended by the family he had left in 1839. The strong heart of this passionate young man stopped when he was thirty-four.[17]

Although Urbain had left the Congregation of Holy Cross, in one sense he never did. Thoroughly devoted to religion, he remained essentially a religious as he made his way around the gold mines of California. He never accumulated wealth and established no homestead, content with a peripatetic life as sparse as any missionary's. He remained devoted to his local church, was in charge of collecting money for a new house of worship in Placerville, corresponded with the archbishop, remained convinced that moral rectitude is essential and must be enforced for salvation. He never married, and his call to obedience kept him tied to his previous religious superior at Notre Dame, if only to offer occasional advice and reminisce about life at Notre Dame. He was obedient to his heart, trudging the California landscape and ultimately returning to his earthly French father just before he returned to his heavenly Father. If his love for his students was too strong, it was still love that made him a great teacher, and his students reveled in the attention, both those who suffered the lash of his tongue for their laxity or boyish pranks and those who touched deeper recesses in his heart where the carnal twines with the altruistic, the one feeling absorbed into the other. Gatian took himself out of Holy Cross, but Holy Cross never really took itself out of Urbain Monsimer. What entered his soul, when he was a perky farm boy of twelve sitting in the classroom of Brother Vital, was ossified by the Brothers in Le Mans where the combined spirits of Jacques Dujarié, André Mottais, and Basil Moreau created in the boy a religious sensibility he would never shake loose. Whatever moral commitment his parents instilled in him was further shaped by the great men of Holy Cross into an unshakable sense of what was right and what was wrong, even when his anger blinded him or his passion shook him to his roots. He did not die dramatically like Robespierre for the history books of France, but he died as much a man, dedicated to the fire that burned within.

CHAPTER NINE

Theodulus Barbé: Reluctant Martyr

All too often history focuses on the lives and exploits of famous people, and if ordinary folk figure at all in history, they are background for the limning out of memorable personages, but if we have learned anything from Studs Terkel, it should be that the little people (for him the foot solders in World War II) are every bit as deserving of coverage in history books as emperors and kings and politicians and bishops who have generally ended up hogging the limelight. In Holy Cross too we have had hundreds of heroic little people who have been by and large overlooked: Hilarion Ferton, Leonard Guittoger, Sister Mary of the Five Wounds. Then sandwiched in between the great and the little are the middle folk who are also awaiting their turns in history: Victor Drouelle, Alexis Granger, Lawrence Ménage. One person who can no longer lie neglected, if only because his letters still complain to us from the grave, is Brother Theodulus Barbé, a reluctant martyr for the orphans in New Orleans.

Like most entries in the *General Matricule* of the Congregation of Holy Cross, the entry for Brother Theodulus is succinct:

> [Number] 347. Brother Theodulus (Francis Barbé), son of Francis [Barbé] and Anne Chardon, was born February 20, 1818, in Jublains ([in the department of] Mayenne); he entered [at Ste. Croix] on July 2, 1838, became a novice on August 19, 1838, was professed August 22, 1843; [he] left France for America with Father Sorin in 1846; [he] died June 25, 1853,

in New Orleans of yellow fever, having been commissioner at the [St. Mary's] orphanage.[1]

The Lower Normandy town in which Francis was born in 1818, just sixteen years after Napoleon's welcome Concordat with the Church, is an ancient town dating back to pre-Roman times. Conquered in the first century CE, it was called Noviodunum by the Romans and also Civitas Diablintum, City of the Diablintes, an ancient Gallic tribe. Eventually the name was corrupted to Jublent and finally Jublains. Located six miles from the Department capital Mayenne, a city of 14,000 people, Jublains itself has today a population of only 700. Its present attractions are the Gallo-Roman ruins, including those of a fortress (apparently more for grain storage than battle), an amphitheater, temple, and baths. The city Laval is about fifteen miles distant, and the town of Saulges, where that most interesting pioneer Brother Gatian Monsimer was born, is on the other side of Laval heading towards Le Mans. Jublains lies fifty-three miles south of Mont St. Michel and fifty-five miles from Rennes.

When Francis Barbé showed up at Sainte-Croix in 1838, the little religious community was undergoing a drop in new vocations after ten years of energetic growth. Although many had their formation cut short by apostolic needs in the diocese, Francis (now named Theodulus) apparently enjoyed a solid period of formation. It was not until three years after his profession that he was sent from his homeland in the company of Father Sorin for ministry in America. Father Moreau was not always so careful with his young recruits: Anselm Caillot was shipped out to America at age 16 and Gatian Monsimer at age 15. However, once in America Theodulus was taken almost immediately from the relative stability of Notre Dame south to a new venture after Edward Sorin had been asked to staff troubled St. Mary's College in Kentucky.

Opened in the spring of 1821 by a diocesan priest, Father William Byrne, at the request of Bishop Flaget twenty miles south of Bardstown and three miles west of Lebanon, Kentucky, in an old stone building, St. Mary's College was twice destroyed by fire during Byrne's time.

Between 1821 and 1833, the school educated 1200 students, many of whom came from Louisiana and Mississippi.[2] One of the first fifty boys to enroll was Martin John Spaulding, who would later become bishop of Baltimore. In 1833 Byrne turned the institution over to six Jesuits. Two more were added in 1836. The Jesuits remained until 1846 when they withdrew from Kentucky because they needed men to run St. John's College, Fordham. Locally St. Mary's was always overshadowed by its sister school St. Joseph's in Bardstown, although a December 5, 1849, letter from the Jesuit president of St. Joseph's, Father Peter J. Verhaegen, to Father Benedict Spalding, brother of Bishop Spalding and vicar of the diocese of Louisville, notes, "St. Mary's could not injure St. Joseph's, because it was a school for Catholic boys only,"[3] implying that St. Joseph's accepted Protestant students as well as Catholic students, a fact demonstrated by a walkout of some Protestant boys over a rule that students had to kneel during mandatory chapel services. There was, at least from the Jesuit point of view, no feeling that two institutions so close together on the frontier would jeopardize each other. Sorin was of a different opinion.

In his *Chronicles*, Sorin begins his Kentucky St. Mary's account (written years after the events themselves) with the 1846 Jesuit pullout. Bishop Guy Chabrat of Louisville had written to Sorin offering him the school, and Sorin in reply offered to take over the institution and also possibly start a Brothers' novitiate and a trade school on condition that the bishop would transfer ownership of all four hundred acres to Holy Cross. According to a note in Brother Aidan's *Extracts*, Sorin intended to use St. Mary's as a novitiate site in order to have more liberty than he enjoyed in the Vincennes diocese.[4] Chabrat accepted the terms and so informed Sorin with a letter addressed to Sorin in New York as Sorin was leaving for France. Sorin in turn asked Father Julian Delaune to leave his parish in Madison, Indiana, and go to St. Mary's to assess the situation. Delaune, without permission, bought the place for Sorin. Some dawdling from Propaganda Fidei complicated the transition for four months. Meanwhile by spring of 1847 Sorin remained in France and Delaune remained in limbo.

Desparate, Delaune had opened the college in January 1847, with the help of some local teachers, and convinced fifty students to enroll. In retrospect Sorin opined that Delaune had hoped to be named permanent president of the college.[5] By October 1847, Moreau ratified the deal. Tension at St. Mary's, however, mounted between Delaune and Father Auguste Saunier, who was Moreau's representative at the college. Into the middle of the muddle four Sisters and Brother Theodulus arrived. Then the vicar of the diocese, Martin Spalding, stepped into the fray, and to make matters worse the Jesuits returned to Kentucky and reopened their Bardstown college.[6]

The first letter we have by Brother Theodulus is postmarked February 18, 1848, from St. Mary's, Kentucky, and as is typical with his writing, the organization is haphazard. He does not like Father Saunier and keeps returning to that theme. He has high regard for Father Delaune, who apparently was doing an excellent job holding the college together before Moreau's emissary Saunier showed up. With between forty-five and fifty boarders,[7] the school does seem to be thriving, but the tension between Delaune and Saunier continues to threaten the entire facility. On this matter of dissension between the two priests, the Cattas are painstakingly detailed, and no one comes off very well.[8] Delaune and Saunier are characterized as energetic and well-intentioned, both wishing to head the school, but Delaune acted too hastily in piling up debt by buying all the departing Jesuits' furniture. Then Saunier came muscling in on this promising enterprise armed with the self-assurance that he should head the institution with Moreau's blessing. Sorin had placed his trust in Delaune who acted precipitously, and Moreau with his usual caution, unwittingly fanned the flames from afar.[9] Apprised of Saunier's machinations, Martin Spalding, at the time vicar-general of Detroit, labeled Saunier "a big blockhead."[10] What Theodulus made of this imbroglio we do not have to guess because his February, 1848, letter to Sorin clearly indicates he is a Delaune advocate:

> Saunier and Mr. Delaune can agree on nothing. One day Mr.
> Delaune said to Father Saunier, "I wish they'd send me a man

with whom I can agree so we could move on." Father Saunier replied to him that he was the most capable. Mr. Delaune replied to him on this occasion, "There's nobody in your Community capable of running a college." … Father Saunier has eight postulants, one of which heads the farm. He's a man with the worst insolence for Mr. Delaune. I also found him so when I arrived here. He hardly works and doesn't push those whom he was told to make work on the farm. Mr. Delaune wished that they'd leave.[11]

Both priests at St. Mary's actually had their strong points: Delaune could attract boarders and Saunier could attract postulants. But the chemistry between the two was irreparably bad. When Bishop Spalding paid a visit to the school in January 1848, he sided with Delaune.[12] Theodulus, lost in the squabbling, tells Sorin he wishes he were back at Notre Dame.

Two weeks after his February letter to Sorin, Theodulus writes again in less confusion than before, although he does say, "I don't know if you can understand the sense of my letter. I don't have the sense to arrange my paragraphs."[13] Moreau has written to Delaune annulling all arrangements at St. Mary's. The news, apparently, has not daunted Saunier whom Theodulus quotes as saying, "I'm the great president of St. Mary's." Moreau, meanwhile, has despaired of authorizing either Delaune or Saunier and yet is preparing to send four Brothers and four Sisters to St. Mary's, with no mention of any other priest than Saunier to guide the establishment. Why Moreau had such confidence in a man whom other men, including a bishop, considered incompetent, is beyond explanation, but while the powers tussled, the little people, like Theodulus, suffered. We can only imagine what the townsfolk thought of the situation.

By the following summer we do know what the locals thought because Theodulus writes in a letter to Sorin (July 9, 1848) that they are saying, "The Lake [Notre Dame] is falling apart; they're going to disperse one of these days."[14] It is true that at the time St. Mary's and St. Joseph's were both able to attract more boarders than Notre

Dame could, a state of affairs that would be no secret either in Indiana or in Kentucky. In this same letter Theodulus notes that Saunier handed over his Holy Cross rule book to Theodulus the night before as well as other Notre Dame material, his intention being to leave the Congregation, although he passed off his action simply as a need for a thirty day retreat with the Jesuits. The truth is that Saunier probably either did not know what he wanted to do with his life or he wanted to use this gesture as a way to rally pity and support. In any case, off he went to the Jesuits, who were thriving in Cincinnati. Theodulus reads the situation in an interesting light: "The loss of this college is a blessing." [15] In fact, he concludes, it would have been a blessing if Holy Cross had never undertaken this Kentucky venture in the first place.[16]

In July 1848, Sorin came to St. Mary's and took Theodulus away with him to Notre Dame, leaving only the four Sisters. Saunier left Holy Cross abruptly, taking two southern Indiana Brothers with him, one of whom was the brash Brother Mary Joseph (Samuel O'Connell) who never backed off from a good fight. When Sorin confonted the three renegades in Cincinnati, where he bumped into Saunier on the street by chance, Sorin told them he would never take them back. Brother Bernard (Patrick Leo Foley) did, however, return to Holy Cross in 1855,[17] taking the name John de Matha and teaching at Notre Dame until his death in 1895, two years after Sorin's own death. Although Sorin and Saunier were seminary classmates, the mess in Kentucky poisoned their relationship. Sorin, in fact, wrote to Moreau of Saunier: "You sent here to represent the Congregation *a child who does not even have common sense.* I think he is diseased in the brain."[18]

Theodulus was, however, not quite finished with St. Mary's because we have evidence in a letter to Moreau the following spring (April 16, 1849) that he returned to Kentucky. He reports to Moreau the details of a very interesting interview he had while there with the bishop of Cincinnati, John Baptist Purcell:

There was in his tone, his manners, and his words so much hatred against us I was surprised. We are a "Community of children and headless folks so as to make all the bishops reject us and send us packing." He's so tired of us that he can no longer stomach us. Nevertheless, he says that if the affair of the Sisters interests him, he'll sooner take you to court than let them go, because they are too difficult to replace. He compares you to one who renounces his signature.[19]

So we know that the Holy Cross Sisters did not leave St. Mary's when Delaune, Saunier, and Theodulus did, and we know that they were valued for their work. But the Sisters did eventually leave Kentucky, reassigned to New Orleans, and it was Theodulus who had to come to St. Mary's to make arrangements for their trip south by boat in late spring 1849: Sister Mary of the Nativity, Sister Mary of Calvary, Sister Mary of Providence, and Sister Mary of the Five Wounds are all named in Theodulus' April (1849) letter. In her blunt manner, Five Wounds says to Theodulus of the decision to include Providence on the trip: "What bad luck; I never would have decided to go there and live with her."[20] They are all, however, getting out of Kentucky just as cholera is moving in. They probably did not know cholera would be waiting for them in New Orleans.

In April 1849, five Brothers and three Sisters traveled to New Orleans to take over direction of St. Mary's Orphanage, which had been floundering since the death of its founder, Father Adam Kindelon, a brave priest from Mississippi who had died as a result of typhoid contracted saving orphans and cattle during a 1837 hurricane on the property at Bayou St. John. The Brothers in New Orleans were directed by Brother Vincent Pieau, whose signature can be seen clearly in the orphanage log (May 1, 1949) now held in the New Orleans Archdiocesan archives. With Vincent came Basil, Francis de Sales, and Louis. Brother Theodulus, according to minutes of the Notre Dame local council for December 6, 1847, was to have the title "steward."[21]

Theodulus' first letter from New Orleans (June 6, 1849), addressed to Sorin, is anguished. The complaints are not petty, and there are many: every morning at 5 AM he has to drive three miles in a small cart into the city to get provisions, and he has to cook for the orphans and staff in an overheated kitchen under the supervision of a bossy old German with the help of only one old black woman. It is not a good situation. Not only are the climate beastly and the working conditions harsh, there is no common prayer life for the Brothers even though good old Brother Vincent Pieau is in charge. Two months later (August 24, 1849) he writes again to Sorin. He has been put in charge of the boys' dormitories, but he gets directions and criticism from both Brother Vincent and a man he particularly has no respect for, Brother Francis de Sales, a very outspoken man (as is attested by the letters Francis de Sales wrote to Sorin earlier in his American career). Theodulus begs Sorin to send a priest to New Orleans (he mentions Father Francis Gouesse by name as unsuitable) and requests a visit from Sorin himself to see how bad things are. By September he is still exasperated and writes (September 9, 1849) to the Chapter at Notre Dame to push Sorin to visit New Orleans. Everyone, including Bishop Blanc, is expecting Sorin to come down. Things would improve, Theodulus writes, if Sorin came. If he does not come—here Theodulus turns darkly ominous: "If you don't want to see some disagreeable things, consider Father Superior's trip necessary—I won't return to any details on this subject."[22] Then Theodulus turns the letter to a less than subtle attack on Brother Vincent:

He [Vincent] knows he's not loved and approved by all of us here. Not that I'm saying he's wrong. He's right in many instances. I don't tell him that any more. He's beginning to get a little old too. Be so kind, my very dear friends, to send us Father Superior. I make this prayer in the name of everyone here, and I make it to you because I know that you'll give permission.[23]

So much for Vincent, the American patriarch of Holy Cross! Then Theodulus cannot resist bragging a bit: "As I'm sacristan, I spend money quietly to decorate the chapel. And Sister Mary of Calvary does everything as I want it." He must indeed have been a delightful Brother, tied to his work but not afraid to grumble. His postscript to this letter is, however, sadly foreboding: "I'm in good health. Yellow fever is in town but will amount to nothing." Four years hence it will ironically be yellow fever that does him in.

The following summer Theodulus again writes an impassioned letter (June 10, 1850) to Sorin stressing Brother Vincent's increasing inability to hold up as director. Complicating the matter, although Theodulus does not refer to it, is the tussle between Sorin and Moreau over the official position of Father Gouesse, who has been appointed by Sorin for New Orleans. Sorin had sent him as "Visitor" to get rid of him (both Gouesse and Brother Gatian were his nemeses in council meetings at Notre Dame), but Moreau named Gouesse "Superior" and separated the orphanage account book somewhat from Sorin's control. Theodulus appraises his own ability to be Vincent's replacement and concludes he could do it if he had to, although he says Gouesse has told him if he took over, "the place would fall apart." This may seem an odd statement because in fact he had been appointed director of the orphanage a month earlier, on May 22, 1850,[24] but obviously the news had not yet reached New Orleans. For the next three years Sorin wrestled with Moreau over the superiorship in New Orleans, Gouesse remaining in limbo and declared merely a "Visitor" by the former and declared officially "Superior" by the latter.[25] Brother Theodulus, meanwhile, went on with the day to day running of the orphanage after Brother Vincent returned to Notre Dame in 1850. One of his biggest headaches was Brother Francis de Sales, about whom he writes to Sorin, "The greatest saint in heaven wouldn't be smart enough to give an order that wouldn't be criticized by Brother Francis de Sales."[26]

By January 1853, Theodulus seems comfortable in his role as director. In the last letter we have by him (to Moreau January 1, 1853), he tells Moreau how busy things are at the orphanage and he outlines what he would look for in a new Brother assigned to New Orleans: neither too young nor too old, adept at organization, able to speak both French and English. In this letter he attacks Sorin and has nothing but praise for the patience of Father Gouesse. Given this epistolary blessing from a man on the ground, we should reassess all the bad press Gouesse has received.[27] It is good to know, at any rate, that director and superior were working well together in New Orleans, no matter how nastily the feud continued between Notre Dame and Le Mans. Then tragedy struck the orphanage in the summer of 1853.

There are only two extant letters from New Orleans in the 1853 Sorin correspondence in the Holy Cross United States Province Archives, both letters by Father Gouesse, neither of them mentioning Brother Theodulus. However, two interesting New Orleans letters in the Notre Dame Archives do mention Theodulus' death: one by Bishop Blanc and one by Francis Gouesse.[28] For this same year there are four letters in the US Province Archives by Sorin, only one of them consequential since it pertains to his refusal of the Bengal bishopric and his considering a five year leave from the Congregation. There is, naturally, no mention of the death of Theodulus in this letter to Moreau: Sorin had more ominous matters on his mind than the passing of one Brother. He did not apparently write to Moreau of Theodulus' death because Moreau in Circular Letter #55 (August 27, 1853) notes that word was received of the death from Father Gouesse by way of Father Rézé:

> It is but a few days since I had the consolation of seeing most of you at the general retreat. At that time, I announced to you the sad news which is the subject of this present letter. Nevertheless, I believe I ought to mention the matter again for the benefit of those who were not present and have not yet learned of it. It concerns the sad loss of one of our members, whose death was announced to me by a letter from his Local Superior to Father Rézé, our Provincial in America:

New Orleans
June 25, 1853

Reverend Father:

I have the honor to inform you that Brother Theodulus, who was Director and Commissioner in our Orphan Asylum in New Orleans, fell asleep in the Lord, on June 25, 1853, at six o'clock in the morning, at the age of 37, after receiving the Sacraments of Penance, Holy Eucharist and Extreme Unction. His funeral was held that same day at five o'clock in the afternoon.

Kindly inform the Very Reverend Father Rector so that he may order the usual prayers for the repose of this dear soul. Ask him, likewise, to send someone to replace this good Brother, since we have no one available at present.

I have the honor, etc.

Gouesse, Salvatorist

This is brisk enough reportage, and it would characterize Gouesse as rather cold if we did not have another letter by him to Moreau dated July 8, 1853. This letter (held in the General Archives, Notre Dame) follows a strong letter by Bishop Blanc (June 30, 1853) to Sorin scolding Sorin for prolonging his squabble with Moreau to the detriment of the New Orleans orphanage. Of Brother Theodulus, Blanc writes, "I don't know if I told you about the death of good Brother Theodulus, who was buried three days ago. He was sick for four days. It is a real loss to the orphanage—a loss all the more felt because the other Brothers are few and not healthy!" He then uses the death of the Brother to further pummel Sorin for the quarrel with Moreau. It is a very strong letter from a good bishop friend of Holy Cross.

On July 8, 1853, Gouesse, in writing to Moreau about the troubles with Sorin, includes touching details about Theodulus' final days. Were it not for this letter, we would know nothing about the four days Theodulus struggled with yellow fever:

Brother Theodulus was taken away at the moment he least expected. I never saw a man so frightened of death during four days of sickness, twelve hours of total loss of consciousness, and fifteen minutes of agony which ended his days. By a stroke of luck some weeks before, he sent you or his family his will or his power of attorney. Forty-eight hours before his death, on his formal request I promised him in order to save his life I'd send him to either Canada or France. That made him very happy that I hoped I'd be able to keep my promise to him.

It is good to know that Theodulus on his deathbed did have the benefit of a Holy Cross priest at hand, a priest, in fact, whom he trusted and admired, as we know from his final letter to Moreau six months before his death.

With the death of Theodulus began a rash of deaths in New Orleans (Brother Athanasius, Brother Eleazar, Sister Alphonsus): four days after Moreau's Circular Letter #55 came his Circular #56 (August 31, 1853), reprinting another letter from Gouesse:

I have the honor to inform you that Bother Athanasius, professed, who was tailor in our house at New Orleans, fell asleep in the lord on August 2, 1853, at the age of 26, after receiving the Sacraments of Penance, Holy Eucharist, and Extreme Unction. His funeral was held that same day.

Kindly inform Very Reverend Father Rector in order that he may have the usual prayers said for the repose of this beloved soul. Request him, likewise, to send someone to replace Brother as soon as possible.[29]

Athanasius was born Martin Kline in Germany in 1827, came to Holy Cross in 1851, and was professed on Christmas Day, 1852. Less than a year later he was dead. Although this second letter from Gouesse sounds formulaic (the order of the sacraments, the request for a replacement), it was accompanied by an impassioned cry titled "The Week in New Orleans":

> Farewell to business, farewell to the noise and the gaiety of other days. On the streets we hear nothing but the grim rumble of hearses on their way to the cemeteries; everywhere the eye sees naught but mournful processions. New Orleans is a Necropolis where death reigns supreme.
>
> All who could do so have left the city. It is sad to witness the heart-rending spectacle offered by every passing day. Many outsiders have left the city to escape the scourge, but the number of those who are obliged to remain here, as on a battlefield, is still too large. Death mows them down mercilessly, and the spade of the grave-digger is constantly echoing from the ground. A hundred victims a day is large, even an enormous figure, when we consider that the foreign population of the city is now reduced to almost nothing.[30]

These are the responses of a poet to a catastrophe, and they are the words of Father Gouesse, not Father Moreau. Moreau is less passionate, as can be seen when he announces less than two weeks later in Circular Letter #57 (September 10, 1853) yet another death in New Orleans:

> The scourge of yellow fever which is decimating the population of New Orleans still rages frightfully. Now, no more than before, does it respect the Brothers and Sisters in charge of the sorely tried asylum which is directed by Father Gouesse. You will have suspected from this observation that we have suffered a new loss, and that we must redouble our fervor to appease the wrath of Heaven ... My greatest worry now is to know who is still alive after the death of those we already mourn. Great indeed would be my joy were I soon to learn that the good Brother whose death I am about to announce to you is the last victim.

This is a dispassionate analysis of the situation, and the letter from Gouesse which Moreau reprints is also cool, very formulaic, announcing the death of the novice Brother Eleazar, 35 years old and a teacher in New Orleans.[31]

The list of deaths ends eleven days later with the announcement of one more death in New Orleans: Sister Mary of St. Alphonsus, a thirty-year old novice "employed in the clothes room."[32] She was herself a novice when she contracted yellow fever and was professed on her deathbed. Born Mary Therese Sheehan in Ireland, she entered the Sisters at Bertrand in August of 1850 and received the habit a year later, two months before she was sent to New Orleans on May 3, 1852. Thus she had just over a year in the South before she died. She is buried in St. Patrick's Cemetery, New Orleans.

Basil Moreau learned of four deaths in New Orleans within three months, the deaths occurring June 25, August 2, August 18, and August 23.[33] The effect on the local community must have been devastating. Sacrificed for orphans in New Orleans, these four religious would not be the only ones to die working for Holy Cross in the Crescent City, but their tragic ends so clustered together made a great impression on Moreau's religious Communities, and among them Theodulus stands out because he left us vivid letters about his work and trials in two locations: Kentucky and Louisiana. And if we remember him in the future, we should remember him as the generous soul that he was, helping in his last years to transform a miserable orphanage into an institution that the city and the diocese would be proud of for a century after his death. He died a tortured death that made him a reluctant martyr in New Orleans. Able to assess personalities and to size up unworkable living conditions, he stayed nonetheless true to his vows and labored intently in two inhospitable locales. When religious Titans battled over his head, Theodulus took care of day-to-day matters, making life tolerable for boarders in Kentucky and little orphans in New Orleans. What more could be expected of a religious martyr?

CHAPTER TEN

Alexis Granger: Sorin's Softer Self

Born in Daon (Mayenne), France, June 19, 1817, to André and Marie (Bourdelet) Granger, Alexis Dominic Granger was home-schooled until the age of fifteen. Daon, a small village, today has a population of about five hundred so we can presume it was considerably smaller in 1817. Located thirty-two kilometers from Angers and ten from Solemnes, the town is not a tourist attraction. With some Latin already to his credit at age fifteen,[1] Alexis Granger entered school ten kilometers distant at Chateau-Gontier, a secondary school that had already trained Basil Moreau and Edward Sorin. It was Sorin who was instrumental in getting Alexis into Holy Cross.[2] After five years, Alexis went to the major seminary at Le Mans, and on December 19, 1840, he was ordained by Bishop Bouvier and assigned to parish work in Le Mans. Encouraged by his classmate Edward Sorin, however, Granger came to Basil Moreau's religious community of Holy Cross in early October, 1843, and began his novitiate training there a month later.[3] He had initially hesitated taking this step out of concern for his sister Marie, who was apparently planning to be his housekeeper, and he had some reservations about being sent by Moreau out of the country. It was Sorin who allayed his fears in a letter dated August 31, 1840:

> You can rest assured that you will not be sent out of France during the lifetime of your relatives or indeed during the

whole of your own life except at the will of the Superior coupled with your own request. Nobody is ever obliged to go.[4]

How ironic, therefore, that Granger was chosen within one month of his profession (August 15, 1844)[5] to leave for Indiana under Brother Vincent Pieau's leadership. They boarded the steamship *Zurich* on September 10, 1844.

From a rhapsodic letter that Granger posted in New York City to Moreau in October, we learn that the crossing took a month and was quiet until they reached Newfoundland. There all hell broke loose:

> The whistling of the wind and the roar of the waves struck terror into my soul. I imagined that the waves were going to wash over the ship … That very night I had quite a narrow escape when I fell headlong near the opening of a trap-door some ten feet deep.

That terror happened on October 3. On the next day a strong wind started to rock the ship:

> At noon, the main mast was broken into three pieces, along with the main yard … At two o'clock we were getting ready for dinner when a strong wind pitched the vessel on her side for a full minute. The rebound hurled a heap of copper against one of the partitions, and the copper rolled up against it with a great crash and shattered it. For a moment we thought we were lost. We feared the ship had been ripped open.

As bad as these moments were, worse were to come on the following Sunday night and lasting all of Monday:

> About six in the evening a storm broke. We got up at nine when the rocking of the ship threatened to throw us out of bed … We were dreadfully frightened; at times we rolled about the ship with the objects we grasped to steady ourselves.

The ship, riding now on one side, now on the other, seemed at every moment on the point of being swallowed up by the waves. An entire row of beds was thrown out into the middle of the ship and all those in the upper berths were pitched out ... The storm abated about six in the morning, after lasting twelve hours.[6]

With the ship damaged, the voyage took eight days more than anticipated. Thereafter, the trip overland to Notre Dame, Granger thought, would take one week. October would have been a pleasant time to travel to Indiana. Sorin, of course, was anxious to have Granger settle into the work at the little college in its first year, although Granger's personality had none of the vitality and drive of the Notre Dame superior. In fact, Granger was a somewhat laid-back missionary: O'Connell on several occasions refers to him as "diffident."[7] Nonetheless, Granger would have found in the first brick building a welcoming community of young and middle-aged Holy Cross personnel, along with a half-dozen or more American novices.[8] Granger became Sorin's right-hand man, named assistant superior and vice-president of the college soon after his arrival. He also was master of novices off and on (more on than off) from 1847 to 1867 and pastor of the campus church. In 1868 when Sorin was elected Superior General, Granger was elected provincial of the American Province. At those times when Sorin was in France or Rome, Granger was in charge of all religious.

The tendency to dismiss Granger as a useful but unimpressive administrator began early.[9] Victor Drouelle, in a letter to Basil Moreau, characterizes Granger as "good little Father Granger."[10] But Granger was a man who held an important position as American Provincial for a generation, passed judgment on scores of religious personnel, and enjoyed the confidence of important churchmen, including prelates. Even Stephen Badin, original owner of the Notre Dame property, characterized by Sorin as a man "who never agrees with anybody, began now to criticize and condemn everything that he himself had approved and admired at Notre Dame du Lac,"[11] wrote a rather strong letter to Granger in 1846 that bears quoting in full:

> The road leading to Niles from Mr. Metzsger's Tavern is now blocked up, by the ploughing lately done by Br. Laurence greatly to his injury and to that of his family and property. In as much as the road now destroyed, naturally throws the custom [business] of Niles and S. Bend, on the other road, leading to the other tavern, owned by a violent anti-catholic.
>
> The sooner your orders and instructions are given to repair these acts of ingratitude and violence to his rights, the better, because the road runs upon a piece of land which does not belong to you, and for which you have no legal title, nor even a Bond. The proprietor of it is resolved to prevent any further trespass whatever, and he cannot possibly fail in the fact.
>
> To prevent scandal and to save this worthy and charitable catholic man "who does good to all men especially to the household of the Faith," whose house has been open at all times to visitors from the Lake, priests, brothers, postulants, and even students, and who, besides has been the largest donor of the Church here, to prevent the continuation of such an act of ingratitude and injustice, the usual road should be left open in a way suitable for travelers, immediately and without one day's delay ...
>
> I beg you to send this letter to Fr. Sorin that he may be aware of the blunders of that great and sapient Brother Laurence who is the laughing stock of the Country, and consequently no credit, but rather a great injury to your Institution, for people through him think they can cheat you as they please.[12]

The sentiments in this letter are not only phrased in a bullying manner to a man who apparently could withstand bullying by Badin, but the requests are made in such a way that the author (Badin) fully expects

Granger to be capable of carrying through on the demands to rectify the road situation. At this time, Granger was not yet provincial, but he was expected to be a strong replacement for Sorin in Sorin's absence.

While Sorin was in Europe in 1846, Granger was left in charge. On returning to Indiana, Sorin found that three of the five seminarians had left and the Sisters were suffering a public relations crisis as a result of their not having a Sister-leader for fifteen months. Yet Sorin did not blame Granger for the Notre Dame disasters:

> Not that Fr. Granger, who took his place, was negligent or spared himself in any way, but being overburdened with duties and having daily to fight against bad will, which took advantage of the superior's absence to heap difficulties in the way, he could not oppose a sufficiently strong resistance to the passions of others which had become more exacting, nor maintain everywhere the spirit of submission and of peace.[13]

We should remember that in 1846 Granger had been a professed member of Holy Cross only two years, had been in America fewer years than that, was still learning English, and had been ordained a priest only six years. In 1846, he was actually doing a remarkably fine job, given his lack of experience. From his own Brothers, out serving in various grade schools around the country, Granger also enjoyed respect and inspired confidence. From Brother Boniface in Cincinnati, Granger received a confidential update on the teaching men:

> Bro. Damasas has caused me a great deal of trouble and anxiety. Ten days ago he seemed to make up his mind for the best, but yesterday morning he left for good. However, before dinner already he returned, when I gave him to understand that I would have no more to do with him. This rude treatment on my part broke the poor man's heart; it was the right treatment for him. Broken hearted he went to the Rev. Supr. of the Franciscans, who at last brought him back,

after humbling him a great deal. I consented to admit him again under conditions that he, Br. Damasas, would give public satisfaction, which he did, by asking publicly pardon of the Bros. The Bro. has a good lust for governing children and gives full satisfaction in school, otherwise I would have shown no indulgence to him. He is now determined to hold out for good. I hope for the best. Please, tell Rev. Fath. Ruthmane to write to him sometimes. I too will do for him what I can. Bro. Constantine is now teaching Br. Leo's class. Poor Bro. Leo cannot get along at all. I am fully convinced that he will make no teacher. With all his learning he can keep no order, and it would be better if the poor brother move again to Notre Dame, since he is of no service to us here. He has great ideas in his head but cannot carry out his plans. He wants to be a Priest—and this keeps the poor man divided; he dislikes the school.[14]

Not a micro-manager, Granger has invested responsibility in his Brother-superiors and counted on informed reports to help him stay aware of conduct out in the schools.

Similarly with Holy Cross priests out on assignment, Granger used "visitors" to report on his men in the parishes. Of the "reporters" none was more dramatic than Peter Cooney. In one twenty-page report from 1874, Cooney feeds Granger information on an alcoholic priest. The language is so vivid Cooney could almost be writing a short story:

The pastor put wine on the table—Father Spillard was present. I remarked that as long as we were hearing Confessions "we should drink no wine or the people could not help smelling it." Father O'Mahony commenced immediately to pour wine into his tumbler saying, "O pshaw"! When he had half the tumbler full poured out, I said in a firm tone without excitement, "do not drink it." He pushed the tumbler away from him saying, "Very well—just as you say." He told me that they accused him of drinking in Canada. He does not know that V. Rev. S. General knows it. At any rate, this knowledge, together with the reason given above, make me anxious to protect him.[15]

A reader will not soon forget the details of this wine encounter, and we can imagine the effect they had on Alexis Granger.

As far as the local Indiana ordinary is concerned, Granger developed so fine a relationship with Maurice de St. Palais (successor to Celestine de la Hailandière) that the prelate could write openly to Granger:

> I believe that if Mr. Sorin had limited his efforts to the founding of Brothers schools in Indiana & if he had sent out only well-formed Religious & had often visited these, the work would have succeeded admirably. By sending them to a distance, he lost many subjects, & if he continues as he begun he will lose many more.[16]

The St. Palais comments are so incisive one can see that he was close to the on-going problem of the poor training young Brothers received before being shipped to grade schools in order to make money to support Sorin's main institution.

Another churchman, the vicar general of Alton, Illinois, wrote to Granger in confidence about the abusive punishments some Brothers were using in one of the schools:

> Please excuse me for troubling you, but I think it my duty to give some information concerning the Brothers. Br. Edmund, our second Brother, had the habit to whip the children very severely. The parents commenced to complain bitterly and consequently the Pastor went to speak to Brother Edmund. He did not deny the charge and mentioned that he had learned this habit from Brother Gregory, with whom he was at Springfield last year. For a little while the Brother did do better, but then he fell back into his old habit. I have seen myself a boy that

had yet the marks of the whip on his hands and legs six days after the whipping took place. At the time Brother Gregory was here, many times parents came to me complaining of the severe whipping their children received from the Brother. Several times I heard myself from our garden that the Brother was whipping the boys and looking up I could see through the open windows that the boys standing in a long line had to come, one by one, before Brother Gregory and then receive one slap on each hand. I am not opposed to it, that the boys be punished if they deserve it, but I do not like it, that they be whipped too severely, and that they be whipped too often and get a slap or two for every fault they commit. Besides there are other kinds of punishment.[17]

It is obvious that Janssen looked to Granger as the man who would do something to control the teachers. How anyone could characterize Granger as an ineffective administrator is belied by letter after letter sent to him about conditions in the schools.

Bishops treated Granger with the same decorum they afforded Sorin. Bishop Luers of Fort Wayne was particularly forthright with Granger over the matter of separating the Bertrand Sisters from the Le Mans motherhouse, and he is withering in his comments on Basil Moreau, the Superior General:

Father General in his circular or letter acts in a rather highhanded manner, but before he is through, I think, he will find that if he had acted more conciliatory he would have done better. Religious Communities never gain anything by quarrelling with the Bps in whose dioceses their institutions exist; or when they throw difficulties into their way.

Has he ever reflected upon the consequences of withdrawing jurisdiction immediately from his Priests over the Sisters—or of refusing their services? Will not the world, who cannot understand those things, come to the conclusion, that there is some awful immorality existing between the

Priests, Brothers & Sisters of your community & that therefore the General, or Rome, or I myself were obliged to put a stop to it?

I have no desire to separate the Sisters from France, all I desire is: that they have peace, so that they may live as religious should & pay off the debts upon their different establishments ...

Please tell Father Sorin to send me the letter to which your Supr General refers, "*I will answer it.*"[18]

The sentiments against Father Moreau are particularly pronounced in this letter as Luers has obviously chosen which side of the Sorin-Moreau struggle he is going to support. Two weeks later he writes a follow-up: "There can be no lasting peace & union for the Sisters with France, but that in this Country they should form one body ... it appears your Supr General knows neither prudence nor conciliation."[19] Luers considers Granger to be of one mind with Sorin and treats him, in Sorin's absence, with the same steely will against Moreau that he would have used with Sorin. It was, of course, to an American bishop's advantage to have the Bertrand Sisters out from under Moreau's jurisdiction—the bishop would have more influence over a local religious community when it would not have ties to a superior in a foreign country on the other side of the Atlantic.

Alexis Granger rarely left Indiana once he arrived. In September 1847, however, he had to relocate with his novices to Indianapolis at Bishop Halandière's insistence. They all returned to Notre Dame in June 1848. When Father Cointet was appointed master of seminarian novices, Granger remained master of novices for the Brothers in the building on St. Mary's "Island," today part of Columba Hall. In 1849 Granger accompanied the Brooklyn Brothers to New Orleans but returned quickly to Notre Dame. He was apparently a man who was quietly devoted to both Notre Dame and Edward Sorin. He traveled when told to, but he did not like being separated from either home or superior for very long.

A smudge in Granger's life surfaces in June 1852 when Moreau wanted him to go as superior to Bengal. Sorin protested vigorously in a letter to Moreau dated July 14, 1852, claiming that to transfer Granger would be a deathblow to Notre Dame. At the same time Moreau and his Council wanted Sorin also to go to Bengal as bishop-elect, ordering the move in a letter to Sorin dated September 13, 1852. In this battle of two giants, Sorin won, Moreau retreated, Granger stayed at Notre Dame. There is no evidence that Granger reacted as violently as Sorin did at the prospect of transfer to Bengal, but the effect was the same: he got his own way.

Sorin's own turmoil continued to seethe and by 1868 in a letter to Bishop Fillion (December 13, 1868), his vituperation was manic. The upshot was Moreau's removal by the General Chapter from the office of Superior General, eventually supplanted by his nemesis Edward Sorin. Granger then, on being elected Provincial in 1869, proved to be an "ineffective administrator"[20] and was replaced by William Corby in March 1870. But Granger was again provincial two years later when Corby was assigned to a new foundation in Watertown, Wisconsin.

There were four Sorin crises in which Granger played a role: in 1852, Sorin's being ordered to Bengal; in 1862, Sorin's threat of autonomy for Indiana; in 1863, the movement toward separation of the Sisters away from France; and in 1868, Sorin's role in the resignation of Moreau. In a letter to Moreau dated October 9, 1852, Sorin refused Moreau's directive to move to Bengal to become bishop-elect there. Granger supported Sorin in the matter and received a letter from Moreau on June 22, 1852, months before Sorin's adamant refusal. In 1862, Granger made a special trip to Le Mans to argue for autonomy of the American province. The following year (by April 1863), Granger had organized the opposition to keeping the Notre Dame Sisters tied to the Marianites in France. He was abetted in this regard by a staunch Sorin ally, Bishop Luers of Ft. Wayne. Finally for the 1868 chapter, Granger stayed faithful to Sorin as Sorin orchestrated (with Drouelle and Champeau) the resignation of Moreau as Superior General, a move calculated by Sorin to save Notre Dame at the expense of Moreau's school adjacent to the motherhouse church in Le Mans.

In late October 1852, Granger writes to Moreau saying he does not have the energy, intelligence, or aptitude to be a superior. He prefers to stay novice master, a position in which he feels a good degree of success. Moreover, he is confessor to almost everyone at Notre Dame, including the students. He suggests Moreau choose Father Cointet instead. Turning his attention then to Father Grouesse, the man named by Moreau to be superior in New Orleans over Sorin's objections, Granger says he has no confidence in the man whom he considers a hypocrite, and he pitied any young priest who would have to live with Gouesse because that young priest would lose his religious spirit. This is an unusually harsh judgment on Gouesse, but it shows that Granger not only feels strongly about the priest but also has the courage to raise a sensitive issue with Moreau. He is, of course, doing all he can to abet Sorin's preventing Gouesse from being named superior in New Orleans. Granger suggests that Moreau have Gouesse stay at the Motherhouse in France so he could see for himself Gouesse's true nature.

Early in November, 1852, Granger writes again to Moreau, this time strongly condemning the actions of Father Baroux, whom he names a Judas for defaming Notre Dame from the pulpit in Pokegan. He wants Moreau to do something quickly with Baroux. Again he turns to the impending removal of Sorin from Notre Dame and the disastrous consequences it would have on the institution. Propaganda Fidei, Granger says, would be horrified at the loss of a place like Notre Dame, sure to go under should Sorin leave it. Again, Granger begs that Moreau not consider him as a replacement for Sorin because the position would be too much for him.

Less than a month lager, Granger writes to Moreau in early December, asking forgiveness for the frequency of his letters. He assures Moreau that his vocation is solid and has indeed grown stronger over the years. But he says he must repeat things he has already stressed—notably that Gouesse is not suitable for the Congregation, at least not in America, a statement he reiterates at

the end of the letter. Throughout, Granger is very subservient to
Moreau, using language that shows he has a great reverence for the
Superior General. He makes his points about Gouesse and about his
own (Granger's) good work with the Notre Dame novices, letting
Moreau infer that Granger is the right man in the right place. The
letter is a testament to Granger's confidence in and love for Moreau.

So already by the early 1850's, Granger was supporting Sorin in
his quest for separation from France, but Granger argued his case
more often than not with a gentleness quite contrastive to the steely
bombast of his Indiana superior. One example will help show the
difference. On February 13, 1853, Granger wrote the following letter
to Bishop Lefevere in Detroit:

> Thank you sincerely for the response your Grace deigned
> to give my last consultation. It appropriately calmed some
> qualms of conscience that circumstances had heightened
> because it was necessary to make a definite decision
> according to the sense you suggested in your letter. These
> steps are extremely important and ought to be made with total
> maturity in order to leave me no scruple in my spirit and leave
> everyone the energy and vigor that future circumstances will
> demand. Here is what made me submit to you all the pieces
> that concern this important act before it came to fruition. We
> sincerely wish separation as a reality and a true necessity,
> and we have finally determined to do so by the enclosed
> letter from Father Rector [Moreau] dated January 13. The
> subject it concerns is one of my priests who sadly cannot
> merit our confidence. It's the same one whom Father Sorin
> told you about some years ago when your Grace first visited
> N D du Lac. In your response you express the desire that
> the Motherhouse declare our emancipation as the best way,
> but we shouldn't wait around to do it. You were inclined to
> counsel us to ask him for this declaration. This would work
> if it had a chance of success, but you easily will understand
> the thing is not feasible in present circumstances and that the

response to a similar demand would be a command in virtue of holy obedience either to remain submissive or to leave the Society immediately. We have therefore believed we ought to take a common ground and declare independence in at least five years, leaving either reunion or perpetual separation to arbitration from a wise and holy canon in Le Mans who has our total confidence, so that experience would show either side the advantages or disadvantages of separation.

As this formal separation, demanded by circumstances, would seem opposed to our vows of obedience that many among us made at the hands of Father Rector [Moreau] and that serious scruples would probably arise in many, if the Father Rector commanded something by virtue of obedience after receiving these pieces, I would be infinitely obliged to you if you would 1) deign to respond with your customary frankness, 2) if you think our approach is licit and if we can act in good conscience independently of the Motherhouse, 3) if it would be necessary to obtain dispensation of our vow of obedience to Rev. Father Rector and to whom we would owe obedience. Here simply the formula of our vows: [vow formula included in Latin]. This last promise was, I believe, fulfilled by our long patience.

I know, Monseignor, I'm asking much of you, more than you are obliged to do, but the glory of God so dear to you and the peace of the community which doesn't want to beg a favor through a sin makes me hope from your Grace a satisfying response.[21]

There is a graciousness in this letter, an almost obsequious graciousness, that indicates a writer capable of fine sentiments of diplomacy. The situation of the priest in question was Francis Gouesse, whom Moreau had appointed superior of the orphanage in New Orleans. Sorin opposed the appointment. This disagreement is simply the catalyst for Sorin to pursue his real goal: emancipation from Le Mans. Of course, a local bishop would be only too happy to have the separation effected because he would then have tighter control over the Notre Dame foundations. Perhaps Granger's gracious language can be ascribed to the fact that he is not the major player in the tug-of-war, but he is Sorin's softer side in the drama, which is all too evident in the letter.

The troubles between Notre Dame and Le Mans did not begin in 1853. Granger, in an August 1853 letter to Father Champeau says that the problems have been going on for five years, which timetable would put their origin around 1846 or 1847, nascent years for Notre Dame. By 1853, the embers were still smoldering in spite of Sorin's visits to Le Mans. Therefore, the Gouesse matter was not the spark that ignited the fire—it merely fed the existent flames.

Writing to Moreau on October 2, 1853, Granger tells Moreau that visits to Le Mans are fruitless. Rather, he wants Moreau to visit Notre Dame to see for himself the work going on there, in a land so different in climate and customs from those in France. He accuses the Motherhouse Council of thinking the Notre Dame men are sitting around doing little when in actual fact each Indiana missionary is doing the work of three or four men. He argues for new foundations in America being undertaken without prior approval from the Motherhouse. Granger concludes this rather long letter by itemizing the steps necessary for a reconciliation: 1) Moreau must visit Indiana, 2) the Indiana superior must be free to start new foundations, 3) Moreau should reserve judgment on Indiana, 4) rules should not be changed as often as they are, 5) Moreau must visit Indiana. This last point is a simple repetition of the first point as, apparently, a way of emphasizing its importance.

Throughout the Granger-Moreau correspondence, Granger writes respectfully to Moreau, and if he has to make strong points, he backs up his assertions with good reasons, e.g., the differences in cultures between France and America. He never loses his temper (unlike Moreau in a letter to Granger dated September 9, 1863, as the separation of the Indiana Sisters was moving forward). Granger never compromises his role as a religious subject.

Granger was a man of the people, a man, in fact, not afraid to get his hands dirty. In 1853 when he was assigned to be novice master of the seminarians, he himself cut the underbrush away on the north side of St. Mary's Lake for St. Aloysius' Novitiate, a building of fourteen private rooms and a chapel.[22] After the Main Building burned, Granger helped clean away the rubble, although the *Scholastic* noted, "Regard for historical accuracy compels us to state that Father Granger would scarcely command a large salary among the horny-handed sons of toil."[23] The same campus magazine had noted years earlier that when Sorin's newfangled two-wheeled velocipede showed up on campus mid-January in 1869, students took turns riding it as Granger shouted, "Watch out! You break zumpsing!"[24] He was a man among men, much beloved.

Another testament to Granger's competence and virtue was his supervision of the Sacred Heart parish at Notre Dame, best felt today in the great church that started to go up in 1871 to accommodate a huge bell Sorin was bringing to the campus. The church actually never attained its final form until 1892, one year before Granger's death. The six apsidal chapels were added in 1879, the Lady Chapel was added in 1888, the steeple in 1892. Granger did say the first High Mass on August 15, 1875, in his church, officially known as Our Lady of the Sacred Heart of Jesus. In that same year the old church, sitting behind the new church, was demolished. To fund the building (O'Connell calls him a "reluctant fund raiser"[25]), Granger advertized in June 1869 that daily Mass would be said for fifty years for anyone who donated fifty dollars. Such a scheme does not seem out of the ordinary even today, but unfortunately Granger added that "any offering less than $50 will entitle the giver to the fruits of the daily Mass *pro rata* of the amount contributed."[26] One can imagine little angels in heaven with their pocket calculators trying to figure out what percentage of the merits would be divvied up for what percentage of the fifty dollars contributed. Granger noted one could also contribute on an installment plan.

Sacred Heart Church was Alexis Granger's last great act. He died at Notre Dame on July 26, 1893, aged 76, and rests with the American provincials in the Community cemetery on St. Mary's Road at Notre Dame. At news of Granger's death, Sorin wept and said, "Mon cher Alexis! Who next?"[27] Twenty-five years before his death, Granger was characterized in the following way:

> Father Granger is of a very retiring disposition, never coming forward into notice unless when duty strictly obliges him to do so; and hence his merit and real worth are not known except to those whose occupation or spiritual wants bring them in contact with him. We would be glad here to speak of his excellent qualities, especially as a priest, but we refrain from doing so, through respect for his wishes to remain unknown, except in the field of his duty. When he has gone to his reward, his virtues will be appreciated and praised by men.[28]

Everyone seemed to like the man. Even Victor Drouelle, who was quoted earlier as condescending in his description of Granger, had this to say to Moreau of the Indiana priest in a letter dated November 1, 1848:

> Do not form an idea of his sacrifices or of his mortification by the expression on his face. To look at him you would think he were living in the midst of all the pleasures and satisfactions of life. But you would be very much mistaken. His bed is nothing but a very poor cot, and his furniture consists of a small table, one chair, and three boards with a few books on them."[29]

Granger had the bad luck to die within a week after Thomas Walsh, the president of Notre Dame. Thus the Notre Dame *Scholastic* devoted most of its July 29, 1893, issue to Walsh, who had died on July 17. A short article on Granger appears on pages 10 and 11, but it says little about the man beyond a sketch of his life. Perhaps it is best that Granger left Notre Dame without much fanfare since he served

Holy Cross and Notre Dame most of his life without much spotlight. Sorin's prop, he lived his life quietly but effectively, leaving a gentle mark where Sorin left a crater.

The finest evaluation of Granger's character comes from Arthur Hope:

> Alexis Granger was strictly a students' priest. For nearly fifty years he had been identified with the college, and when he died the thousands of boys who had been to Notre Dame exclaimed with one voice: "What a saintly priest!" For fifty years he had been the confessor to the boys. He was amiable and understanding: a bit timid, with none of Father Sorin's daring: retiring, strictly honest, devoted. He rarely made a speech, could not bear to appear on public platforms, made no journeys, except the one Father Sorin forced on him. His peculiar powers in the confessional were ascribed to his genuine humility … Fifty years in the confessional, listening to the faults and sins of Notre Dame boys, might have tended to break his gracious spirit. His kindness was not soft. Rather, it inspired true penance.[30]

Hope then quotes from a letter from an alumnus who arrived at Notre Dame in 1887, just six years before Granger's death:

> I went to confession to Father Granger in the chapel in the basement of the church. He gave me as a penance, a decade or so, of the Rosary. He asked me if I had a Rosary and I told him I had lost mine in a fire which consumed our home two months before. He immediately reached in his pocket and handed, around the outside of the confessional, a rosary and told me to keep it with me always. Whether he handed me his own rosary or not, I do not know. I always obeyed his injunction to keep the rosary with me.[31]

Hope ends his remarks on Granger by saying, "When anyone lay dangerously sick, it was for Father Granger they always asked."[32] A priest could not ask for any better testament to his life and work. No matter how embroiled Granger became in Sorin's intrigues, he remained faithful to his pastoral calling: as Sorin's softer side, he was a priest par excellence before he was anything else. Or so Hope would have us believe. Hope ignores Granger's important role as Sorin's right-hand man in four crises because Hope wants to read Granger as a pious projection of priesthood. But it is time at last to appreciate Granger the way Sorin appreciated him—as a worthy assistant and administrator able to take Sorin's place when Sorin was out of the country. He was not a mousey man hiding out in a confessional or avoiding his administrative duties. He made decisions. He was a confidant to his Brothers and priests on assignment at Notre Dame and outside of Notre Dame. He had the ear of bishops. He was an effective religious who used his talents well to help build Holy Cross in America, especially in early formative times. The strength of Notre Dame remains today a testament to his hard work and good will.

CHAPTER ELEVEN

Rémi Mérianne: A Voice of Reason against Separatists

The amalgamation of two organizations is rarely accomplished without wrinkles and heartache, especially if one of the two organizations is fifteen years old and the other is fledgling. Add to this mixture a hierarchy of education, and the result can be less than conflict free. So it was with the amalgamation of Jacques Dujarié's Brothers of St. Joseph and Basil Moreau's auxiliary priests in 1835, the Brothers fifty strong and teaching in thirty schools, the priests six in number with four seminarians. The joining of two such religious organizations was, however, accomplished with minimum chaos thanks to the gentle sanctity of Dujarié and the charismatic energy of Moreau, at stake a revolutionary idea of joining as equals (more or less equals) clerics and non-clerics. Originally the apostolates of the two groups were to be separate and complementary, the Brothers as teachers, the priests as pastoral substitutes in parishes, but rather rapidly the priests moved into school management and teaching, thus threatening some of the Brothers trained under Dujarié to manage their own schools. It did not help, of course, that the priests generally enjoyed a lengthy and deep education-preparation for apostolic work while the Brothers cobbled together one or two years of study before being shuttled out to the primary schools.

At the 1835 church ceremony in which Dujarié formally entrusted his fifty Brothers over to Moreau, most of the Brothers present in the

Ruillé church were unaware that they were being shifted from the care of one priest to another, and they were unaware their headquarters was being moved at Moreau's insistence from little Ruillé to a suburb of Le Mans. Umbrage rose and fell among a minority of the Brothers in the following years, some of it very vocal as in the case of Brother Leonard Guittoger, a respected old man of the Ruillé Community who merited censure in 1871 for his maneuverings to separate the Brothers from the priests.[1] The underground ferment never really settled until the definitive separation of Brothers and priests into separate Holy Cross provinces in 1945.

The majority of Holy Cross men, of course, both Brothers and priests, never agitated in Moreau's lifetime to separate the two groups. Moreau sent Brothers and priests together as units to found settlements in Africa, Indiana, Canada, and Bengal, and most of these missionaries valued each other, respected each other, and worked deliberately together to extend Holy Cross abroad from France. In Indiana, for example, Brother Vincent Pieau and Father Edward Sorin had a smooth working relationship based on mutual trust for half a century as they labored side by side to mold Notre Dame from a boys' boarding school into a university. In France, one of the most respected voices for a united Holy Cross over the same length of time was Brother Rémi Mérianne, who labored for sixty-three years in education, supported his priest-supervisors, and on occasion counseled provincial superiors. We can appreciate him today as a man who entered Dujarié's group when it was moving toward Moreau's stewardship and who recognized that groups evolve like any other organic being. Rémi accepted that evolutionary movement in Holy Cross as inspired by the Holy Spirit for the betterment of Church work. He did not fight to preserve the old ways, the old order, the old system of community used under Dujarié. Rather, he saw that change for the Brothers, and at the same time for the priests too, was a dynamic change envisioned and nurtured by Moreau, who based his vision on earlier visions for a mixed community, visions by both Dujarié and his primary director Brother André Mottais. We would do well, therefore, to study Brother Rémi Mérianne's correspondence to understand how beautifully the dynamic of Holy Cross worked in its first half-century.

Brother Rémi was born Etienne Mérianne in La Quinte (Sarthe) February 10, 1809, the son of Etienne Mérianne and Marie Ivon. The town was named for its distance (five leagues) from the cathedral in Le Mans (St. Julian's). The population of La Quinte in 1800 was 504. Today it is 801. Its most famous attractions are the church, the Château d'Eporcé, the fifteenth-century manor house La Roselle, and an outdoor shrine of the crucifixion dating to 1763. The shrine was erected just two generations before Brother Rémi's birth. The first schools in La Quinte date to 1773, half a century before schools were mandated for towns having more than 500 inhabitants. In November of that year, the pastor (Father Lejoyant) founded not only a school for boys but also one for girls, the latter an unusual step for eighteenth-century France when schools for girls were not common. We do not know what Rémi's father did for a living, but he was probably a small farmer in the La Quinte area. Likewise we do not know what motivated Rémi to join Jacques Dujarié's Brothers of St. Joseph in Ruillé, a group he joined when he was fifteen, one month before his sixteenth birthday.[2] He became a novice on September 21, 1825, nine months after entering, but did not profess final vows until August 19, 1838, ten years after he had received his teaching credentials on October 7, 1828. By the age of nineteen he was considered by the government to be prepared to teach French children. Throughout his years as a religious Brother, he apparently excelled in the teaching profession.

Our earliest record of his teaching career is a receipt dated September 3, 1839, from the town of Poncé in the department of Sarthe. The school there was staffed by Holy Cross Brothers from 1834 to 1860. Subsequent to the 1839 receipt extant in the Holy Cross General Archives today, we have four Rémi letters posted from Poncé between 1845 and 1847. We can conclude that his tenure at Poncé lasted from 1839 (or earlier) until 1847 (or later). By 1850 he was a member of the General Council so that position would have kept him in Le Mans, and in 1851 he made a trip to Rome, quite possibly for the General Council, to report on the Holy Cross Vigna Pia and Santa Prisca properties there.[3] For the 1847-1848 school year, Rémi, teaching at Poncé, was sent a young Brother teacher to assist in the school. Rémi wrote to the mayor about exempting the young Brother from the local road tax because the young man was not yet eighteen-years old. The mayor responded that if the young man were born after May, he would also be dispensed from the 1849 tax because the levy did not take effect until after that month for each year.

In May of 1851 Brother Rémi found in Rome that several of the Holy Cross men in the Via Pigna and the St. Prisca houses were suffering (possibly from Roman fever), and Brother Michael was hospitalized. On May 25 Rémi saw the pope, Pius IX, in an audience, and his account of that visit is covered in a letter full of rapture:

> My heart was beating so fast when the bell reminded Msgr. de Mérode[4] to introduce us. I didn't know where I was. Two big doors opened in front of me, and Brother John of God and I saw the Holy Pontiff standing near a kind of platform. He hastened to come in front of us smiling. In the middle of the room while leaning on Msgr. he raised his right foot high enough for us to kiss it. At that moment I could neither cry nor lower my eyes because I was so overcome.[5]

The pope asks Rémi how long he has been with the Community, and since Rémi is unable to talk, the monsignor says Rémi has been with the Brothers for twenty-seven years, twenty-six of which have been spent in the schools. The pope talks in Italian until he realizes Rémi can't understand a word so the pope switches to French, then reverts to Italian when he asks Brother John of God about the land around Vigna Pia. Apparently it is not all that great and will require more work from the Brothers.[6]

As exciting as it is to read of Rémi's audience, it is more exciting to read in the same letter that the pope made a surprise visit a few weeks later to the Vigna Pia orphanage. Just before supper one of the boys went to ring the Angelus bell and cried out stupefied, "Mio fratello Ste. Padre." The boys gathered and sang a song, but the papal monsignor stopped them because it apparently was the battle cry of the Republican rebels. The pope blessed everyone and asked a few simple catechism questions: How many sacraments are there? How many commandments? Satisfied, the pope offered his foot for everyone to kiss and left.

By 1856 Rémi was teaching in Le Dorat in Haute-Vienne. He may have been assigned there by 1853, soon after his mission to Rome. The Community worked in Le Dorat from 1853 to 1860, and Rémi's first letter from there to Basil Moreau is dated April 25, 1856. In the letter he tells Moreau that the pastor at La Souterraine had asked him to let Moreau know how well preparations were going for the arrival of Holy Cross.[7] Four classrooms would be furnished by September 1, the opening day of school. The pastor hoped Holy Cross personnel would be in place by August 20. The new priest in charge of the establishment would receive a thousand franc stipend for saying Mass and would have no other duties than supervising the Community. The Holy Cross personnel would have a beautiful chapel, four classrooms, a courtyard for the older children and a separate one for the smaller children, a recreation room, and a lovely vegetable garden. The pastor would make 4000 francs available for good furniture, a kitchen, a changing-room, a dining room for the Brothers and postulants, a separate dining room for the boarding students, a wine cellar, a woodshed, a dormitory, and four or five bedrooms, the latter undoubtedly for the religious staff. The Holy Cross Sisters would be given the presbytery to live in. At the time the parish school was served by a layman who taught primary classes but also gave lessons in French and Latin. Obviously the pastor had expansive plans for his school.

From his correspondence we can tell that Rémi was an active and respected member of the Brothers' Society. In 1847 in a letter thanking Moreau for the rules and constitutions, he states that the superior of the Brothers' Society should be elected before the superior for the priests' Society. He does not elaborate on his reasoning, but he adds this very telling sentence: "The Rector [Moreau] will always have more rapport with the priests than with the Brothers because he lives with them."[8] If we have ever wondered about the living arrangements at Sainte-Croix, this letter should not only illuminate for us the physical separation between the two societies by way of living conditions, but it should also hint at the psychological separation between the two societies as well. Moreau's two societies did not live together in one group as we may have thought, and the Founder chose to live with his fellow priests rather than with the Brothers. I do not think that Rémi is simply referring to the fact that the majority of the Brothers were away from Le Mans living singly or in small groups in various parish schools around Sarthe. There actually were Brothers living at Sainte-Croix—teaching in the school there and supervising the Brothers' novitiate—but Moreau did not physically (or psychologically) live with them. He lived with his priests. Such an arrangement surely fed the fires of separatists like Brother Leonard Guittoger, who had to be confronted now and then for outspoken critiques of Moreau's vision that two societies (one clerical, one non-clerical) could be joined in one community.

In a letter to Edward Sorin on February 14, 1878, a good ten years into Sorin's tenure as Superior General, Brother Rémi himself addressed the matter of separating the two societies and comes down firmly on the unity of the two societies in one community:

> From its foundation right up to the present day I see Providence at work. In our Congregation nothing has changed, yes, given direction from above, spiritual direction conferred not on regular ecclesiastics. Enemies of the status quo, more numerous than your Reverence could imagine, are working to separate religious priests from lay religious, as per the Christian Brothers, the Marists, the Delaménais Brothers, the St. Gabriel Brothers before their rule was approved by the Holy See. For us the matter is over, and thanks be to God really over, and curses on him who wants to put his hand on the holy ark.[9]

For Rémi obviously the subject has been settled once and for all—
he is happy with the structure of Holy Cross uniting priests with
Brothers.

We should note, however, that the illogical yoking of two groups
based on different identifications has not crossed Rémi's mind.
The religious vows taken by priests at Sainte-Croix were identical
to those taken by Brothers, and thus the priests were basically
religious Brothers. To discriminate them further on the basis of their
ministry (priesthood) or sacred character makes as little sense as
discriminating another group (e.g., the teachers) on the basis of their
ministry (education). When Basil Moreau amalgamated his band of
auxiliary priests with Dujarié's Brothers of St. Joseph, he was not
amalgamating religious with religious because no auxiliary priest at
Sainte-Croix took religious vows until 1841, six years after Moreau
had brought to Sainte-Croix Dujarié's Brothers, most of whom had
taken at least a single vow of religious obedience. By 1838 most of
these Brothers had taken perpetual vows, with Brother André Mottais
in the first position, three years before any of the auxiliary priests
took any religious vows. The priests, of course, followed the practice
of celibacy and obedience to the local bishop, but they had professed
no vows to a religious community. One could argue, I suppose, that
they were living at Sainte-Croix in a kind of extended novitiate from
1835 to 1841, but novices are never categorized as religious per se
and enjoy none of the protection that professed religious enjoy. Such
reasoning apparently never crossed the minds of most Holy Cross
men in 1878 when the Congregation had had Vatican approval of the
Constitutions for a generation. Brother Rémi was quite satisfied with
Holy Cross as constituted, and if he ever thought about the separatists
(e.g., Brother Leonard Guittoger), he condemned their thinking and
their tactics as evidenced in this 1878 letter to Edward Sorin. What
was not to like in Holy Cross? The Congregation was working and
thriving on three continents (not four since Louis Champeau, the
French provincial, had pulled all Brothers out of Africa in 1873), so
it was obviously blessed in its organization, i.e., Brothers and priests
united in one religious unit.[10]

The relationship of Holy Cross Brothers and priests was very much on Rémi's mind when he wrote to his French provincial Champeau in February 1878. He outlines six points on the matter. First of all, he notes that the Congregation was inspired by the Holy Spirit and birthed by Bishop Claude-Madeleine de la Myre-Mory[11] at the annual clergy retreat (presumably in 1820). Its apostolate was to give religious instruction to boys in the Le Mans diocese and surrounding dioceses. It was first to be composed of Brothers and later joined by priests who would teach in secondary schools. We should notice two things in this first point: Rémi does not date the "beginning" of the Congregation to Moreau's assuming its direction in 1835 so in his mind the Congregation started with Dujarié and merely continued under Moreau.[12] Rémi's second point to Champeau says as much: "the addition of priests joined to the Brothers was not a second beginning but simply the complement to Dujarié's original plan, which Dujarié tried to start." It may be news to some that Dujarié actually did try to attract priests to his Community. We know also that Brother André Mottais tried to move on this vision.[13]

Thirdly, the plan for the Brothers of St. Joseph was not the same as that for the Christian Brothers, the Curé Delaménais's Brothers, or the Marists of St. Gabriel. Curious in the wording of Rémi's fourth point is the following: the Holy Cross priests' society and the Brothers' society are "two sisters who must walk together, animated by the same spirit although their functions are different." That choice of the word "sisters" is telling because it enables Rémi to skirt the issue of priests as "brothers"—call them all "sisters" and you do not have to stumble over the awkward idea that priests and Brothers walk together as "brothers," using the same word for two different meanings. What this suggests is that early in the Congregation, members struggled to mix a ministry (priesthood) with a lifestyle (brotherhood) in the same Congregation by isolating one ministry for separate treatment over other ministries. Surely in his subconscious Rémi and others wrestled with this odd organizational principle.

Fifthly, Rémi says that the two societies need each other to fulfill the destiny that Divine Providence wanted in creating this one unified Congregation. And finally he avers that neither society could break off without ruining the plan sanctioned by God through the approbation of the rules and constitutions under Pius IX. Rémi probably represents the majority opinion on this matter of unity, i.e., a unity that persisted in spite of the majority of the members being defined negatively as "non-clergy" instead of all members being defined as "brothers" in various ministries.

Rémi apparently enjoyed a close and cordial relationship with the French provincial Louis Champeau. After a circular letter by Edward Sorin in 1878 had made its rounds, Rémi wrote to Champeau (March 23, 1878) to express surprise. Waxing poetic, Rémi notes that the Sorin letter was like a lead ball dropped on an anthill (Rémi's image): "it broke through the roof and went as deeply as it could into the living quarters." The Brothers, Rémi adds, have been similarly affected by the circular letter, and, although some calm has returned, the anthill "of separatist ideas" has been destroyed, undermined at its base before it could ruin the Congregation. Rémi was particularly concerned about novices who had been infected by separatist ideas.[14]

In another letter to Champeau the same year (October 8, 1878), Rémi comments at length on the lack of direction afforded the young Brothers working out in the schools after their novitiate training. In a house of two or three men, a young Brother is just put under the spiritual guidance of an older man in the house, a man who may or may not have the necessary expertise to give spiritual direction. Rémi suggests that the situation is acute enough to need the provincial's immediate attention. The letter is quite long and quite impassioned, indicating that Rémi had Champeau's ear and was convinced enough of the present danger that it needed quick attention.

By 1877 Rémi was teaching at Le Bignon in the department of Mayenne. The Brothers taught at the school from 1858 to 1878 so Rémi was there for the last two years of the Brothers' tenure. Curiously a letter by Rémi in 1879 to Louis Champeau is posted from Le Bignon so one chronology (*Sainte-Croix en France*) may be in error. The letter is dated, however, September 1, 1879, at the time of year that schools generally opened in the French countryside. Rémi may have been simply cleaning out his things before he headed into retirement at Angers. Rémi would have been seventy-years old at the time. He would live another nine years.

By 1877 Rémi was a trusted source for the history of the Brothers. In September of that year the General Administration (through Brother Gregory LeRoy) wrote to Rémi asking him about his memories of the old days under Father Dujarié. Rémi replies that he no longer has copies of the circular letters that summoned the men to the annual end-of-summer retreat year by year under Dujarié, but as he recalls, those convocation letters were not well written, as he put it, "not a masterpiece of enscribed eloquence" ("n'était point un chef d'oeuvre d'éloquence écrit"). We see here Rémi's gentle sense of humor, an ability to size up the past in a matter-of-fact way without garnishing the truth. The memoirs, covering his entrance up to the death of Dujarié, are completed, but he has to make a copy of them before he can forward them. His hope, he confides to Gregory, is that the other elder members of the Community can correct or add to his recollections.

An important letter dated September 1, 1879, by Rémi to Champeau is the last letter we have by him, written nine years before his death in 1888. In it he gives details on the early days of the Brothers whom he asserts were founded as "The Brothers of St. Joseph," not "The Josephites." Why he insists on this point is not made clear in the letter. What is important early in the letter is his recounting the visit of two priests (Maigret and Richard) from the diocese who came to Ruillé at the end of April 1825 or at the beginning of May by order of the bishop to discuss the possibility of Dujarié's founding a group of priest-missionaries dedicated to the Sacred Heart and joined to Dujarié's Brothers. The news was bruited to the novices, and Rémi notes that he himself was present to hear the news.[15] Unfortunately, the plans were never realized, but it is interesting that this discussion took place ten years before Basil Moreau organized his band of auxiliary priests, men who would eventually be dedicated to the Sacred Heart and joined to the Brothers of St. Joseph.

According to Rémi, around 1825 Dujarié gave direction of the Brothers over to three men: André Mottais, Henry Taupin, and Leonard Guittoger.[16] Thereafter, Dujarié tried to interest three priests to take over the Brothers: one named Duclos, the second a Norman priest (no name given in Rémi's letter), and a Breton (also unnamed). This third priest was, with Brother Leonard, trying to start a novitiate on the property of the Duchess of Montmorency in the Chartres diocese sometime in 1834 or 1835, an enterprise that never came to be. Finally at the annual retreat in 1835 at the end of the summer, Bishop Bouvier turned the Brothers over to Basil Moreau. Rémi states definitely that there was no talk at the time of having a Brother direct the group—the Brothers always thought in terms of a priest as director. Curiously Rémi attributes the actual founding of the Brothers to Bishop Myle-Mory, who initially told Dujarié to start a group of brothers. Rémi may only raise this point in the letter to Champeau to show that the bishop's successor (Bouvier) could therefore be the only one to decide the fate of the Brothers. It is hard for us to imagine a successful group of male religious not wanting to direct themselves, but Rémi insists that no one, not even any of the four Brother-directors (he here includes Vincent) wanted a Brother as a replacement for Dujarié.

A certain frustration comes with the reading of Rémi's letters because just as he is about to give us some wonderful details about the history of the Brothers, he launches into exultation over the unity of the Congregation or the excellence of priesthood. He must have been a philosopher of sorts, armchair of course, who thought through fact to idea. Would that he had stuck more to fact! How wonderful it would be to have from him a physical description of André Mottais or some insight into the personality of Henry Taupin or the layout of a typical classroom or even a few lesson plans. As a scion of the early Community, he can be treasured for his endurance, but we wish he had been more particular in his details. Of course, who knows what has been lost in his correspondence, his dozens of letters to fellow Brothers, men in the field who never kept their correspondence for the sake of history because, unlike provincial superiors, they never felt the need to preserve a paper trail of their apostolate. For Rémi then we must be content with what we have—a handful of letters and a legacy of respectability. Brother Rémi died at Angers on February 12, 1888. He had given all but the first fifteen years of his life to the Brothers first known as the Brothers of St. Joseph and later known as the Brothers from Holy Cross. He was a champion of Brothers and priests united in one religious community, never wavering in this heartfelt vision.

Conclusion

The early men of Holy Cross were a brave lot. Their parents, having lived through the horrors of the French Revolution with its momentous upheaval in government, church, and educational system, were saddened, heartened, and energized by the atrocities and the wonders attendant upon traumatic change. Thus the early men of Holy Cross learned second-hand from mother and father, from grandmother and grandfather, and from heroic curates like Jacques Dujarié that the embers left from the catastrophic fires of Robbespierre and Danton could be stoked into new fervor for country, family, and church. How the Brothers managed to infiltrate their dreams into the dioceses of Orléans and Le Mans is a joy to visit in retrospect. In spite of their meager beginnings in little towns like Ruillé and Poncé and Larchamp, the Bothers of St. Joseph worked singly or in pairs to bring rudimentary learning to children of farmers and tradespeople. They earned next to no salary but worked with high hopes in their hearts.

A man like André Mottais brought stability to this burgeoning group of religious men. He nurtured their nascent spiritual lives in Dujarié's rectory, and he followed their progress as teachers around the countryside, yearly checking on their progress as teachers in far-flung parish schools where they usually were the only educators in the vicinity. Men like Vincent Pieau and Leonard Guittoger and Rémi Mérianne grew into solid teachers, forming the core of the little community, which gathered as a unit only once a year—at the end of each summer before the next school year would begin. At their annual retreat Dujarié would preach to them and they could renew their ties of brotherhood with one another, trade teaching techniques, and swap stories about their students and their experiences. Gradually they were molded into a beautifully cohesive group.

Their energies, of course, extended beyond France. Vincent Pieau led two young novice-teachers to America where they lived first near Vincennes, Indiana, and later at Notre Dame du Lac to the north. Hilarion Ferton brought the Brothers back into Africa where they worked tirelessly in conditions that ranged from tolerable to desperate. Everywhere in their correspondence back to France is evidence of their youthful enthusiasm and their commitment to the religious ideals of their founders. Even today, at some two hundred years distance, we can sense in their letters a healthy élan that explains why their characters matured grace-filled into what today remains the Congregation of Holy Cross. They were born in the ashes of revolution, but they matured in the wisdom and intrepidity of their mentors Jacques Dujarié, André Mottais, and Basile Moreau. Today we study them to learn of their heroicity, and we use their biographies to inspire young people in Bangladesh, Ghana, Uganda, India, Brazil, throughout, in fact, all the countries where the ministries of André, Vincent, Leonard, Hilarion, Rémi, and their confreres live on in new faces and new hearts.

APPENDICES

Appendix I

Chronology for the Early Brothers of St. Joseph

1767 Jacques Dujarié born

1789 French Revolution begins

1793 Reign of Terror begins

1799 Basil Moreau born

1800 André Mottais born

1802 Concordat

1804 Sisters of Providence founded at Ruillé-sur-Loir

1820 Brothers of St. Joseph founded

1831 Alliance Formula

1831 Separation of Brothers' finances from finances of Sisters of Providence

1835 Brothers move to Le Mans (Sainte-Croix)

1837 Pact of Fidelity (Brothers and priests)

1840 Arriving in Algeria

André Mottais	died 1844
Alphonsus Tulou	left Holy Cross 1862
Ignatius Feron	dismissed 1855
Louis Marchand	drowned 1841
Julian Le Boucher	left Holy Cross 1843
Victor Drouelle	died 1875

1841 Arriving at Vincennes: St. Peter's at Black Oak Ridge

Vincent Pieau 44   died 1890
Joachim André 32   died 1844
Edward Sorin 28   died 1893
Lawrence Ménage 26   died 1873
Francis Xavier Patois 21   died 1896
Anselm Caillot 16   died 1845
Gatian Monsimer 15   died 1860

1842

Holy Cross religious leave Algeria

Holy Cross religious move to Notre Dame, Indiana

Group 1: Leaving St.Peter's November 16, arriving at Notre Dame November 26

Edward Sorin   died 1893
Francis Xavier Patois   died 1896
Gatian Monsimer   left 1850
Novice Patrick (Michael) Connelly   died 1867
Novice Basil (Timothy) O'Neill   left 1850

2nd part of Group One: arriving Notre Dame December 6

Novice William (John) O'Sullivan   left 1847
Novice Peter (James) Tully   left 1847
Novice Francis (Michael) Disser   left 1846
Etienne Chartier   left 1843

1843

3rd group: Leaving Black Oak Ridge February 13, arrive Notre Dame February 27

Vincent Pieau   died 1890
Lawrence Ménage   died 1873
Joachim André   died 1844
Novice Joseph (Charles) Rother   left 1850
Novice John (Frederick) Steber   left 1846
Novice Thomas (James) Donoghoe   left 1852

Novice Ignatius (Thomas) Everard   died 1899
Novice Celestine (Lawrence) Kirwin   left 1843
Novice Paul (John) de la Hoyde   died May 27,
                                       1844
   first pioneer recruit to die at Notre Dame
   first name in act of incorporation for Brothers of
   St. Joseph in South Bend, January 15, 1844 (with
   three other Brothers)
Postulant Peter Berel (Br. Francis de Sales)   died 1862
Postulant Samuel O'Connell (Br. Mary Joseph)
   first postulant to become a novice at Notre Dame
   left 1846 from St. Mary's, Kentucky

1844

Holy Cross returns to Algeria

Aloysius Gonzaga Galmard	died 1893
Liguori Guyard	left 1846
Victor Catala	left 1845
Hilarion Ferton	died 1849
Basil Gary	died 1888
Marcel Coupris	died 1896

Appendix II

Alliance Formula of the Brothers of Saint Joseph

Ruillé-sur-Loir   September, 1831

We, James Francis Dujarié, priest superior and founder of the Society of the Brothers of Saint Joseph, established at Ruillé-sur-Loir, and we members of the said society, considering the present evils which threaten all hope of our enduring for much longer, but aware that the government will no longer suppress congregations like ours, but will encourage and sustain them, and moreover convinced that the goodness of God will not permit this state of affairs to be fixed forever in our Christian country, but will lead us to peaceful days and true freedom by which our Institute will be able to appear in its former glory and advance, together and as one, to assure its continuation for the greater glory of the Lord and the salvation of souls, we pledge ourselves by the present act in the strictest obligation that we can make so that violation of it will constitute sin:

1) To live attached to our holy Institute.

2) To sustain each other until death.

3) To remain united in the body of the Congregation and the Community as long as possible, following the same practices and rules that we have practiced up to now.

4) And in case we have to dissolve, to remain united in heart and affections, sustaining and assisting each other reciprocally.

5) To assemble as a body in community as time and place permit.

6) We Brothers of Saint Joseph will continue our submission to and dependence on Father Dujarié, our founder and superior general, assisted by four Brothers of his council, who are presently Brother André Pierre Mottais (Chief Director), Brother Léonard Francis Guittoyer (Second Director), Brother Henry Michael Taupin (Third Director), and Brother Vincent Ferier John Pieau. In case it is possible to reunite us, or if impossible, he will give all of us orders, following the circumstances below.

7) Conforming to the dispositions of the preceding article, he will be able to innovate and abrogate in our rules and customs everything he judges necessary for the time and circumstances.

8) Near our superior we have our rallying point.

9) If we have the misfortune to lose him, we will rally around the bishop of Le Mans.

10) If one of the members of the council is lost, the superior with his remaining counselors will elect another.

Made at Ruillé-sur-Loir, at the house of St. Joseph, September 1, 1831.

Brother John Baptist Verger

Brother André Pierre Mottais, Chief Director

Brother Vincent Ferier John Pieau

Brother Romain Francis Bouvier

Michael Coupine

Brother Henry, Third Director

Brother Leonard Guittoger, Second Director

Brother Stanislaus Lorian

Joseph Gregory Derve

Brother Francis-Mary Tulou

Brother John Climacus J.C. Coutamin

Brother Onezime Maturin

P.F. Pilard

Brother Martin John Varger

Brother Rémi Mérianne

Brother Stephen Gaufre

Brother Anthony Peter Le Fevre

Brother Vincent de Paul

Brother Mary Joseph Peter Rene Duval

Appendix III

Brother André Mottais' Final Letter from Africa

[Moustapha]   [December 1, 1841]
My Reverend Father [Basil Moreau],

Such sad news you've sent by your circular letter of September 29: I was unaware of the death of the excellent Brother Louis. The circumstances which accompanied it, that Father Drouelle has since set out to me, hit me in such a way that I can hardly believe it. My God! Our existence is fragile here below! I am not delaying to have Mass said for the repose of the soul of this dear confrere and to carry out myself the other prescribed things.

I received with great joy your very wonderful letters of August 24 and September 23. I admired your goodness which does not disdain the least and the most miserable of Brothers. Oh! How I admire you, and I bless the Lord for having saved our poor failing Institute. And the result is the children of Our Lady of Holy Cross are established in America. May the Lord preserve them and make them successful in their work in that faraway place.

I envy the good fortune of those who helped at the ceremony of the exhumation of our venerable founder [Jacques Dujarié]. Also, happy are our novices to whom is given the chance to be formed in the religious life under the holy Father Chappé, so full of light. I would think myself happy if I were allowed to go spend a year with them. This would not be without my own need, I who know nothing and who never knew anything about virtue but the name. They [novices] have only to put roots down deeply into virtue because the chances to fall abound, especially in this country where there is so little morality, where so many people came, it is said, to amass riches and were not concerned about their moral health. We're in Africa. This is the usual response they give to those who push them to live as Christians.

Nevertheless, although outwardly Philippeville may be difficult to handle, there is no lack of doing good work there; and religion, which is not yet practiced there, is at least honored generally by the military and civil authorities. A dead captain was accompanied by those of his own rank to church. Each of the subordinate officers, customs-house officers, Italians, do likewise for their dead. The parish priest ordinarily gives them a little speech in this circumstance. Almost no one refuses the succor of religion for the dead. The mob and the fortune hunters who make up the major part of the population for the most part are merging little by little into the people of better means and reputation who are coming every day to settle in this country.

You ask, my reverend Father, what I think about the African brothers: God has elevated for us it seems the best, except Brother Alphonsus, for the good life. The others appear to me to be what they were in France: little trained and having character faults still rather obvious. I would have to remark first of all on myself, then on the lack of propriety by Brother Victor, on the negligence of Brother Ignatius in his refectory work, and on the mobility of Brother Ligouri. I don't think he'll be in Africa for a long time. About the rest, each of us had his work and answered for it to our priests. I have noticed some misunderstandings among some. My work did not allow me to spend time with the brothers. They just found me in recreation sometimes. Brother Eulogius seemed to me lazy, talking much, fearful of his health … Father Le Boucher ought to have reproached me for giving some dissatisfaction to the brothers on the subject of the letters which were addressed to me; he wants me to show them to them: for those which concern them, yes; but I vow that I am repugnant about a similar constraint when it is a matter of those which I receive from my family or friends. I would hope, my reverend Father, to be instructed about your wish on this matter. I will submit myself without difficulty because I wish peace at whatever the price.

All my adventures will end up enriching me. I realize now that my mood and a certain depth of vanity, which I've allowed in myself, without any zeal and conserving my honor, have permeated all my ways. I have come back, thanks be to God, like everyone came back to the prophecies of 1840.

I am very grateful to your Reverence for concern about my deprivations, which continue apace. About six weeks ago I informed Father Drouelle that the parish priest didn't change our clothes; he wrote to him and made him agree to give 200 francs as salary to the brother in charge of cleaning for him; then he hasn't given even a word of response to two or three letters that I wrote to him. I believe he is sick. I'm ashamed to go out in our habit: if news doesn't reach me by the next post, I'll buy one and make do with it as I can; then I'll wait for all the other things I need except for shoes.

My ringworm is healed. Heavy blood continues to give me pimples, even sores when I'm not careful about removing wool on my skin. Hemorrhoids, which have developed in me for ten years, have greatly increased this year. I have had them three or four times this past month: thus for three or four days each time that I go to the toilet, blood flows like after a blow from a needle put in the arm of a sick person. When relieving myself, I have to apply a sheet of paper in my crack to stop the blood which would run down my legs. My headaches are as frequent as they were in France, but less sharp.

My soul is languishing more than my body. I have to tell you, my reverend Father, that I often miss my regular spiritual exercises. The sacristy work is the usual cause; I do the exercises without fervor. I have above all neglected to read and prepare for prayer. I've observed Grand Silence badly. I have neither meditation book nor particular examination. Most often I do these exercises while walking to avoid the torment of my sores.

I confess to the parish priest every week. I'm very happy with my confessor: he knows how to drive scruples away. My confessions are short and precise. He doesn't want me to fast. Up to now I've had the good fortune to take Holy Communion twice a week. The same temptations that I had in France I still fight: and I'm no better than before. Please pray for me, my reverend Father, because I'm not winning the game of life and I'm afraid of death.

A sickness, which the parish priest experienced because of arguments with several people, put him in a bad humor against me; he reproached me on the subject of the sacristy. He didn't want to furnish classroom furniture. He complained to me without giving me reasons … He has not yet given money for the children: thus I have nothing to give them but additional tasks.

It's also a chore to obtain underwear: he refused me and left me with me the same ones for more than three months. I've worn a shirt three weeks. There are no agreements about towels. I am disgusted with this lapse in cleanliness. Water was purchased for a week: it was muddy. I saw some in which there were little critters … Meanwhile I drink only prepared water because of the color of my blood.

I teach three hours of class before noon and three hours after. I have about thirty-six inscrutable students. I meet with twenty-two to twenty-eight of them for each class. Here the major defect among students especially in the summer is their lack of hard work. I believe the teacher should meet with only eight to ten of them. It's not that he'll leave his job: it's charming for him and worth 1500 francs. I have twenty writing students. I give a half hour to learn prayers and catechism each day. Almost all know their prayers. I teach reading the same way. The most advanced in computation are beginning long division. I give dictation each day for which they correct the spelling; no other way of teaching penmanship because we have no beginning book, not even catechisms. I'm happy with progress in general. The school is free.

The church, the rectory, and the school relocated on July 15 and are in one building as before. The church is much bigger and more beautiful. The classroom is small, poorly lighted, having only a medium sized opening on a street much frequented by soldiers and civilians, who look in on us incessantly, stopping often to listen to the teacher and the students through this opening. We keep it open to have some air: the door opens onto the corridor, inside; people come to the classroom many times during the day to ask for the parish priest and to make me deliver their messages to him. Everything is spoiled in this classroom by the dust and water which falls from the parish priest's bedroom by boards poorly joined together in his floor. Thus in falling on me, dust falls on dust. More and more I'm obliged to sleep in it, to make and unmake my bed evening and morning and to rise from it. What is disagreeable are the public women who come and go during the evening by my window. I can't sing a verse of a hymn because the parish priest is bothered by it in his bedroom as well as the people in church. There is no bathroom: for my calls of nature I have to leave town and go into the mountains. The parish priest has a bedpan that the maid empties at night. I make Thursdays a holiday. I have only that day in the week because especially on Sunday I don't lack for work in preparing the church and the altar, carrying and straightening two to three hundred chairs for the two masses and vespers. I sweep the church and the pulpit two or three times a week, then we have burials, baptisms, marriages, the clock to wind, Holy Mass to prepare for each day. I assist with the students, even on Sundays.

I taught catechism in church to both boys and girls when the parish priest was sick; I've done home baptisms ... I've helped a sick servant, and took him to the hospital where we count on going, the parish priest and I, when we get sick. Father Drouelle tells me to aim at becoming a public school teacher. I'm going to tell him that I no longer think about it for two reasons: the first, because there is no indication that the present teacher will quit, and secondly, even if he were to quit, I would be in no state to sit for the exam which the inspector told me about in his visit here. I know little and I forget this little because I don't have a minute to study.

We have two meals per day. Since I arrived, the lunch hour has varied from ten o'clock to one o'clock, the dinner hour from five to eight PM.

In the morning I take a piece of bread and what I can grab to eat ... Some dried fruit or a small piece of sugar. The parish priest has his coffee or his chocolate. Then our first meal is in the afternoon. For a long time we ate everything cold, and we had scarcely a glass of soup each day. These details make me ashamed, but I believe it is up to your Reverence to judge the position of his subjects in Africa. The parish priest is edifying to the highest degree. His daily occupations are visiting the sick, especially the soldiers, at the hospital and in town, visiting families and in particular the poor. He gives what he can: everyone comes to him, and he succeeds, from what I can tell, in procuring places for the newly arrived and others who have need, in getting bread for families, in legitimizing a great number of marriages, etc. He is simple and the spirit of Jesus Christ lives in him.

Our vacation lasted from July 15 to August 19. During this time I took several days to recoup myself and visit Hippo. Among the ruins of the basilica of peace I tasted virtue, I read, I meditated and prayed alternately. I have not forgotten you nor very honorable Father Le Boucher in my feeble prayers. Thoughts came to me about Saint Augustine who so often preached in that cathedral and who meditated on the mystery of the very Holy Trinity on the seashore not far away. It now serves as a park for cattle. The place that the town occupied is a flat plain covered with olive trees, fig trees, and carob trees. Immense Roman wells are some hundreds of meters from there by the Mainelon River, and several meters below is the monument erected to the glory of the Doctor of grace. But this monument in the form of a rotunda is poor and going nowhere. The walls were only to the height of my chest.

Now, before finishing, please let me, my reverend Father, let you in on the prayers that I offer incessantly to the Lord for you on the occasion of the New Year and your feast. The days are near that your large family will come joyfully to pay homage to you out of their gratitude and devotion. Yes, you are the true father of the Society of Holy Cross. We are happy to be your children and to obey you, hoping the Lord will keep you forever among us.

The memory of your holy priests, brothers, etc., that I know and who edified me at Holy Cross [Le Mans] is precious to me. May the Lord give them an increase of spiritual goods, which will make them more and more worthy of the names they carry. For me, my reverend Father, I beg you to obtain for me from God the grace of dying in his love.

Please accept my profound respect and perfect gratitude, and so I have the honor of being, my reverend Father, your very humble and very obedient servant,

Brother André

Philippeville   December 1, 1841

P.S. The mailman just came: I happily accept your New Year's spiritual gifts. You had the greatest goodness, my reverend Father, to send a copy of a book to my parents last year: would I dare ask you to do them the same favor this year? My mother above all will be very grateful to this attention from your reverence, and I would be obliged to you.

Finally Father Drouelle has responded to my letters: he leaves me but a glimpse of the trouble at the minor seminary caused by the bishop's absence. I had already guessed at that. From many indications, I've thought for some time that our Congregation this year has been put to many tests and that Our Lady of Sorrows is making her children drink from her chalice. He tells me to buy some clothes. I have already bought shoes for five francs (sandals). I have 50 francs for a habit; I'll be asked 25 francs for the tailoring and lining. If the parish priest can't get around to advancing me something, I'll look pitiful. I just bought some cloth at four francs 50 per meter. That's too expensive because it's not worth anything. So what? It's better to appear before God in poor clothes than in rich.

Our poor church in Philippeville was also unfurnished: it's going to be well furnished: the military engineer used all his talent to make a magnificent altar, which is now being installed. He made a pulpit that is said to be of better workmanship than the altar and will soon be in place. Finally the Minister of War sent a painting by the mailman for our church; it is enormous (about five feet by eight). The first communion of our children will take place on Christmas Day. I recommend them for prayers at Holy Cross [Le Mans].

Here in the space of two months many scenes and sad events have occurred. Duels, suicides, assassinations, communications with Constantine disrupted by the enemy, two unsuccessful expeditions. Moreover, from October 2, the feast of the Guardian Angels, there was for several days a hot desert wind so strong that I had to let the class go. The children couldn't work because of the heat. Fire that started on our mountains on both sides at once in twenty-four hours ate up myrtle trees, cork trees, green oaks, and bushes that had covered the immense region. The fire came up to the walls of the town. The smoke covered the land and sea. We thought we had come perhaps to the end of the world.

Appendix IV

Letter by Brother Hilarion Ferton at Oran to the Scholastic Brothers at Sainte-Croix

January 17, 1847

Gentlemen and dear friends,

It will undoubtedly please you to relax with me for a moment. I would like to recount to you everything from when I went to Sainte-Croix last September. Undoubtedly in the shade of your laurel trees, in the comforts of your families, you are free to relax, the way one savors living at your age, especially after spending a year studying very hard. I had the pleasure of recounting to many of your co-disciples my old ideas, and they taught me many good and beautiful things. For example, your sparkling musical military parades, but above all your remarkable awards ceremony, which brought joy and wonder to all the spectators. And finally, gentlemen, your co-disciples made me promise to write to you, and I hope, more than just holding to my promise, it will bring sweet memories back to me.

First, don't be surprised that I will not wish you a Happy New Year. That's useless. I believe they are like all the past ones—beautiful and good. You really know how to align piety and knowledge with cheerfulness. I swear to you that I scarcely feel disposed to give you a scientific narration today. I don't have the courage to make you yawn nor to make myself the torturer. So, gentlemen, I will not talk to you about philosophy, nor chemistry, nor astronomy, nor hydrography, nor zoology, nor geology, not even math, botany, politics, history such as it is, nor belles lettres, because I admit I know a bit about only three letters and these are ETC. I will not lecture you. "But what are you going to talk about," you would write to me a little impatiently. Just a minute, please. Let me catch my breath, let me trim my pen, let me wipe my sweaty forehead, and I'll be with you in a minute.

An important visit just distracted me. Unhappy, I lead it humbly toward the door, which stayed open, thank goodness, confusing me with greetings. All the while it offers me its snuffbox, and contrary to habit, I slowly introduce my thumb and forefinger into this orbicular cavity, and I lift out a pinch of the best Moroccan tobacco and perfume my hydropic brain. The effect is quick: two or three long and healthy hadehiiii. … gives me a delighted head, a brain disengaged from all swampy humor. I joyfully start my introduction. Attention!

Since it will soon be noon, and for some time I have been watching a thick smoke escaping in gloomy flocks from a cylindrical vent in the gutter. Arriving at Mers el Kébir, a dinghy takes me on the Tenare River. The weather is magnificent, the sea as calm as a vast blanket of sleeping water. "Sir, my couchette, please." "Your name?" "Someone." "Take number 2." A couchette is a nice, small alcove, as long as a medium sized man, as high as an elbow and a half, and as wide. There we are, all safe for the night. The captain commandant is on his quarterdeck. The bell gives its final rings, ladders are raised, the anchor pulled up. The wheels churn the foamy sides of the vessel. "Starboard," cries the captain with a thunderous voice. "Yes, yes," replies the quartermaster. Already a long furrow can be seen. We have left Oran on our right. "We'll have good weather, captain."

"Yes, a tail wind. Raise the standing jib, unfurl the fore-sail." Everything gets done by the chirping of the quartermaster's terrible whistle. "Always south-south- east," says the quartermaster to the helmsman. Soon two or three blasts on the whistle are again heard. Two sailors and some poor cabin boys rush in. The flag is struck, the log is heaved. "How many?" "Ten and a half, captain." "So, gentlemen, we proceed a little more than three leagues an hour. Long live Neptune!" It's 4 o'clock. The quartermaster takes over, and that's how it will happen every four hours. At that moment, the maitre d', fully dressed in white with a napkin on his left arm, laughing, rings the bell inviting to dinner the officers and the passengers admitted to that table. Sea air so dilated my stomach that it was not without feeling a gastronomic need that I went down into steerage to sit at a table. To my great satisfaction, food was served copiously but didn't do the least credit to the cook. For whoever was slightly gourmet, the time passed quickly at the table. When I went up on the poop deck, the sun offered but half of its golden disk. Soon it left us for the other hemisphere. At that moment the whistle, hanging by a ribbon at the quartermaster's buttonhole, made itself heard. The sailors understood. They come in order, split up at starboard and port, and out of the gunwales take their hammocks that they hang in designated places in order to sleep there until a harsh voice will wake them up with a start to go and relieve others from their maneuvers. The passenger, wrapped in his cloak, walks for some time on the bridge. Then he goes to snuggle in his couchette or in some corner or another of the vessel if he prefers fresh air. Two lanterns are lifted to the top of poles. They also hoist a lantern, which lights up the compass of our guide, the helmsman. A light breeze wrinkles the surface of the bitter waves and the tranquil night begins to spread its veils, sprinkled with thousands of stars. The log is thrown, always the same speed.

It is 10 o'clock. We pass Cape Ferrat. Then we are in the Gulf of Arzew. Here is our first stop. A dinghy is going to carry dispatches to land. The port captain also arrives with his dispatches. The dinghy having returned, the two captains clasp hands in a sign of affection and say adieu. We leave. Now I go down to visit my couchette. I say my prayers. Scarcely have I finished when very faithful Morpheus comes to touch my eyelids with his poppy flower, the effect such that I open my eyes only seven hours later. The noise of the engine is no longer heard. The vessel has stayed in the harbor of Mostaganem. "Waiter," I cry to myself, "a little cold water and a white napkin." Then, my washing finished, my prayers said, I casually go up to the poop deck. Dispatches are exchanged. We move on. Everyone is active on the bridge. Each thinks about his individual washing as the young cabin boy, dressed simply in large grey canvas trousers smeared with some archipelago of tar, endeavors to get an enormous piece of Marseille soap to lather his naked shoulders, even as an old captain quietly seated in front of his wash stand tries to rejuvenate himself with the help of Thousand Flowers soap and sharp steel. All this happens as the sun rises. Dawn just pushed the night back into its somber abode, and then she fled at the approach of her father Phoebus, overflowing like rubies reflecting the marvelous scarf of the beautiful Iris. From personal cleanliness, attention turns to that of the vessel: at that moment the quartermaster's whistle blows, splitting the air across a thousand ropes. "Hold tight to the rails," cries the quartermaster, and each sailor carries his hammock rolled longitudinally, places it orderly around the gunwales. Then eight or ten sailors ranged symmetrically, each armed with a handleless broom, scrub with uniform movements the bridge soaked with dirty water thrown appropriately at two or three other sailors. Everything susceptible to sparkle receives polishing more or less and soon shines with a new luster from the cabin boy's hand.

The sun, continuing its ascension, begins to make us feel his hot rays. The foresighted captain gives orders to tighten the poop awning. "Hold on tight," says the captain to a cabin boy who seems a novice. "Don't get thrown into the sea—one hand for the king, one for yourself." That done, some whistle blasts are sounded. Sailors arrive silently on the bridge and line up in two lines, straight as grenadiers of the empire, all wearing off-white linen pants, blue shirts with a collar bordered in white, head uncovered, no shoes so as to better reveal body cleanliness. The quartermaster advances, followed by a mail orderly, notebook in hand. Head to toe nothing escapes the eye of Argus, the terrible prefect of discipline. "This collar is not folded properly," he says to a sailor, and the mail orderly writes down the name of the individual and the noted fault. The officer continues his review. It should end without any other incident. Suddenly he stops. He holds the long lobe of the right ear of a poor cabin boy. "They are not washed behind," he says. "Pardon, if—" "How, a thousand ports ..." The reply, "I ... yet." "Into shackles." And the mail orderly writes the name of the individual, the defect in hygiene, the reply, and the punishment to be inflicted. The review finished, the officer orders, "Left flank, forward march," and he goes back up on the poop deck while the sailors go to work, except for the poor cabin boy whom the quartermaster, after putting him in handcuffs, forces down into the hold where he will be kept for at least twenty-four hours.

It's 9 o'clock. The likable maitre d', dressed in his stunning outfit, hits his bell a few times. Few people wait for a second invitation. Their stomach says, "Go." The table, although a little less sumptuous at breakfast than at dinner, honors the cook, however, by its very appetizing morsels. After being sufficiently restored, each one goes happily back up to the bridge. The log was just thrown, always at the same speed, never a more pleasant passage. All the sails are deployed and fairly well filled. The serenity of the sky is reflected in all our faces, and some passengers, giving in to the light swaying of the boat, turn in for a satisfying, digestive nap. Others, more lively, taste another pleasure—drinking the most exquisite nectars. The captain, who also partakes in this drunken foolishness, laughs up his sleeve seeing them raise a toast in honor of favorable Neptune because he, old wolf of the sea, knows by experience that Neptune is also called "Breeze-boat." "It seems to me," says one of these anti-water-drinkers, "I see Neptune on a chariot made out of a huge seashell and pulled by four dolphins skimming rapidly along the surface of the waves, impressing the seas and me." Says another, "I think I see this triple ruler of the seas, rivers, and fountains changing all the water into nectar with the power of his trident."

From the other side, sailors on the bow, patching their clothes or repairing some other ruined thing, start up some drinking songs. You see, gentlemen, that there is not much sadness on board the Tenare, a name, however, of bad omen. But here we are in the harbor of Ténès, our third stop. Dispatches are exchanged, and some of the curious step out on land. The captain, not seeing them come back, begins to murmur oaths, but, silence, here is the dinghy bringing them back by quick oar strokes. The captain looks at his watch. "Three and a half hours," he says, "one hour late." A thousand curses. His menacing face shows how much he is ticked off. Soon we veer to starboard. Then the log is thrown. It's off by only seven knots. The wind shifts to the southwest. The sea is less calm, and the rolling, that is, a rocking from starboard to port, begins to be felt. The physiognomies formerly so happy are imprinted with something troubled. 4 o'clock has just struck. Here is our knowledgeable maitre d' who shakes his little bell and invites us to dinner with a complaisant air of ho-hum, even though no one is hungry. "Nevertheless, let's go down," says one passenger to another. "No, I don't feel like eating," says the other one. "I'll see about the second seating," says the other. And both cheer each other up. As for me, I go down. "Are they sulking?" says the maitre d' pleasantly. "Waiter, you haven't invited all those gentlemen." "Pardon, they are waiting for a table, in spite of efforts to go breathe fresh air on the bridge."

The sumptuously furnished table has a good number of delicacies. There are even a few extras. But I let these good gentlemen take what is vulgarly called "thumb coffee," and I go off to breathe fresher air on the poop deck. The horizon begins to wear a veil of reddish clouds, which, developing rather rapidly, soon hides us from the smiling azure of the sky. The whistle of the quartermaster is sounded and the sails, falling softly on the yards, are brailed up. Steam alone propels the boat. Five or six passengers walk at large on the bridge because "we have to walk," they say, "to avoid seasickness." Others, on the contrary, dare not rise from the seats where they are seated because, they say, they'd soon have seasickness if they walk around. "Oh well, that's how it is," says a promenader to one of those seated. "I feel a little bothered in my stomach," responds the other. Another says, "My head is turning around. I have to sit down." A few minutes later, both of them, imitating others, suddenly empty their stomachs, throwing to the fish with some effort what they couldn't digest. From all over is heard, "Waiter, a cup of tea. Waiter, a lemon." And to satisfy the barrage of requests, the waiter is all legs, but in vain is sweetened tea drunk, the acidic juice of a lemon humectated, the hermetic ether enclosed in precious flasks surreptitiously sought, any care taken before debarking: nothing can stop a sickness which has no other remedy but terra firma. Suddenly a gust from the open sea is too much, and most of the sick men try again to leave like firecrackers for their sleeping bunks so that in a blink of an eye the bridge is almost deserted.

All preparations to get through the night are done orderly. The two lamps hoisted to the top of the masts indicate by their vivid light the night's obscurity. It's 10 o'clock. Let's continue on our voyage. Alone, I go down, having said my prayers on the bridge. I leap into my maritime bed. My neighbor below snores admirably. The one on the first berth often hangs his head over a bucket to get some relief.

I soon rise up from a confident sleep. It is broad daylight up on the bridge. A rather thick fog prevents us from seeing the land we are not far from, but the sun finally dissipates these somber mists, and we can enjoy the picturesque life of this fertile land we will soon be on. We're near Sidi-Ferruch. You are acquainted with it, gentlemen. It's where the French first landed in 1830. The whole crew is in motion. The flag floats out behind the vessel. For some time a large pallid stain surrounded by mountains covered in greenery can be seen, but as this large stain is approached, an enormous rock of white chalk appears, not hesitating to divide in stages and take on the aspect of a multitude of superimposed blocks. Finally one can guess that these very white rocks are houses, rising up and climbing, so to speak, one on top of the other. Together they form a large triangle, the base of which stands on the bank, and the summit of which touches the top of a rather high mountain. You have probably guessed, gentlemen, we're soon going to enter the port of Algiers. We have already overtaken Cape Maxime.

All the passengers are on the bridge to enjoy this unique spectacle. The port of Algiers at a glance looks like the port of Marseille with its multitude of boats and looks like the port of Toulon surrounded by fortifications. Here's the fort on the right. If it were night, we would see different fires projected in different colors. Here is the pier covered with magnificent batteries. The captain is on his seat in order to give orders. We lean to port. They throw the anchor overboard, and the vessel, now in the middle of lots of other boats, comes to a halt. A number of dinghies vie for the honor of bringing us to land. As I have no other baggage, I have to wait only for a sailor to retrieve my trunk from steerage. I greet the quartermaster and get into a dinghy with three or four other folks. The Turkish devil doesn't have enough people so he fights with another to get a poor passenger already half sick who without the help of a strong arm would have pitched himself into the sea. "My trunk, my hat," he cries. "Here they are, mister, here." And he is forced to leave the dinghy so he can go into the one with his trunks. Only by insisting, even threatening, does our funny wretch of a boatman consent to take us to land in exchange for 50 cents each. As I had a set time for my trip, my intention not being to run around Algeria like a tourist, I would profit by being in the same boat that would take me the next morning at 5 AM to Bône. After being rather refreshed, I take my notebook and profit by a few hours excursion.

Soon I am in the upper section of the city. With some trouble I walk the steep, narrow, dirty, dark streets, with houses having no exterior windows but some rare barred openings in the upper floors, going one on the other as if two opposite sides of the street touch. The street is even vaulted sometimes. This section is Old Algiers, but it disappears everyday under the traffic of civilization, and some years hence the city will be totally European in architecture. Finally I arrive out of breath at the Casbah. From this citadel, surrounded by high crenellated walls in the Moorish style, a magnificent panorama stands out. The square house is there, forts of the Emperor Bad-a-Zoun, etc. Then the smiling plain of Mustapha, the green hills of Bab-el-Oued, and six mills, and a multitude of houses surrounded by gardens, trees, etc. The city is surrounded by a long ditch and fortifications, which are not yet finished. Leaving the Casbah by the back section and going toward the east, I tumble into the suburb Bad-a-Zoun. Bad-a-Zoun, Bab-el-Oued, and the Marine are three beautiful streets in Algiers. Running along the first two, which are really only one street, one can imagine it's Paris, nothing as elegant as these arcaded houses, these wealthy stores, etc. They look like a street in Chartres where there's a beautiful plaza in the middle of which is a beautiful fountain surrounded by orange trees. The government plaza and the Muslim plaza are also nice to walk in when military music is played every Sunday to entertain the elite of Algerian society.

It was night when I got to the hotel. My head was turning from having seen so much in so short a time. I had also visited St. Philip's Cathedral, some bazaars, some mosques, etc., and I particularly regretted leaving without being able to walk in the magnificent garden of the cobblers, nor visit the library, the museum, etc. The governor's palace is a magnificent Moorish place full of oriental opulence. What seemed strange to me, on returning to the hotel at night, was to see men wrapped in their bournous, sleeping on the ground in the streets. I won't tell you about the inhabitants. You already know that people from every nation can be found here, people of every color wearing all kinds of clothes. I get to my hotel, happy to throw myself on a sofa. My window opens onto a courtyard. A noise makes me open my eyes. I see eight or six Arabs grouped around a wooden bowl. They're eating, served by women. It was couscous they were eating. Couscous is much favored by the Arabs. It's a mixture of oil and farina formed into lumps the size of grains of millet and steamed. It's eaten with milk, butter, etc. Arabs use no fork other than their fingers. They wash their hands only after a meal. But that reminds me that I've eaten nothing since morning. I go down to the dining room thinking one is served in Algiers as in Paris. Supper over, I ask the waiter to awaken me at 4 AM.

The next morning this nice waiter knocked on my door at the requested time. I got on board by 5 AM, and half an hour later we left the port of Algiers. Since one has lots of time at sea, I'll observe here only that we had beautiful weather, beautiful, nothing but beautiful, and hot. But passing the Matifar Cape, I remember that last year here the Sphinx, a government steamboat, broke apart. Its engine has not yet been recovered from the sea. It's noon. We stop at Delys. Dispatches are exchanged at 1:30. We continue our voyage, and at 4 PM we are in the harbor of ancient Bougie. This city is very picturesque. High mountains rise up behind it. The sea bathes houses surrounded by masses of orange trees, pomegranate trees, fig trees. The getting off and getting on of a crowd of passengers stalls us for two hours. It starts to get dark when we leave Bougie. Soon camp blankets are given out to the soldiers on board, and they settle down as best they can on the bridge to spend the night.

The next day I learn we had stopped for an hour in the harbor of Zizelli (Dzidzelli) for dispatches and the getting off of some passengers. The serenity of the weather let us enjoy a truly magnificent spectacle. The sun glistened in all its majesty, and we saw an immense horizon. Here and there dazzling white sails seemed to have reached the final limits of our hemisphere and appeared on this vast sea to other people, observers like ourselves. A multitude of fat, silver fish leapt from the depths to play on the surface of transparent waves and seemed to parry the rapid movement of our vessel. We were soon near enough to land to discern rich vegetation rendered all the more lovely by the rays of the rising sun. We could even discern some houses scattered in the mountain gorges on the seashore. Nothing is more unusual than the view from these rocks bordering the coast. It seems nature has showered down the most varied and grotesque shapes here.

It's 11 o'clock and we've been moored for a quarter of an hour at Stora, three quarters of a league from Philippeville. There we will exchange dispatches. At noon we leave Philippeville, and at the close of day we'll be anchored in the gulf of Bône. Here on this formerly inhospitable land a Brother waited for me, a comfort that can't be defined. He came into my open arms, and for twenty-four hours I was his guest. I was delighted at so happy a reunion. The day after my arrival we visited the Casbah and the Danoir fort. Then we went to walk in the plain that the Boudjimah River covers with its water most of the year. We visited the numerous ruins of the celebrated Hippo, in the middle of which grow masses of olive trees, myrtle, and red laurel, indicating the passing of a great people. Near these ruins Bishop Dupuch raised a monument in honor of St. Augustine. The circular monument consists of a white marble altar surmounted by a bronze statue of the saint about a meter high. The rest is surrounded by an iron grill. The evening of the same day, I prepared to leave, after having crossed almost the entire coast of Algeria. This time I hazarded a visit to the interior of the country. Brother consented to go with me. Around 4 AM we are afoot. Our first hike is to visit some tribes in order to get animals to ride, but our Bedouins bargain too well. We found the price too high for their mule. Unfortunately, our purse didn't respond to our too happy faces, and regretting we couldn't stand on the honor of our reputation, we left these gentlemen behind and decided to travel on foot. Since in this country the only inns encountered are tents far apart, and since the Kabyles are not very hospitable people, we armed ourselves with everything our wise guide suggested, pockets filled with all kinds of ammunition, a cudgel in hand. Our ever present coats thrown over our shoulders, we resolutely undertook the road from the Dréan camp, leaving the Seybause River on our left and Lake Fetzara on our right. At 7 o'clock the sun shows his golden disk proudly and menaces us with one of the hottest days of the season. The area around Bône is rich and fertile, but scarcely two leagues away we are surprised to find an immense empty plain. The only thing encountered are some green shrubs to make a traveler regret leaving Eden behind. The heat grows intense. From time to time we have to turn backward to breathe rarefied air in our shadows. Then we start to use our provisions. Our liquid refreshment is soon gone. Our shadows almost disappear. We sweat blood and water.

But here is Dréan. We've done our six long leagues. Brother Basil, a bit asphyxiated by the heat, is happy to find a seat to rest on. I go on to greet the camp officer and inform him of our goal. I have the good fortune to encounter a man of extreme kindness. Two Turkish troopers receive orders to find us two mules and to serve as escort and guide all the way to the camp at Mesmélia, and at the invitation of the officer who is waiting for the visit of a general also going to Constantine, I am served a buffet dinner. Scarcely have we finished when a noise is heard in the camp. Everyone is on horseback to receive General Charron, the engineering inspector. I hurry to greet him. I had the honor of traveling before with him from Algiers to Bône. This general meets me with the kindness generally afforded higher officers in Algeria. He puts two mules and two Turkish officers at our disposal. He even invites us to take advantage of his escort. We accept this last offer and had no occasion to regret it. So, Gentlemen, here I am on horseback surrounded by thirty French or Arab cavalrymen, our black dress, our large hat augmenting the strangeness of this kind of caravan. We arrive around evening at the camp at Mesmélia. The general gives us the honor of dining at his table and invites us there throughout the trip. We accept without further ado. When we look for shelter for the night, we learn the general has two beds prepared for us. Truly Providence is looking over us.

At 7 AM we take our coffee. Then we mount on horseback. We do not follow a direct route. Our guides alone know where we are, sometimes on the crest of a mountain, sometimes in deep ravines. It seems we're wandering, but for the Arab one mountain indicates another to him, and in this way we come to our goal. It's 10 o'clock. We halt. Here's an organized camp, officers and soldiers, all at work, soup made. But here's where neighboring tribes of Arabs rush to this new sight, and Chief Ab-el-Kerim at their head greets the general, passing his right hand under his and then kissing it. From all over come chickens, butter, milk, couscous, crepes, honey. Everything goes on the general's table. Then the soldiers go about their business. While we eat, 50 Arabs are grouped around us, delighted to see us. To better entertain us, they bring in some musicians who flay our ears with the horrible sound of a kind of flute and the noise they make knocking their fingers and drum sticks on skin stretched tightly on a cylinder which somewhat resembles a pipe put under our chimneys to stop smoke. They accompany this music with a chant so monotonous that we would gladly have left to go to sleep if the impatient general had not given marching orders. The Arabs make their horses gambol in front of us, and we let them gather up what the soldiers can't carry with them.

Towards nightfall we camp in a place called Alteia on a hill near a source of water. Tribal chiefs still honor us. We eat supper. Then a guard is ordered for safety during the night. This time we are to sleep under the beautiful stars. Two beautiful tents are put up for the general and his aide-de-camp. To our great surprise we're invited to use the second one, as the officer wants to have the celestial vault as a sky for his bed. The earth serves as our mattress and our coat is our cover. I assure you, gentlemen, our sleep was interrupted only by the cries of hyenas and jackals common in this country. In the morning, we break camp to get on the road. This countryside seems richer than what we just came through. We encounter rather extensive forests. The cork oak is very common here. At 11 o'clock we get to Guelma. Today this camp resembles a very pretty little city. Its position in the middle of beautiful and vast plains is giving it rapid growth. A number of Roman ruins are here. This place, neighbor of the regency of Tunis, is a short distance from Bône and Constantine. The general goes down to the hotel. We are lucky to encounter a pastor who is happy to have us stay with him. He said he hadn't seen a black habit in two years, other than his own which he doesn't always wear. Out of his bed he makes three beds, and out of his dining room a common dormitory.

The next day at 6 AM we left this generous host to follow the general. After three or four hours of marching we come to Haman-Escoutin. Nothing more admirable than this charming place. On the edge of Raz-el-Akba, smiling vegetation of rose laurel, arbutus, jujube trees, wild vines or other climbing plants growing in natural abandon. We walk on acanthus, angelica, even the violet underfoot, but on the side of this rustic place many conical domes five to eight feet high bubble up with sulfurous water 80° Réaumur [100° F]. Its water, in escaping from this crater, forms a number of silvery and graceful waterfalls on the limestone sediment deposited there. Its boiling water comes out below the ravine to mix with the water of the Seybouse River and acquires by this mixture a temperature conducive to ordinary bathing. Curiosity swept me away in the middle of these marvels and forgetting the people I was with, I went to see it all, so that Brother Basil and the two Turkish officers, believing I had become the prey of ferocious Kabyls, wandered looking for me. I didn't meet up with them for two hours. I had stopped to visit the preserved ruins, which show that the Romans had a considerable foundation at this place. Finally we left Haman-Escoutin and its thermal waters to take the Constantine el-Mérich road. The simoon, a terrible desert wind which shrouded the army of Cambyses entirely in dust, dried up our lungs. We had no more provisions, and we came upon no place to refresh ourselves. The soldiers grumbled. The horses couldn't. We had to march on. At 10 PM we got the gates of Constantine to open up. I had not put my feet on the ground since noon! Here we are in Constantine, this city that you sing about sometimes in your recreation periods. Constantine is ours. Yes, it is ours, but it runs with French blood, and in examining the deep ditch surrounding it, its fortifications bristling with fiery mouths, one is frightened by what the taking of this city cost the French. Constantine, Cirta of the ancients, sits at the small Atlas mountain near the Oued-Rummel River. This city of four gates is built on a plateau surrounded by rocks. It is separated from the heights of Mansourah Sidi-Mècid by a deep crevice from where are seen four successive gates forming natural bridges 50 to 100 meters long. The Casbah dominates the city. The church is the most beautiful mosque I've seen in Africa, and Mohammed's rostrum has become a rostrum of truth. Houses have by and large three floors. There are two public plazas, but the streets, although paved, are narrow and torturous. The population is estimated at 25,000 men including 2000 Europeans. After thirty-six hours we left Constantine to take the road to Philippeville.

This time we had to leave the general. We borrowed mules, and a Bedouin served as our guide. We had supper at the Smindore camp and slept at El-Arrouch. At 6 AM we were on our way. You would have really laughed if you had seen me riding pillion with my Bedouin, eating his dates deposited in the hood of his bournous. Finally we get to Philippeville at noon. Here a Brother received us. We stayed eight to ten days. Philippeville, ancient Russiade, is today a city totally French.

I'm stopping here, Gentlemen. I've forgotten that I wanted to spare you. A thousand pardons I have been so long. I returned alone to Oran. I learned just now that the Ténare, on which I had made so many beautiful trips, went down across from Ténès. Fortunately no one perished. I end with two Arab distichs: Greetings! Similar to musk perfume and the suavest amber on which those far away from me and in which my heart is the dwelling place. I groan for him every hour, every moment. As Jacob groaned for the tender dweller of the Cistern … Oh, my document! When you reach their presence, kiss the earth a thousand times, then after that their hands. Tell them that they are the light of my eyes, and give them my greetings. Adieu, love to everyone, Gentlemen and dear friends.

Brother Hilarion

Appendix V

[Copy of a letter written by Brother Leonard Guittoger at Easter, 1868. This copy was made by or for Father Pierre Dufal and was referred to when Leonard was denounced at a General Council meeting held at Précigné August 15, 1871.]

June 8, 1868

To his Eminence Cardinal Barnabo, Prefect of the Sacred Congregation of Propaganda.

Most Eminent Lord,

The men who signed below call themselves respectful and submissive sons of the Holy Apostolic Seat, most faithful to our very holy Lord and royal Pontiff, the august Piux IX, and it is thus that they submit to your Eminence the following matter: they have been members of the Congregation of Holy Cross in the diocese of Le Mans for twelve, twenty, thirty-five, forty-two years or more. Two were masters of novices in their society, and, like the others who sign below, directors of houses of two, three, and five brothers. The oldest [e.g., Leonard] saw the beginnings of the Congregation of the Brothers of St. Joseph which the French government approved in 1825 and which the Holy See recognized, under the jurisdiction of Bishop Bouvier around 1840 or before joining with the priests from Holy Cross.

They have observed different phases of the entire Congregation with a religious and sincere attitude. They were never opposed to this union, nor the one with the Sisters, established a little later near the Holy Cross foundation, but they saw, not without regret, that after a few years the original spirit of the Brothers degenerated by the overly prolonged stay in the Mother House of men lax or of doubtful vocation, not sufficiently formed. The new spirit and the new law of the day came along with independence and the purported freedom to question facts and acts of all authority, a most deadly thing in the Church as well as in Religion.

It is thus that the highest clergy in the country, the archbishop of Tours, the bishops of Le Mans and Blois perceived this change in the Brothers' spirit, and the celebrated wise Dom Guéranger, Benedictine of Solesmes, could predict, before 1844, that the Holy Cross priests would suffocate the Brothers.

The fact is that among them are found subjects offering few guarentees by their past actions and, instead of loving and respecting the rule, being faithful to the vows of obedience and poverty, are only giving contrary example, proved by their abandoning religious life.

While those signing below do not wish to criticize either the institution or individuals, their society has lost touch with religious and civil authorities and with benefactors, and numerous establishments have been abandoned to the great sorrow of many people and almost all the brothers, who have weakened considerably in public opinion.

If one adds to this manifest defect, the plan of certain members of the provincial administration to suppress various houses of two or more brothers to sustain or develop secondary institutions, the men signing below in this case declare conscientiously that this would depart from the original purpose of their humble institution, and from the first moments of their existence many novices lost their vocations from contact with teachers and students of similar houses, where they had been considered auxiliaries, and which today sadly takes place in houses directed by Holy Cross priests. The idea has come to many brothers to leave their first state for the sacerdotal state where they could not succeed or would not be particularly brilliant, thus warned without harming them … while the situation was already known, around 1830 the archbishop of Tours, cited above with the bishops of Le Mans and Blois, announced that their seminaries would no longer be open to these kinds of applicants; it didn't take that many catastrophes to make the brothers sense that they were no longer being recruited as before, and that very likely, what would happen to them is what happened to the Christian Brothers at Nancy, to the Brothers of St. Lawrence at Vendée, to the Little Brothers of Mary, founded in 1817 by Abbé Champagnet, all of whom had begun united to priests from which they separated—without being annihilated—and who have flourished as time and circumstances permit.

The sum total of these facts would have sufficed for many of the men who signed below to awaken in them the wish to separate, but the debts of the Congregation seemed to them an insurmountable obstacle, if the result would be the liquidation of their society.

Nevertheless, in view of the demotion of two Superiors General in less than two years and general unrest that is growing in the spirit of the Brothers, and many novices taking the opportunity to return to the world, and even professed religious being weakened by a situation in which they are discomfited by one or two urgent or pushy creditors who could turn up momentarily, the men who signed below ask themselves what they can do or say, and they believe themselves authorized to save their religious society or their name and the name of many other professed and novice confreres, whose sentiments they know by recent letters or entreaties, but whom they don't have the leisure to consult in their haste, they believe themselves obliged consequently to communicate these various givens to your lordship and hope for help from the Sacred Congregation of Propaganda.

With this hope, they fervently pray that the all powerful God will preserve in the church the sovereign and well loved Pontiff who leads with so much wisdom in the midst of perils so imminent, and that they have more than other Faithful the right and duty to call upon the Holy Father, His Holiness who has honored them with approval as a religious body.

Consequently, they beg very humbly Your Eminence to accept the most respectful and submissive sentiments with which they have the honor to be, Most Eminent Lord, the most humble and faithful servants of your Eminence in Jesus, Mary, and Joseph.

Flers, in the diocese of Séez, Holy Saturday in the year of grace June 8, 1868.

[Signed] Brother John Baptist Brother Leonard Brother Leontian The house of Oisseau, diocese of Laval: Brother Macaire Brother Ariste Brother Elisée

Brother Eulade Brother Moses Brother Germain Brother Raphael
I unite myself to all those who wish sincerely the health of the
Congregation:

Brother Francis Xavier, director of the school at Bouére (Mayenne)
House of Gennes, same diocese: Brother Zachary
House at Ernée, same diocese: Brother Valery
At Bourgneuf-la-Forêt, same diocese: Brother Sixtus Brother Basilide
St. Denys-d'Angou, same diocese: Brother Adolph Brother Frederick
Brother Sosthènes Brother Julian Brother Vincent-de-Paul
At Rasnes, diocese of Séez: Brother Octavius Brother Claude Brother Ives
Brother Matthew

Instead of twenty-four signatures, there would be more than
sixty, if this supplication had been presented to them. If the Sacred
Congregation of Propaganda wishes, we will procure the addition
of all the brothers that we know hold our views. All the Brothers
who have signed did so freely and voluntarily, with no pressure
or exertion, and all did it with the sincere desire to continue their
association with the Brothers of St. Joseph, if the Congregation of
Holy Cross cannot survive.

Brother Leontian　　Brother Leonard　　Brother Matthew
Brother John Baptist

Rome, St. Brigit, June 8, 1868, from a copy faithful to the original,
P[ierre] Dufal

Appendix VI

Order of the Day in the Sainte-Croix [Le Mans] Novitiate [in Alexis Granger's own hand from his novitiate notes]

1. 5 AM   Recitation of Little Hours.
2. 5:30 AM   Prayer for an hour, the last half-hour in the chapel for Holy Mass, or after Mass thanksgiving for those who say the Mass at 6 AM.
3. 7:30 AM   Breakfast.
4.   Study or classes until Particular Examen.
5. 11:45 AM   Particular Examen on the Savior's five wounds.
6.   Lunch followed by recreation until 1:30.
7. 1:30 PM   Singing class until 2 PM.
8.   Vespers in common.
9.   Study or classes until 4 PM.
10.   Matins and Lauds in common.
11.   Visit to the Blessed Sacrament in common for quarter of an hour.
12.   Conference until 6 PM.
13. 6:15 PM   Spiritual reading for half an hour, followed by rosary.
14.   Supper followed by recreation until 8:30.
15.   Prayer.
16.   Bed at the designated time.

Sunday: Rising at 6 AM. Recreation until 2 PM.
Monday: Conference on dogma.
Tuesday: Conference on morals.
Wednesday: Conference on liturgy in place of spiritual reading.

Walk at 1 PM. Return at 5 PM. Reciting as much as possible Vespers going and Matins/Lauds coming back with the rosary. Taking care starting out together from the chapel and meeting there on the return. The usual route of the walk will be visiting Catholic places.

Thursday: Conference on the Constitutions. Prayers at spiritual reading time.

Friday: Sermon. Chapter on spiritual reading.

> Confession if possible every week at a fixed time.
>
> Spiritual direction every two weeks.
>
> See your monitor every month on the retreat day, usually the last Sunday of the month.

Appendix VII

(Sermon by Alexis Granger, August 18, 1848)

I have been commissioned by Father Superior to take his place this morning. In compliance therefore with his request I will continue the series of instructions he has delivered you till now. Please grant me all your attention and think rather of the ideas and considerations I will suggest you than of the form under which they might be presented. The Christian soul has then departed from the world and has already made her appearance before the awful tribunal of God. A sentence has been pronounced that eternity is fixed forever, an eternity of happiness or of eternal misery. Shall I speak of the eternal glory and joy of the Blessed. How could I express what according to St. Paul the eye of man has not seen nor his ear heard, neither his mind understood! And besides the consideration of heaven is rather fit for the last days of a retreat, when the soul purified by a salutary confession is less heavy and able in consequence to appraise the delights of heaven.

Shall I speak then of the everlasting punishment of the damned, of the horrors of hell? Should I speak to worldly men. To common Christians such matter would be fit for them, but before you, before religious men who once perhaps were sinners given to criminal habits, but are no longer the slaves of sin, before men who I hope are now strangers to mortal sins, before such men a more suitable matter ought to be treated. I mean the punishment of the venial sins in Purgatory. Yes, the punishment of venial sins in the other world is a matter which ought to be frequently meditated upon by religious men who too often committed venial sins without any remorse almost because its punishment is not eternal illusion. Illusion! May God make you understand what I intend to tell you on the subject. I will repeat what the saints have said before. Hear St. Catherine of Genoa speaking of this matter. I will quote but a few of her words. God, she says, kindles the soul with a love so burning, and so strongly draws it towards him that were it not immortal there would be enough to annihilate it. The soul then sees that the stains of sin are as a bond which hinders it from following this attraction in opposition to the perfect union with God. It conceives also perfectly how great a loss is the least delay of the intuitive desire, the most ardent possible to see the obstacle vanish which hinders God from drawing it to himself. But, adds the saint, from the furnace of the Divine love I see rays of fire dart like burning lamps which penetrate the soul in purgatory with so much violence and impetuosity that had they their bodies they would be consumed and that they would destroy their very souls, were they not indestructive. These rays have a double effect for they purify and they annihilate. Consider how a material which melted repeatedly becomes always more pure, may be so often melted that there remains at length no mixture of dross. This is what fire works in material things. Now this operation produces in the soul the same results. Kept a long time in a state of fusion, so to speak, in the crucible of Purgatory, it is so disengaged from all impure alloy that it at length becomes as it was at its coming forth from the hands of God. It is said that gold may be purified to such a degree that fire has no longer any action upon it because it has nothing to consume but foreign substances which dim its purity. This is precisely what the Divine fire works in the soul for God keeps it in the fire till all its imperfections, all its impurities are destroyed. Afterwards, when it is perfectly pure, love transforms it entirely so that there remains to it no more of itself and that its being is God. Then, having nothing more that can be consumed becomes impossible; so that should it continue to swell in the fire instead of causing it suffering would become for it the fire of Divine love, which would make a heaven of this punishment. So far St. Catherine. Now do you conceive an idea of the punishment of Purgatory? What an awful transformation ought to take place in the place of purgation! The soul ought to be restored to its primitive purity, to the life it received in Baptism, ere as a single venial sin made it to depart from the state of perfect innocence, removed it in as much from God, it follows that the torment of Purgatory ought to be proportional with the number of its sins and imperfections, and since the soul shall be kept in the fire till all its imperfections are destroyed. Oh! How long then, how painful, how violent the fire reserved by divine justice to those worldly Christians whose life is but a series of negligence, omission, and sins without any penance and mortification! We live in an age where fervor and mortification are almost unknown so for that the Church not to expose her children to transgress her precepts and so compromise that eternal salvation has deemed proper to relax that discipline in many points. Do not rejoice at it. The condition of the Christian is no better under another point. Ah! What an awful purgatory is reserved for them. How violent ought to be the fire which would transform into God those [] souls departing from this life absolved, it is true, from eternal death, but overcharged with the immense debt they have contracted by so many sins they have never tried to make atonement for: but how awful also the fire reserved to the religious tepid, negligent in his duties. Alas! We performed many actions good in themselves, but melted with numberless imperfections. His meditations were all of willful distractions, his attendance to the holy sacrifice of Mass cool, indifferent, his confession unprepared, his communion without fervor, his obedience deficient, all his exercises without a true spirit of piety, his study, his work melted with vanity and idleness, without speaking of his immortification, his infidelities to the grace of God, his numberless omissions. Ah! let everyone excite his fervor, let the consideration of the necessary satisfaction we have to pay for our sins, even after they have been forgiven, and influence each one with a real and ardent desire of mortification and penance. Let us anticipate here below this transformation of our being into God which has necessarily to take place before we should be admitted into heaven. Ah! Let us be more zealous to go benefit ourselves with the indulgence of the Church, a means so simple and [] to shorten our purification in Purgatory, and yet so little appreciated and valued among Christians and even religious. Ah! This leads me to recall a thing quite consoling for those who have already made their profession. It is that by this very fact, according to St. Thomas and after him to the generality of theologians that a full remission of the temporary punishment is remitted, so that it is as a second

Baptism. What a consolation! You will have to expiate in Purgatory the debts contracted only since your profession provided it was made in a true spirit of love, with pure intention, and with fervor!

Our resolution then is never to commit willfully a single venial sin, and to practice mortification as far as possible.

NOTES

Chapter One
André Mottais: the Second Founder

1. Charles Edward Smith, CSC, *Documentation for Preserving the Memory of Canon Jacques François Dujarié* (Montreal: n.p., 2003), 167.

2. Philéas Vanier, CSC, "Brother André's Project," in *Canon Dujarié* (Montreal, 1948), rpr. *Brother André Mottais, Pioneer of Holy Cross: "Remove my name every time it appears,"* ed. George Klawitter, CSC (Austin: St. Edward's University, 2001), 46. Hereafter the Klawitter edition will be cited as *Mottais*.

3. Various references to Brother André give his birth name as simply "Pierre," but the General Matricule lists his legal name as "André " with no mention of "Pierre." His birth is officially recorded in Larchamp as "Andrée pierre" [sic]. Why the feminine form of "André" appears in the official birth record is a mystery. It is probably an error that only the recorder would have noticed and would not have considered important enough to emend. All of the material on André's relatives was discovered by M. Yves Guilimeau, who has generously shared all of his work on the Mottais heritage.

4. Jean Mottais's father was also named Jean, and it was with his second wife Marie Laize that André's father was born. André's grandparents were married on July 10, 1743, five years after the grandfather married his first wife Julienne Lepentier on February 11, 1738. André's great-grandfather was likewise named Jean Mottais, and his second wife was Michelle Davy. André's great-great-grandfather, Olivier Mottais, died January 1, 1701, a century before André was born. Olivier married Julienne Sibelle on October 10, 1674, one month before the English poet John Milton died and thirty-one years into the reign of Louis XIV, who reigned until 1715. André's own father died at the age of 78 in Larchamp on July 12, 1847, three years after his Holy Cross son. André's mother had died earlier than her husband, on August 30, 1845, one year after her son André. She was the daughter of François Blot and Jeanne Caillère.

5. André's brother Jean died on March 6, 1830, long before his Holy Cross brother or their parents. He was married twice: first to Marie Fleury on May 8, 1815, and then to Louise Lottin on January 21, 1826. André's sister (named for her mother and possibly the first wife of her grandfather or the wife of her great-great grandfather) married Jean Grégoire Chevillé on October 25, 1834, when she was twenty-nine, ten years before her brother André's death. She died in 1879. André's younger brother Joseph died December 14, 1878, one year before his sister. He was married to his cousin Michelle Caillère on November 10, 1841.

6. Philéas Vanier, from notes of Brother Rémi, *Rec. Doc.*, 544. Brother André, according to Ephrem O'Dwyer in *The Curé of Ruillé* (92) was the fourth recruit to show up, the first being a former Christian Brother whom Dujarié dismissed as unfit for religious life. This young man is not listed in Bernard Gervais' *General Matricule* where, however, André is still listed as the fourth member of the Community because Gervais lists Father Dujarié as number one, even though Dujarié never took religious vows.

7. Dujarié managed to get André presented to the prefect of La Sarthe, Count de Breteuil, by General Coutant's uncle, the pastor of the historic Le Mans church Notre Dame de la Couture. See *Extracts from the Chronicles of Notre Dame de Sainte-Croix*, 10, in *Mottais, 39.*

8. *Mottais*, 16.

9. Ibid., 16.

10. Ibid., 16.

11. The *Chronicles of Notre Dame de Sainte Croix* (Notre Dame, IN: General Archives) gives the date as November 25, 1821. Since André wrote these early *Chronicles,* we can trust his memory for the precise date.

12. Brother Stephen (Etienne Gauffre) was born in 1792 and was the fourth man to join Dujarié's group. He came to Ruillé in November 1820 at the age of twenty-eight, one month after André. He received his teaching license in May 1822 and persevered through all the troubles that visited the Brothers of St. Joseph. He died in 1851 in Le Mans two days shy of his fifty-ninth birthday.

13. The event has been captured in an oil painting by Brother Harold Ruplinger, CSC, who put three Brothers (plus Dujarié) in the picture. He used as models three Brothers of the Midwest Province (Bernard Platte, Michael Becker, Thomas Moser) because there are no photos of any of the earliest Brothers. Photography was not invented until 1829 and did not come into any wide use for another two generations. For Dujarié, Ruplinger used Brother Raymond Dufresne as model. In Ruplinger's painting one brother is actually taking off his habit because Ruplinger wanted to show that the man would not persevere as a Brother of St. Joseph. Ruplinger tried to depict three types of Brothers: the Brother to the left is intellectual, the Brother in the middle a farmer, and

the Brother on the far right unsure of his vocation. There were, of course, only two Brothers at the actual event in 1821.

14. *Chronicles*, 11, qtd, in *Mottais*, 39.

15. Ibid., 11, qtd. in *Mottais, 39.*

16. Ibid., 12, qtd. in *Mottais, 39.*

17. André Mottais, "Renewal of Vows (Formula)," September 11, 1830, in *Mottais*, 7.

18. *Chronicles*, 13, qtd in *Mottais*, 39.

19. Brother Adrian (Louis Legeai), the son of Louis Legeai and Françoise Maillet, was born February 26, 1803, at Rahais. He came to Ruillé on January 1, 1925, was professed in 1839, and died in the community April 14, 1873, an elderly man.

20. Brother Francis (Pierre François Blanchet) was born February 3, 1793, at La Chapelle Genson. He came to Ruillé on December 15, 1821, and left the community in 1832. He had been the tenth man to join Dujarié's Brothers and thus knew André for eleven years.

21. *Mottais*, 1.

22. *Mottais*, 1.

23. Of the first fifty young men to join Dujarié's community, only ten received teaching diplomas: 1822 (André, Etienne), 1823 (Augustin, Vincent), 1825 (Dominique, Marie-Joseph), 1828 (Pierre, Martin, Marin, Romain). Dujarié may not have accepted "non-teaching" Brothers, so the other forty of the first fifty would have been sent out to teach without licenses (or left before being assigned).

24. Etienne Catta and Tony Catta, *Basil Anthony Moreau*, 2 vols. (Paris: Fides, 1950), 1.292.

25. The two lost were Brother Jérôme (René Porcheré), twenty-six years old, who had been with the Brothers two years, and Brother Jean-Marie (Jean-Marie Gauchet), twenty-seven years old, who had entered the community not quite two years before his death. The former died in Ruillé, the latter in Mayenne.

26. *Chronicles*, 16, qtd in *Mottais*, 39.

27. Philéas Vanier, "Brother André's Project," rpr. *Mottais*, 46.

28. *Chronicles*, 22, qtd. in *Mottais*, 42.

29. *Mottais*, 11.

30. Tony Catta, *Jacques Dujarié* (Milwaukee: Bruce, 1960), 202.

31. Ibid., 212.

32. *Mottais*, 8.

33. Catta, *Dujarié*, 238, n. 5.

34. It may seem that Moreau was influencing such matters four years earlier, and André's document may hint that Moreau was already determined to headquarter the Brothers at Le Mans, not at Ruillé, but the sale of the Ruillé boarding school was not effected until 1835, so André must have amended

his 1831 letter years after it was written to reflect the fact that M. Laguette from Masle-sur-Sarthe would buy the property four years after the financial separation of the Brothers from the Sisters.

35. *Mottais*, 11.

36. *Chronicles*, 42, qtd. in *Mottais*, 43.

37. Rpr. from *Mottais*, 12.

38. André died in 1844 at age 44, Leonard Guittoger in 1887 at age 84, and Vincent Pieau in 1890 at age 93. Henry (Michael Taupin) left the Community at age 42, a few years after signing the oath of allegiance.

39. *Mottais*, 18.

40. Ibid., 18.

41. Ibid., 24.

42. Ibid.,19.

43. Ibid., 20.

44. The most thorough analysis of André's plan is that by Philéas Vanier. He has carefully reconstructed André's plan and compared it point by point with both Dujarié's plan for an organization of auxiliary priests to work alongside his Brothers and Moreau's plan that eventually became the Congregation of Holy Cross. See "Brother André's Project," Philéas Vanier, in *Mottais*, 47-53.

45. See *Mottais*, 45.

46. Catta, *Moreau*, 1.326. Bouvier had in fact pledged himself to join such a group when he was a seminarian. See Catta, *Moreau*, 1.320.

47. Catta, *Moreau*, 1.343. Thomas Maddix suggests ("Breaking the Historical Amnesia," 79) that Dujarié never had manual labor Brothers and that Moreau created the practice of using them, but Dionne notes that Dujarié did use Brothers for manual labor, following the practice of both de Lamennais and Deshayes, founders that Dujarié had consulted in the establishment of the Brothers of St. Joseph. (See Dionne, "Book Review," 96.) What is not clear is if Dujarié had Brothers who were devoted totally to manual labor or if he simply used the novices part time for manual labor before they went out to teach in parish schools. André's reference elsewhere to "brother carpenters" (*Mottais*, 43) suggests that there may have been Brothers who did indeed do manual labor full time and never taught. André names, for example, one Brother-carpenter: Alphonsus, who was eventually to accompany André to Algeria where Alphonsus worked as a joiner, not a teacher.

48. Moreau left La Chesnaie after three days, but Brother Leonard stayed several days longer in order to visit the schools run by the Ploërmel Brothers. Leonard then went back to Ploërmel itself where he spent three weeks at the motherhouse. See Catta, *Moreau*, 1.345.

49. In one volume Catta notes that Brother Vincent was left in Ruillé to run the boarding school there. (See Catta, *Dujarié*, 268.) In another book Catta writes that Brother Vincent was put in charge of the new school at Sainte-Croix.

(See Catta, *Moreau*, 1.353.) Vincent could not be in two places at once. André must have been in charge of one of the schools. As the *Chronicles* mention that André was novice master in both Ruillé and Sainte-Croix, he probably supervised the Sainte-Croix boarding school, and Vincent stayed behind in Ruillé.

50. Catta, *Moreau*, 1.353.
51. Ibid., 1.351.
52. Thomas Maddix, "Breaking," in *Mottais*, 78.
53. Catta, *Dujarié*, 259.
54. Qtd. in Catta, *Moreau*, 1.369.
55. André could not even comment on his own role in saving the Brothers without Moreau's finding fault in him. When André in the *Chronicles* writes about his own work to save the Brothers as Dujarié weakened, Moreau writes in the margin: "I am pained to see this note by Brother André, which is not the fruit of humility." See *Chronicles*, 42, qtd. in *Mottais, 43.*
56. Catta, *Dujarié*, 261-262.
57. *Chronicles*, 265, qtd. in *Mottais*, 44.
58. Brother Léopold (Pierre-Nicholas Putiot) was born in 1804 and entered at Sainte-Croix in 1830 at age twenty-five. He died in 1864 at age fifty-nine. Silvin-Auguste De Marseul was born in 1812, was ordained in 1835, and became a novice at Sainte-Croix in 1836 at age twenty-four. He left in 1842, re-entered in 1857, but left again in 1868 at age fifty-six. Pierre Chappé was born in 1809, entered at Sainte-Croix in 1837, and died in 1880 at age seventy.
59. Another chore André had was to travel to Auvergne where the bishop of St. Flour wanted to start a community of Brothers. The bishop had sent three young men to Sainte-Croix to make their novitiate under Brother André, but when André took them to Auvergne, the planned community never did materialize. See *Chronicles*, 147, qtd. in *Mottais*, 43.
60. Catta, *Dujarié*, 281.
61. The novice Ignatius (Théodore Feron) was born October 20, 1820, making him nineteen at the time of the Algerian announcement. Julian Leboucher left the community in late 1843. We do not know the date of his birth. He came to Sainte-Croix as a priest in October 1839 and was sent six months later to Africa. The Cattas spell his name "Le Boucher," but the *General Matricule* spells it "Leboucher." The other priest sent was Victor Drouelle who was born in 1812 and entered the community as a priest in 1837 when he was twenty-five. He turned against Moreau in the Le Mans debacle of 1865 and died in 1875, two years after Moreau.
62. *Mottais,* 23.
63. Ibid., 24.
64. Ibid., 25.

65. Helen Metz, *Algeria: A Country Study* (Lanham, MD: Office of the Federal Register), 22.

66. Mahfoud Bennoune, *The Making of Contemporary Algeria, 1830-1987* (Cambridge: Cambridge University Press, 1988), 35.

67. Louis Veuillot, *Les Français en Algérie* (Paris: 1924), 1.234.

68. Jules Fournier, *La nouvelle Eglise d'Afrique. La conquête religieuse de l'Algérie, 1830-1846* (Paris: 1930), 64. In Algeria, however, the European population was transient and mostly military. They were aggressive invaders who had little time for the refinements of religious vocation. And as for the native population of Arabs and Berbers, the hopes of conversions to Christianity were quickly dashed. In fact, not a single vocation to Holy Cross came in Algeria the entire time the Brothers worked there. The soil was not ripe for either conversions or vocations. One cannot help but contrast Algeria to the work of Holy Cross in Bengal twenty years later when Holy Cross worked among the native people from day one and was not perceived as abettors to an invading European force. The Muslims and Hindus of Bengal have worked well alongside the religious of Holy Cross for over a century and a half. If there was a similar dream for Algeria, it was aborted. Holy Cross, however, worked hard to bring religious and social services to the Christians already in Algeria, for whatever reason those Christians were there.

69. Basil Moreau, *Circular Letters*, trans. Edward L. Heston (1943), 1.23.

70. *Mottais,* 26.

71. The king had six sons, and although André does not name the ones he met, we can presume that the two princes were Louis-Charles, Duke of Nemours, second son of King Louis-Philippe, and Henri d'Orléans, Duke of Aumerle, fifth son of the king. These were the only two of the king's sons to serve in Algeria. They were returning to Paris after having taken part in a military expedition against what André calls "the enemies," referring to the native Algerians who defended their homeland from the French invaders.

72. *Mottais,* 26.

73. Ibid., 27.

74. Ibid., 28.

75. Ibid., 31.

76. Ibid., 32.

77. Ibid., 32.

78. Etienne Catta, *Basil Anthony Mary Moreau*, 1.483.

79. *Mottais,* 34.

80. Why the Cattas would falsify primary source material is a matter of conjecture. To excuse them by saying they were working fast makes them sloppy researchers. To say that they were basically interested in writing a clerical account of Algeria in which priests had to be chronicled in the best

possible light makes them suspect historians. Either way, their account of André's suffering in Philippeville is unconscionable.

81. Basil Moreau, *Circular Letters*, 1.46.
82. Etienne Catta, *Moreau*, 1.483, n. 77.
83. The Cattas note the recall was effected in June (1.485), but André in a letter dated May 26, 1843, gives the recall date as August 5. See *Mottais,* 37.
84. *Mottais,* 37.
85. Ibid., 37.
86. Moreau may not have given André the appointments or the title. In his March 20, 1844, letter announcing André's death, Moreau writes that it was the General Council who appointed André, on André's return from Africa, to be Moreau's "Assistant and Counseller in the various transactions of my administration." See *Mottais*, p. 44. The Council, of course, may simply have voted on Moreau's nomination of André and not instigated the appointment themselves.
87. *Mottais,* 37.
88. *Chronicles*, 265, qtd. in *Mottais,* 44.

Chapter Two
Hilarion Ferton: Apostle to Africa

1. Catta, *Basil Anthony Mary Moreau*, 1.486.
2. Marshall Soult, letters to Moreau (May 4, May 27, 1893), in Catta, *Moreau,* 1.487.
3. Catta, *Moreau,* 1.488-489.
4. Why Moreau sent novices on early missions is unclear. He sent two in the first colony to Indiana: one drowned at age 20 and the other left the Community embittered. Victor Catala is not to be confused with Victor (John) Huard, who was on the first Algerian mission, and not to be confused with Louis (Victor) Marchand who died in Algeria in 1841 while swimming with the Algiers orphans.
5. The General Matricule notes that he was born at Boulogne, Pas de Calais. This would place him way north of Paris, near Dunkirk in Flanders. He would have been Flemish. This makes little sense—Father Moreau's band of Brothers in 1837, when Hilarion came to Le Mans, was still basically a diocesan community, drawing its recruits from towns near Le Mans. Some, e.g., Edward Sorin, came from as far away as Laval, but it is doubtful that men would have crossed over half of France, bypassing other religious communities in and around Paris, in order to join a fledgling diocesan community in Le Mans. Furthermore, there is no town named Boulogne in Pas de Calais. There is a town named Boulogne-sur-Mer, but no town named Boulogne. Of

course, the town may have been known as Boulogne in Hilarion's day, but we have no basis for assuming that. Another possibility is the neighborhood of Boulogne-Billancourt, shortened often to Boulogne, a western suburb of Paris, five miles from the city's center. Originally a town named Boulogne-la-Petite in the fourteenth-century (to commemorate a famous shrine north in the greater town Boulogne-sur-Mer), it was later called Boulogne-sur-Seine. The only site in France today named simply "Boulogne" is a small river south of Nantes and connected to Lac de Grand-Lieu, a rather sizable body of water just north of the little Boulogne river. This is more probably the location of the Ferton family, ten miles from Nantes, fifty miles from Angers, one hundred miles from Le Mans. Pas de Calais, the site named in the General Matricule, is two hundred miles from Le Mans. Access to baptismal records, of course, would resolve this matter. It is possible, of course, that the General Matricule is incorrect in giving Hilarion's birth in the Boulogne north of Paris if his family had later moved to the vicinity of Le Mans. The Matricule, of course, would make no note of a family's having moved. The first man in Holy Cross to receive the name "Hilarion" was Jean Lagarde, who was born in 1795 and came to Ruillé in 1824, very early in the history of the Brothers of St. Joseph. Lagarde left the group two years later (1826). Ordinarily religious names were recycled quickly upon death or departure. Why the lapse of eleven years before someone else was dubbed "Hilarion" is a mystery.

The bestowing of names in Holy Cross often depended upon the practice of any given novice master. In the twentieth century various novice masters used different methods for the procedure. For example, Father Felix Duffy had novices draw names out of a hat. Brother Remigius quipped in later years that the first name he pulled out was 7 3/8. Father Robinson used a different method when he was novice master. He simply told each novice what his new religious name would be. One day he called Frederick Hunt into his office and said, "What do you think of the name 'Moses'?" And Frederick replied, "What do YOU think of the name 'Moses'?" Father Robinson laughed and said, "You're right—your name will be Edmund." In the 1950s the practice of changing one's name disappeared from Holy Cross, and by the 1960s most Brothers had returned to their legal names.

6. Letter, Brother Hilarion to Basil Moreau, September 10, 1844, in *Algeria*, 131-134. All the Algerian letters have been translated by George Klawitter, CSC, in *Holy Cross in Algeria: The Early Years, 1840-1849* (New York: iUniverse, 2007). This source will hereafter be cited as *Algeria*.

7. Letter, Brother Basil Gary to Basil Moreau, November 4, 1844, in *Algeria*, 145.

8. Ibid., 146. Hilarion discovered he had left an important portfolio behind containing his teaching certificate, various papers he needed, and letters from Father Haudebourg. Luckily he still had his commissioning letter.

9. Antoine Louis Adophe Dupuch was the first bishop of Algiers, which was erected as a see in 1838. Dupuch retired in December 1845. His encounters with the 1840 contingent of Holy Cross missionaries were not pleasant.

10. Letter, Brother Hilarion Ferton to Basil Moreau, September 3, 1844, in *Algeria*, 129.

11. Letter, Brother Basil Gary to Basil Moreau, November 4, 1844, in *Algeria*, 147. Brother Louis's own account of the visit differs from Basil's and Hilarion's in that Louis focuses on the hard and apparently insalubrious life of the monks. In a letter to Moreau he declares, "One would really have to love God to be a Trappist. Who could stay in a place where one is always sick or uncomfortable or busy with the lowliest, most fatiguing work, where one is badly housed, badly clothed, eats poorly and sleeps poorly?" (letter of Oct. 1, 1844, in *Algeria*, 140).

12. Letter, Brother Hilarion Ferton to Basil Moreau, September 3, 1844, in *Algeria*, 130.

13. Letter, Brother Basil Gary to Basil Moreau, November 4, 1844, in *Algeria*, 148.

14. Letter, Brother Hilarion Ferton to Basil Moreau, September 3, 1844, in *Algeria*, 136.

15. Ibid., 137.

16. Ibid., 137.

17. Letter, Brother Louis Gonzaga to Brother Hilarion, October 1, 1844, in *Algeria*, 139.

18. Letter, Brother Louis Gonzaga to Basil Moreau, October 1, 1844, in *Algeria*, 140.

19. Letter, Brother Hilarion Ferton to Basil Moreau, October 23, 1844, in *Algeria*, 142-143.

20. Letter, Brother Hilarion Ferton to Basil Moreau, October 26, 1844, in *Algeria*, 144.

21. Letter, Brother Hilarion Ferton to Basil Moreau, January 8, 1845, in *Algeria*, 153.

22. Ibid., 157. In this same letter Hilarion tells Moreau that Louis Gonzaga should have been appointed director, not Hilarion (150).

23. Theotime had come to Le Mans two years after Hilarion and never did get to Algeria. In 1853 he studied at the Holy Cross seminary, was sent to New Orleans in the same year, and died there one year later of yellow fever. He might have become an excellent missionary in Algeria, but we will never know.

24. Letter, Brother Hilarion Ferton to Basil Moreau, August, 1845, in *Algeria*, 167.

25. Letter, Brother Louis Gonzaga to Basil Moreau, August, February 4, 1846, in *Algeria*, 175.

26. Letter, Brother Louis Gonzaga to Father Pierre Chappé, April 4, 1846, in *Algeria*, 194.

27. Letter, Brother Hilarion Ferton to Basil Moreau, February 8, 1846, in *Algeria*, 183.

28. This Brother Clement wrote no letters to Moreau in the 1840's so we know little about him except that he entered Holy Cross in 1836 at age 25 and died in Algeria in 1851 at age 42. Hilarion claimed "Clement is African" (*Algeria*, 203), but Clement's last name was Deschamps, and he was born in Changé les Laval (Mayenne), so Hilarion's remark was probably metaphorical and meant that Clement adapted well to the Algerian climate.

29. Letter, Brother Hilarion Ferton to Basil Moreau, July 25, 1846, in *Algeria*, 203.

30. Letter, Brother Hilarion Ferton to the scholastic Brothers at Sainte-Croix, January 17, 1847, in *Algeria*, 212-213.

31. Ibid., 221.

32. Letter, Brother Hilarion Ferton to the scholastic Brothers at Sainte-Croix, August 10, 1846, in *Algeria*, 204.

33. Letter, Brother Basil Gary to Basil Moreau, June 4, 1846, in *Algeria*, 201.

34. Louis Antoine Augustin Pavy was bishop of Algeria from 1846 to 1866. He is best known for an important sermon he preached on Islam and Christian relations in 1853.

35. Letter, Brother Basil Gary to Basil Moreau, September 24, 1846, in *Algeria*, 207.

36. Letter, Brother Hilarion to Brother Zachary Cognet, February 9, 1848, in *Algeria*, 229-230.

37. Letter, Brother Hilarion to Basil Moreau, October 9, 1848, in *Algeria*, 232.

38. Basil Moreau, Circular Letter #37, in *Circular Letters*, 2 vols., trans. Edward L. Heston (Rome, 1943), 1.169.

39. Moreau, Circular Letter #39, in *Circular Letters*, 1.181-182.

40. Letter, Brother Florentine to Moreau, December 19, 1849, in Moreau, *Circular Letters*, 1.182-183.

Chapter Three
Leonard Guittoger: Prophet or Fool?

1. Terrehaut was originally spelled "Terrehault" but assumed its present name at the time of the Revolution.

2. Brother Leonard Guittoger is listed as #106 in the General Matricule of the Congregation of Holy Cross. As with most of the early Brothers, we have no photograph of Leonard. It is not surprising, given the naissance of the art and the attitude of Moreau, for whom we have but one photo because, as he

said, the only photo he would allow would be the one taken "after my death" (Charles Moreau 2.53). It is time to set the story straight about the one Moreau photograph we do have. Years ago at the Le Mans Holy Cross Institute, members were told a story that the severity of that Moreau photo was due not to Moreau's actual visage, but rather was due to the circumstances under which the photo was taken. Community members tricked Moreau into posing for a group shot with two other religious who suddenly bolted out of the way as the photographer took the picture. Their act so startled Moreau that he grimaced. The story is, unfortunately, apocryphal and has been handed down simply to mitigate the harshness of Moreau's only photographic reproduction. Charles Moreau tells a quite different story:

> In his second visit Father Moigne was accompanied by Jules Dubosc, physician and expert photographer from Paris, who obtained the privilege up to then impossible of leaving to the Institute Father Founder's portrait. Several times supplications and all manner of influence had been tried in vain. Basil was inflexible on that point, as inflexible as the Superior General of the Sulpicians, of whom a portrait may not be taken before his death. When anyone spoke to Father Moreau of his portrait, he always gave the same permission, "after my death." In vain he was told that he need never see it, that it would be given only to the Missionaries of the Institute, leaving for foreign countries. Nevertheless, the presence of the photographer who had succeeded in taking several views of the Establishment and of several groups of pupils, furnished an occasion for a new attempt. Father Founder's friend, the Count de Ch— who had his two sons at Holy Cross College, knew of this ardent desire of the Community, which he himself shared. The day of the distribution of prizes, after the departure of the pupils, the Count happened to be with a group of ecclesiastics who took recreation with Basil, and who begged him to have his photograph taken in front of the group. Seeing that they were getting nowhere, the Count himself went to Basil, knelt at his feet, and arose only after having won. The artist awaited but the sign, succeeded to his satisfaction, and from the group picture later made a photograph of Father Moreau alone. (53)

And so is laid to rest another bit of Holy Cross Community folklore.

3. See Bernard Gervais, *General Matricule.*
4. Charles Moreau, *The Very Reverend Father Basil Anthony Mary Moreau, Priest of Le Mans and His Works,* trans: anon. 2 vols. (Paris: Firmin didot et cie, 1900), 3.
5. Charles Edward Smith, CSC, *Documentation for Preserving the Memory of Canon James François Dujarie* (Private printing: 2003), 12.
6. Tony Catta, *Father Dujarie,* trans. Edward L. Heston, CSC (Milwaukee: Bruce, 1960), 115-116.

7. "Pact of Fidelity" (Notre Dame: General Archives), in Catta, *Dujarie,* 225.

8. Brother Henri-Michel Taupin eventually became the black sheep of the four Brother Directors. Although he signed the Pact of Fidelity in September, 1831, by August of 1834 he had become such a scandal in the community that Brother André Mottais complains about him in a letter (August 18, 1834) to Bishop Bouvier. Henri-Michel left the Brothers in October of that same year. We know little about him and have no letters by him or to him. Brother Vincent Pieau, the Fourth Director, went on to become a kingpin in the Indiana colony. The oldest to emigrate there in 1841, he died, a much revered member of the American community, at Notre Dame, 93 years of age, in 1890.

9. Letter, Brother Leonard to Basil Moreau, October 15, 1847. All letters, unless otherwise noted, are found in the Holy Cross General Archives at Notre Dame, Indiana. Trans. George Klawitter, CSC.

10. Ibid.

11. The June 17, 1849, letter may not have been written to Hilarion. Its recipient is conjectural.

12. Letter, Basil Moreau to Bishop Bouvier, August 19, 1849.

13. Letter, Brother Leonard to Bishop Bouvier, May 13, 1853.

14. Letter, Victor Drouelle to Sacred Congregation, 1855.

15. Ibid.

16. Document, December 19, 1855. Notre Dame: General Archives.

17. Brother Narcissus (Jean-François) Hulot was born October 3, 1817, at Pezé le Robert. He entered Holy Cross in December 1835 and became a novice in February, 1836. He received a teaching certificate in 1844. He did not profess vows until August 15, 1872. He died December 29, 1887, in Angers.

18. Leonard gets the year of André's death incorrect. André died in 1844, not 1838.

19. Letter, Brother Leonard to Bishop Nanquette, January 10, 1856.

20. Letter, Brother Leonard to Bishop Nanquette, January 28, 1856.

21. Etienne Catta and Tony Catta, *Basil Anthony Mary Moreau,* trans. Edward Heston, CSC, 2 vols. (Milwaukee: Bruce, 1955), 2.171.

22. Brother Edward (Celestine) Raymond (#598 in the General Matricule), the son of Bertrand Raymond and Jeanne-Marie Dedieu, was born September 4, 1827, at Foix. He came to Holy Cross in August, 1845, was a novice the following summer (1846), and received his teaching certificate in 1850. He professed vows in 1854 and died January 8, 1871, at La Faye.

23. Letter, Brother Narcissus to Brother Leonard, 1856.

24. Minutes, General Council, May 8, 1868. Curiously, the minutes are not signed by Dufal, the Superior General.

25. Catta, *Moreau,* 2.772.

26. Hugh Cleary, CSC, "A Year of Rejoicing and Spiritual Renewal" (Rome: Via Framura 85, 2006), 18.

27. Three 1868 typescripts in the Holy Cross General Archives at Notre Dame are important to Brother Leonard but are problematic. The original letters no longer exist, a situation that could cause some alarm to researchers of the period. The first typescript is dated only June, 1868, and is addressed to "Monseigneur." Someone has written "Dufal" in parenthesis after "Monseigneur." The document is five pages long and has several typed-in corrections.

The second typescript is only three pages long and comes from the lost original that also generated the first typescript. Someone has written in this second document in the top right margin "Petition des Frères [au] Card. Barnabo." It seems to be an earlier typescript of the first document because the errors corrected in the first document are not corrected in the second. Possibly an early archivist (Vanier?) began a typescript (document #2) of the original document, set it aside, came back to the project at a later date, began a new typescript (document #1), completed the typescript, found the earlier one and decided to file both. For practical purposes, it is best to ignore document #2, the incomplete earlier transcript, and rely solely on document #1, the complete transcript of the lost original. A crucial point, of course, is the identification of "Monseigneur." Was the letter addressed to Bishop Dufal or to Cardinal Barnabo? The first paragraph of the document indicates that the document itself was indeed addressed to Dufal: "On the invitation of Your Excellency [Dufal] the Josephite capitulants [of the General Chapter] came together to know the true sense and purpose of the petition which was just addressed by your intervention to His Eminence Cardinal Barnabo."

The third typescript is dated June 8, 1868, and also has a handwritten note that the original no longer exists in the General Archives. This document is clearly directed to Cardinal Barnabo.

28. Brother Leon (Norbert-August) Cotin was born March 16, 1819, in Sérigny. He entered at Le Mans July 9, 1838, and received his teaching license May 11, 1843. He did not profess until August 12, 1888, and died January 21, 1894, at Angers.

29. Letter, Brother Leonard to Edward Sorin, August 20, 1870.

30. Minutes, General Council, August 15, 1871. See Appendix V for letter to Cardinal Barnabo.

31. Catta, *Moreau,* 2.1013.

32. Letter, Moreau, January 2, 1872.

33. Sister M. Georgia Costin, CSC, *Priceless Spirit: A History of the Sisters of the Holy Cross, 1841-1893* (Notre Dame: University of Notre Dame Press, 1994), 78.

34. Costin, *Priceless Spirit*, 132.

35. Sister M. Emerentiana Nowlan, CSC, unpublished chronicles, 2 vols. (Notre Dame: St. Mary's Archives, n.d.) in Costin, 26.

36. Leonard Guittoger folder 1877, xii-12 (Notre Dame: General Archives).
37. Letter, Brothers at Soligny to Edward Sorin, October 12, 1875.
38. Letter, Brother Leonard to Brother Vincent, 1876.
39. At the end of this remarkable document is a note by the copyist that the document is a faithful copy of a report given to the bishop of Laval. The original is in the handwriting of Brother Basil (Michael) Gary, but the main ideas are those of Brother Vital, a capitulant at both the 1868 General Chapter and the 1872. Obviously Vital had considerable compassion for Leonard, although he does not name Leonard directly. Someone opines, probably Brother Basil, at one point that the old maligned Brother in question was Leonard.
40. Letter, Brother Hippolyte Lecointe to Edward Sorin, 1877.

Chapter Four
Vincent Pieau: Patriarch in America

1. The painting cannot presume to portray an event in 1820 because for the first year of Dujarié's little group, the Brothers wore no religious garb. Community records disagree on the date of the first investiture, one record giving November 25, 1821, another giving August 15, but the event was outdoors, probably after a procession to a wayside shrine. Only two young men, however, were invested: André Mottais and Etienne Gauffre. See Ephrem O'Dwyer, *The Curé of Ruillé* (Notre Dame: Ave Maria Press, 1941), 106.
2. Letter, Brother André Mottais to Brother Vincent, May 18, 1840. All letters are held at Notre Dame University in the Holy Cross General Archives.
3. Vow document, Brother Vincent Pieau (Notre Dame: General Archives).
4. Letter, Mother Theodore Guerin, in Anon., *Life and Life Work of Mother Theodore Guerin* (New York: Benziger Brothers, 1904). The Brothers slept on planks for two months. See Sister Mary Borromeo Brown, *The History of the Sisters of Providence of St. Mary-of-the-Woods,* 2 vols. (New York: Benziger Brothers, 1949), 353.
5. Letter, Brother Vincent to Mother Theodore Guerin, January 1, 1842.
6. Letter, Brother Vincent to Edward Sorin, March 8, 1842.
7. Letter, Brother Vincent to Edward Sorin, May 4, 1842. "Unfortunate blacks," of course could have referred to their condition rather than to their conversion.
8. Letter, Brother Vincent to Basil Moreau, April 10, 1842.
9. Letter, Brother Vincent to Basil Moreau, June 6, 1842.
10. Letter, Brother John to Basil Moreau, February 1843.
11. Ibid.

12. Joachim, born William Michael André in 1809, at St. Martin de Connée (La Mayenne District) was a tailor, but in the New World he was used as a cook. His final sickness lasted eighteen months, half of the time spent in his new land. When he died on April 13, he was buried on the island (today the land around Columba Hall) where a cemetery in the form of a large triangle had been set out: one angle for the Sisters, one for the Brothers, and one for the priests. A juxta crucem scene was placed at the center of the triangle. A small octagonal chapel would eventually be built nearby.

13. Letter, Brother Vincent to Edward Sorin, July 14, 1844.

14. Twenty year old Augustus would live to work over fifty years in America, dying in 1900. Justin, almost as old as Vincent was when Vincent first came to America, would die in 1870, a quarter century after his arrival at Notre Dame. Augustine's interest in medicine did not last. He returned to Notre Dame a year later to study for the priesthood. He did not persevere in that endeavor either and left the Community.

15. Anon., *The Metropolitan Catholic Almanac and Laity's Directory* (Baltimore: Fielding Lucas, 1842), 108.

16. Anon., *The Metropolitan Catholic Almanac and Laity's Directory* (Baltimore: Fielding Lucas, 1843), 79.

17. Anon., *The Metropolitan Catholic Almanac and Laity's Directory* (Baltimore: Fielding Lucas, 1846), 122.

18. Ibid., 124.

19. Anon., *The Metropolitan Catholic Almanac and Laity's Directory* (Baltimore: Fielding Lucas, 1847), 115.

20. Anon., *The Metropolitan Catholic Almanac and Laity's Directory* (Baltimore: Fielding Lucas, 1848), 110.

21. Ephrem O'Dwyer, CSC, *The Curé of Ruillé* (Notre Dame: Ave Maria Press, 1941), 108.

22. By the early twentieth-century, the Brother-teachers gradually moved into high school teaching. By 1906 there were no Brothers on the Notre Dame faculty, but in 1943, two years before the separation into separate provinces for Brothers and priests, there were four Brother faculty members: Patrick Cain, James Dwyer, Edmund Hunt, and Columba Curran.

23. Document, Brother Vincent to Edward Sorin, December 29, 1847. O'Connell misinterprets this document in his Sorin biography: O'Connell thinks the document indicates that Brother Vincent was complaining about Sorin out of ill-will. See Marvin O'Connell, *Edward Sorin* (Notre Dame: University of Notre Dame Press, 2001), 265. O'Connell misdates the document as February 23, 1847.

24. The original orphanage set up by Adam Kindelon was on Bayou St. John, but the property was destroyed by a hurricane so the diocese transferred the orphans to the David Olivier plantation on the levee near Chartres Street

where the original house eventually was replaced by brick buildings, which remained until 1950 when they were demolished.

25. Letter, Brother Vincent to Edward Sorin, May 17, 1849.

26. Letter, Brother Vincent to Edward Sorin, June 22, 1849.

27. Letter, Brother Vincent to Alexis Granger, July 8, 1849.

28. Minutes, Notre Dame Minor Chapter, May 24, 1850, Holy Cross General Archives (Notre Dame, Indiana).

29. Minutes, January, 1853, Notre Dame Minor Chapter, Holy Cross General Archives.

30. Letter, Edward Sorin to Basil Moreau, February 12, 1860, qtd. in O'Connell, 429.

31. The artist, Francis P. Miller, was born in Columbus, Ohio, in 1855 and died in New York City in 1930. He was trained in New York, Paris, and Berlin.

Chapter Five
Lawrence Ménage: Pioneer Businessman-Farmer

1. As with many of the early Holy Cross pioneers, the data in records occasionally conflicts. Thus the United States Province archive card on Brother Lawrence gives his place of birth as Bussy, his novitiate entry as August 22, 1840, his profession date as August 22, 1841, and his departure date to America as March 1843. These items do not correspond to the data in the *General Matricule* compiled by Brother Bernard Gervais. The Gervais *Matricule* contains generally the most accurate information we have on early Holy Cross men and should be the preferred source for data. All quotations from original manuscripts are printed here with permission. The translations, except where noted, are mine.

2. O'Connell refers to Lawrence as having been "a successful farmer" on entering Holy Cross but gives no source for the information. See O'Connell, *Edward Sorin*, 54.

3. Edward Sorin, *Circular Letters*, 2 vols. (Notre Dame: n.p., 1885), 1.57.

4. Letter, Sister Francis Xavier to Louis de la Motte, September 1841, qtd. George Klawitter, CSC, *After Holy Cross, Only Notre Dame* (New York: iUniverse, 2003), 86.

5. Edward Sorin, *Chronicles,* trans. William Toohey, CSC, ed. James T. Connolly, CSC (Notre Dame: University of Notre Dame Press, 1992), 90-91.

6. Ibid., 90.

7. Ibid., 90.

8. See Klawitter, *After Holy Cross*, 153-154, 157-160.

9. Letter, Brother Lawrence to Edward Sorin, March 5, 1850, trans. George Klawitter. All Lawrence letters, unless otherwise noted, are located in the Holy Cross General Archives at the University of Notre Dame.

10. Placidus' will is extant in the General Archives at Notre Dame. The document, written in French, is in Brother Vincent Pieau's hand. Placidus (Urbain Alerd) "signed" it with a + between his first and last names. Above the + is "sa" ("his") and below the + is "croise" ("mark"). The name "Urban Alerd" (separated by the +) is in Vincent's hand. Placidus could not even sign his own name.

> In the name of the very Holy Trinity, I declare this is my will that I will be faithful to up to the hour of my death. I'm giving freely to E. Sorin everything that belongs to me at the hour of my death and give him permission to use it any way he deems proper. Done at Notre Dame du Lac in Indiana, United States of America, December 30, 1847.

The will is witnessed by Brother Vincent, Brother Lawrence, and Brother Gatian.

11. Letter, Brother Lawrence to Edward Sorin, March 15, 1850, qtd. in Franklin Cullen, CSC, *Holy Cross on the Gold Dust Trail* (Notre Dame: Indiana Province Archives Center, 1989), 10.

12. Letter, Brother Gatian to Edward Sorin, qtd. Cullen, *Holy Cross*, 20.

13. Letter, Brother Lawrence to Edward Sorin, November 1850, trans. Klawitter.

14. Cullen, *Holy Cross*, 27.

15. Brother Lawrence, Document, June 19, 1868 (Notre Dame: Holy Cross General Archives).

16. See the following chapter, "Brother Francis Xavier Patois: Carpenter-Mortician."

17. Letter, Brother Lawrence to Edward Sorin, November 15, 1869.

18. Letter, Brother Lawrence to Edward Sorin, January 24, 1870.

19. Letter, A. Richardson to Brother Lawrence, March 1, 1858.

20. Aiden O'Reilly, CSC, *Extracts*, on-line.

21. Brother Aidan O'Reilly's *Extracts* are described on-line as follows:
> The Brother Aidan Extracts were compiled by the first Archivist of the United States Province of the Brothers of the [sic] Holy Cross, Brother Aidan O'Reilly, C.S.C. The work was done in 1946 and 1947 and was nearly finished at his death in 1948. The first set of notes was typed by the Scholastic Brothers at Dujarie Institute, but the present three volume set-up provides a slightly edited and more compactly typed edition done by the Archives Department in 1949 and 1950. The letter [sic] was done under the direction of Brother Garnier Morin, C.S.C., archivist from 1948 to 1950. (Notre Dame Archives). On-line.

22. Edward Sorin, *Circular Letters*, 1.56-58.

23. There are at least two wills by Brother Lawrence preserved in the United States Province Archives: one dated January 1, 1848, the other February 27, 1850 (the day before the departure for California). In the earlier document,

written in French, and very obviously in Lawrence's hand, Lawrence wills everything to Brother Francis Xavier (René Patois). In the second document, which is three times as long as the first and written in English, he also leaves everything to Francis Xavier, but he names Sorin as executor. This use of Francis Xavier was simply a formality: governments (especially in France) did not consider clergy as legally capable of "owning" property in the mid-nineteenth-century. Brothers, non-cleric as they are, were a convenience for religious congregations. Even the original 524 acres at Notre Dame were deeded to "The Brothers of St. Joseph," not to Edward Sorin.

24. *St. Joseph Valley Register*, April 10, 1873, 2.1
25. *Religious Bulletin*, January 18 [?], qtd. O'Reilley, *Extracts*.
26. *Scholastic,* April 12, 1873, 244.
27. *Scholastic* 6:31.245.
28. The photo is preserved in the University of Notre Dame Archives and has been reproduced often.

Chapter Six
Francis Xavier Patois: Carpenter-Mortician

1. Today Clermont is part of Clermont-Créans, a union effected in 1842, a few years after Brother Francis Xavier left town. Today the combined towns have a population of just over 1000, so in 1842 each would have had only several hundred people. Clermont can trace its roots to the twelfth century and is located at the foot of a hill on the road between Paris and Nantes. The Clermont church is St. Lambert, named for a bishop of the eighth century. René Patois was undoubtedly baptized in this church soon after his birth in 1820.
2. The Le Mans Francis Xavier's signature is similar to Brother Marie's, with similar flourishes, but such a phenomenon is not unusual, given the importance of hand-writing pedagogy at the time. Brother Marie's handwriting is quite beautiful, even on documents written in his old age.
3. Marvin O'Connell in his Sorin biography has index errors for the name "Francis Xavier."
4. The following matricules from the US Province Archives list Brother Francis Xavier with the name "Reynault":
   a) *Brothers buried in Community Cemetery.* Typescript by last name: n.a., n.d.
   b) *Obituary Register of the Congregation of Holy Cross, Province of the United States 1844-1941.* Typescript by month: n.a., n.d.
   c) Handwritten ledger with names listed by date of entrance (somewhat).
   d) Handwritten ledger of Josephites listed by entrance (somewhat).

The following matricules list Brother Francis Xavier with the name "René":

a) *French Brothers who Labored in Whole or in Part in the United States.* Typscript by religious name, n.a., n.d.

b) *Matricule Generale.* Compiled by Brother Bernard Gervais, CSC. Typescript, n.d.

His family name is given as "Pattoy" in *Table Analytique des Lettres Circulaires des Superieurs Generaux (1836-1976).* Rome: Holy Cross Generalate, 1977. He is listed as "René Patoy" in the French obituary compiled in France by Jean Proust, CSC.

A "last will" Francis Xavier wrote in 1847, leaving all his possessions to Brother Lawrence Menage to be distributed as Lawrence saw fit, is signed "René Patois dit frère Marie" (Holy Cross General Archives). I conclude that the proper spelling of Francis Xavier's family name was Patois. His last will, written in his own hand, is proof enough.

A French genealogy site lists the following variants for the family name "Patois":

PATOIS | PATOUA | PATOY | PATOI | PATTOIS | PATOIT | PATOUEIL | PATOIL | PASTOIS

There is no Patois family living today in Clermont, but according to the mayor's secretary (July 2013), there is a Patoil family living there. That family has a long history in the area but not for the year 1820:

PATOIL Clermont (Sarthe, Pays de la Loire, France) 1698 - 1740
PATOIL Créans,72084 (Sarthe, Pays de la Loire, France) 1687 - 1694
PATOIL Mareil sur Loir 72200 (Sarthe, Pays de la Loire, France) 1569 - 1619
PATOIL Clermont-Créans,72200,Créans (Sarthe, Pays de la Loire, France) 1642 - 1724
PATOIL Villaines sous Malicorne (Sarthe, Pays de la Loire, France) 1664 - 1768
PATOIL Créans (Sarthe, Pays de la Loire, France) 1665 - 1724
PATOIL Clermont-Créans, 72084 (Sarthe, Pays de la Loire, France) 1665 - 1676
PATOIL Mareil-sur-Loir,72200 (Sarthe, Pays de la Loire, France) 1562 - 1699
PATOIL Clermont-Créans, 72084 (Sarthe, Pays de la Loire, France) 1668 - 1759
PATOIL Pdl, Villaines sous Malicorne (Sarthe, Pays de la Loire, France) 1699 - 1722
The Patois family for Sarthe includes only the following ancestry:
depgn3244 1 PATOIS 1699 - 1699 Cures Sarthe, Pays de la Loire, France
The Patoy search includes significantly more hits for the Sarthe region:
http://en.geneanet.org/search/?name=PATOY&country=FRA& ressource=arbre

There was a Patoy living in Clermont-Créans in 1835.

5. George Klawitter, *After Holy Cross, Only Notre Dame,* 85.

6. Letter, Sister Francis Xavier to Louis de la Motte, August 1841, qtd. in Klawitter, *After Holy Cross,* from Clémentine de la Corbinière, *The Life and Letters of Sister Francis Xavier (Irma Le Fer de la Motte)* (Saint Mary-of-the-Woods: Providence Press, 1934), 85.

7. Letter, Mother Theodore Guerin, qtd. Klawitter, *After Holy Cross,* 88 from de la Corbinière, 228.

8. O'Connell, *Edward Sorin,* 84.

9. George Klawitter, *Adapted to the Lake: Letters by the Brother Founders of Notre Dame, 1841-1849* (New York: Peter Lang, 1993), 1.

10. Ibid., 343.

11. Ibid., 21-24.

12. Letter, Edward Sorin to Basil Moreau, December 5, 1842, qtd. Etienne Catta, *Basil Anthony Mary Moreau* (Milwaukee: Bruce, 1955), 1.60.

13. *South Bend Tribune,* June 22, 1895, qtd. Kilian Bierne, *From Sea to Shining Sea: The Holy Cross Brothers in the United States* (Valatie: Holy Cross Press, 1966), 30-31.

14. On the outside chapel north wall is a large white commemorative slab for the pioneer Coquillard family. It reads: Alexis Coquillard / First Permament White Settler / Co-founder of South Bend / September 28, 1795 / January 8, 1855 / Wife / Frances Comparet Coquillard / April 9, 1805 / October 11, 1880 / Son / Alexis Theodore Coquillard / February 13, 1836 / January 2, 1884. The wife and the son would have known Francis Xavier for most of Francis Xavier's life. The son is the little boy referred to in Francis Xavier's notes to Professor Edwards (see n. 23 below).

15. *Notre Dame Scholastic,* 19.1, 7.

16. Ibid., 10.13, 91.

17. Minutes, Notre Dame Council, April 22, 1850, qtd. O'Connell, 252.

18. Aidan O'Reilly, *Extracts,* May 24, 1850 (Notre Dame: General Archives).

19. Ibid., April 3, 1847.

20. Ibid., 1851.

21. Letter, Bother Francis Xavier to Basil Moreau, January 27, 1863 (Notre Dame: General Archives), trans. George Klawitter.

22. See O'Connell, *Edward Sorin,* 470-472.

23. These notes by Edwards were written in pencil, and the manuscript is fading fast (United States Province Archives). The notes also contain a charming story Francis Xavier told Edwards about Charles Moreau's trip to Kalamazoo. When a storm came up and Charles sought shelter under a tree, Charles sat down and prayed all night. Unfortunately, the horse "lay down and squash [sic] the cup of the little relic chalice flat." There is also a story about church bells destined for Notre Dame.

24. Arthur Hope, *Notre Dame: One Hundred Years* (Notre Dame: University Press, 1941), 134.

25. After Mrs. Sherman begged Sorin for another army chaplain, Sorin sent Father Carrier in 1863. See Anna McAllister, *Ellen Ewing, Wife of General Sherman* (New York: Benziger Bros., 1936), 259. Later Carrier proved to be the perfect emissary from Sorin in 1864 to intercede in Washington for

military exemptions for Notre Dame's Brothers after the election debacle fomented by Schuyler Colfax.

26. Hope, *Notre Dame*, 134 n.

27. Sorin, *Chronicles*, 288-289.

28. Minutes, Notre Dame Council, October 17, 1864 (Notre Dame: General Archives).

29. *Notre Dame Scholastic* (University of Notre Dame: General Archives), 8.18.

30. Ibid., 251.

31. Ibid., 10.13, 202.

32. Ibid., 9.40, 634.

33. Ibid., 26.13, 203.

34. Herman Alerding, *The Diocese of Fort Wayne 1857-1907* (Fort Wayne: Archer, 1907), 201.

35. *Notre Dame Scholastic*, 11.31, 490.

36. Three well-worn tombstones twenty feet south of the Cedar Grove Cemetery chapel are the stones of the Dignan family. Two are still legible: one in the center reads "FATHER" and the one to its immediate right reads "MARGT MARY DIGNAN" but the one on the far left of the three is illegible. The spelling of the family name on the Margaret Mary tombstone does not agree with the spelling of Dignan on the accounts document in Francis Xavier's hand: he wrote the family name as "Degnan." The tombstone, however, agrees with the typescript cemetery records held in the Notre Dame Archives (see MCEM reel #2, HIST040D). On this alphabetical typescript, there are seven entries for "Dignan": Annie (March 1901), Catheran (April 1875), Francis (April 1940), Frank (n.m. 1900), Frank (December 1880), Margaret (October 1881), Mary E (September 1881). The three tombstones have no dates. The record by Francis Xavier for Francis Degnan [sic] is dated 1881. Francis' tombstone is the center one of the three in Cedar Grove Cemetery. The puzzle remains for Margaret (d. 1880) and Mary E (d. 1881). Since the one tombstone has the name Margaret Mary, she must be the daughter of Francis. The worn tombstone (illegible) must then be that of Catheran (d. 1875) or possible Mary E (d. 1881). But who is Mary E? And is this her stone? If it is her stone, why isn't it as legible as the stone for Margaret Mary?

37. *Notre Dame Scholastic,* 15.38, 591-2.

38. Francis Xavier would not have known the apostle to the Miami, Benjamin Petit, who died ministering to the Native Americans in 1838, just four years before the first Holy Cross men arrived at Notre Dame, but he would certainly have known Petit's poignant history. For letters written by Petit in his last days see Irving McKee, *The Trail of Death: Letters of Benjamin Marie Petit, 1811-1839* (Indianapolis: Indiana Historical Society, 1941).

39. *Notre Dame Scholastic,* 24.26, 412.

40. O'Reilly, *Extracts*, 1896.

41. Ibid., 1896.
42. William Corby, Circular Letter, November 13, 1896, qtd.in Bierne, 32.
43. *Notre Dame Scholastic*, 30.10, 155.

Chapter Seven
Anselm Caillot: Ready to Serve in Indiana

1. Georges Mace, *Un Departement Rural de L'Ouest: La Mayenne,* 2 vols. (Mayenne: Floch, 1982), 1.15.
2. In population La Mayenne grew from 352,486 in 1831 to 360,290 in 1841; France herself burgeoned from 33,218,000 to 34, 911,000. Ibid., 2.868.
3. The four Caillot children were Perrine (b. May 29, 1819), Constant (b. January 24, 1822), Félicitée-Jeanne (b. March 28, 1823), and Pierre (b. March 19, 1925). Anselm's father and grandfather were both named Pierre. Anselm's paternal grandparents were Pierre Caillot and Renée Deslandes. Their son (Anselm's father) Pierre was born on May 3, 1796. Anselm's maternal grandparents were Louis Chartier and Jacquine Collet. The grandmother died on November 8, 1813. Their daughter (Anselm's mother) Jacquine Chartier was born on April 10, 1793.
4. Garnier Morin, *Holy Cross Brothers: From France to Notre Dame* (Notre Dame: Dujarié Press, 1952), 34.
5. Brother Mary Joseph was born Samuel O'Connell in Ireland in 1819. He joined the Holy Cross group in December 1842 at St. Peter's, Indiana, and went to Notre Dame with Brother Vincent a few months later. He was the first postulant to become a novice at Notre Dame. After teaching in Vincennes, he replaced Anselm in Madison in 1845. When he returned to Madison the following year with Brother Francis (Michael Disser), the new pastor (Maurice de St. Palais) sent them away. Mary Joseph left the Community a few months later (November 1846).
6. Sorin, *Chronicles*, xx.
7. Letter, Brother Anselm to Edward Sorin, July 9, 1843. All the Anselm letters are collected in George Klawitter, *Adapted to the Lake.*
8. August Mary Martin, chaplain at the Royal College in Rennes, arrived in America in 1839. He met the first Holy Cross colony at Logansport, Indiana, where he was pastor of St. Vincent de Paul Church. He was appointed Vicar General of the Vincennes diocese in 1842 and was the first bishop of Natchitoches, Louisiana. He was Sorin's closest confidant among the Vincennes clergy: they shared perceptions of Hailandière. See O'Connell, *Edward Sorin*, 11.
9. Letter, Brother Anselm to Edward Sorin, July 26, 1843.
10. Letter, Brother Anselm to Edward Sorin, October 26, 1843.

11. Letter, Brother Anselm to Edward Sorin, November 7, 1843.

12. Letter, Brother Anselm to Edward Sorin, February 8, 1844.

13. Ibid.

14. Letter, Brother Anselm to Edward Sorin, June 2, 1844.

15. Letter, Brother Anselm to Edward Sorin, August 4, 1844.

16. St. Michael's Church since August 1842, had as its pastor Juian Delaune who opened the school September 26, 1843, first in the church, then in the church basement. Delaune was pastor until 1846 when he left Madison to direct Sorin's ill-fated college in Kentucky. He died in Paris on May 4, 1846, at the age of thirty-seven.

17. See O'Connell, *Edward Sorin,* 220.

18. Letter, Brother Anselm to Edward Sorin, March 26, 1845.

19. Malaria was common on the frontier. See John Hanners, "The Great Wizard of the North," *Traces of Indiana and Midwestern History* (Spring 1990): 30.

20. Letter, Brother Anselm to Edward Sorin, July 10, 1945.

21. Letter, Julian Delaune to Basil Moreau, July 1845, qtd. Klawitter, *Adapted to the Lake,* xxi-xxii.

22. Sorin, *Chronicles,* 57.

23. The original land for the sixty-acre cemetery was purchased in 1837 by the city of Madison. The cemetery is bound by State Road 7, Vine Street, a creek (Crooked Creek), and the foothills of Hanging Rock Hill. If Anselm's grave were inundated in the great Ohio River flood of 1937, it probably would have been inundated by the creek rather than by the river.

24. In 2001 Robert Newland of Indianapolis found the marker lying flat under three inches of dirt and grass. The stone is large and heavy, 66 inches high and 17 ½ inches wide. The top has decorative work and a cross in an arch, but some top decoration has been broken off. Alerted to the concerns of the Midwest Brothers, Newland decided to pursue the quest. He and his wife Janet, who is archivist for the Archdiocese of Indianapolis, travelled twice to Madison to hunt for Brother Anselm's grave, and on Sunday, December 2, 2001, they were successful. With directions from Bob Leach, the new sexton for Springdale Cemetery, Bob Newland went to the far north end of the cemetery near a creek where the oldest stones were said to be located. Previously, the Brothers who trekked to Madison hunted on the west hillside. The creek, which runs east and west, was apparently the culprit in the 1937 flood, not the Ohio River on the south end of the cemetery.

  As Janet Newland tried the hillside, Bob worked in the old section where he found stones covered by dirt and grass. All were flat on the ground. Using garden tools, he uncovered a few stones and saw dates from the 1850's. Knowing he was on the right track, he uncovered a third stone and saw the word "France." He knew immediately he may have found Anselm. The stone was buried under three inches of dirt. Bob Leach and Bob Newland agree that the stone marks the exact spot where the grave is. Such a large stone would have been placed at least two feet in the ground and floodwaters would have affected it little, especially flood waters from a creek. Bob Leach believes that all the stones in this section of the cemetery were intentionally laid flat, possibly to preserve them from vandalism. Although cemetery records were lost in the 1937 flood, Bob Newland has found Anselm in the lists kept by the Daughters of the American Revolution. Anselm can also be found in the lists on the Springdale Cemetery Website. Made of soft Indiana limestone, Anselm's tombstone is not as durable as granite stones. The inscription remains, however, easy to read.

25. In addition to the inscription the postcard reads: "Pilgrimage to this cemetery where the above inscription marks the resting place of one of the group who founded N.D. Bro. Anselm was drowned. Marius." The postcard is half typed, half script, the memorial from the stone being the typed part.

Chapter Eight
Gatian Monsimer: Rebel on the Frontier

1. Eli Sagan, *Citizens & Cannibals: The French Revolution, The Struggle for Modernity, and the Origins of Ideological Terror* (New York: Rowman & Littlefield, 2001), 484.

2. Gatian gives the precise time of his birth in a letter to Edward Sorin. See George Klawitter, CSC, *Adapted to the Lake*, 299. Brother Gatian's grandfather, Urbain Monsimer, was born circa 1770, the son of René Monsimer and Jeanne Chamaret. He married Marie Lebreton, left Chéméré-le-roi, and settled at Préau near Saulges where he died at age seventy-one in 1841, nineteen years before his grandson Urbain's death. The grandfather had two sons: François, who died in 1834 at age 20, and Urbain (Brother Gatian's father) who was born on January 9, 1800, and married (at Saulges) Rose Julienne Joseph Reneaudeau on June 22, 1824. She was a laundress from Saulges.

3. Later as a corporal in the Crimean War, August fought in the infantry, but contracted typhus several months after the war ended (1855) and died in April 1856. The mother of these three unfortunate boys herself died at La Teillerie on March 24, 1837, only thirty-six years old. At the time her sons would have been ten, eight, and three. We do not know what she died of. Although the extended Monsimer family would have afforded some mothering to the boys, the widower Monsimer did not wait much longer than a year to remarry. On June 26, 1838, in the Church of the Assumption in Chéméré-le-roi, he married Frances Viéron. She was twenty-eight, he thirty-eight, and the marriage was fruitful: Henry Clement was born in 1840, Isidore Adolph on May 9, 1841 (died at age 9), Henry Armand on June 15, 1842, Francis Louis on August 18,

1844, and Eugene Adrian on January 26, 1846. When the grandfather died in 1841, the Monsimer family left the farm near Chéméré-le-roi and moved back to the grandfather's farm at Préau near Saulges.

4. This other farm, La Teillerie, near Chéméré-le-roi, is also very beautiful. Many of the buildings from Urbain's days remain standing in fine shape and are still in use: the cow barn, the pig barn, and the main house show little wear for the century and a half between us and him. They are picturesque structures, removed from the paved road by a dirt road some hundred yards long. The well-cultivated fields stretch far into the distance beyond the dirt road. The buildings are constructed of fieldstone and the sloping roofs are tiled with grey slate. The rustic doors to the barns are wooden, and everywhere there are flowerbeds full of color in the summer. The farmhouse itself is to the left of the short driveway off the dirt road, and its far end is the oldest section, probably the only part of the house that dates to Urbain's youthful days there. The house is two stories high.

5. The priest de Marseul was ordained in 1835, joined Moreau's auxiliary priests in 1836 but left six years later. He did return to Holy Cross in 1857 but stayed only until 1868. Brother Euloge went to Algeria in September 1840 with the first colony, but he left Holy Cross in March 1842.

6. Brother Chrysostom (Céleste Maillard) came to Ste. Croix at age nineteen in August 1840, one year after Gatian. He received a teaching diploma in 1843 and left Holy Cross six years later. Brother Hilaire (Pierre Beury) was born in 1817 and entered Holy Cross in 1835. He served in Algeria but left Holy Cross from there in 1846. He returned to the Community circa 1853 and died at Angers in 1890. As there is no Brother John of the Cross listed at this time in the *General Matricule,* the brick layer that Gatian refers to is probably Brother John (Jean-Baptiste Hilaire Diard) who was a fellow novice aged eighteen. He left Holy Cross in February 1842, after Gatian was already in America.

7. Letter, Edward Sorin to Basil Moreau, October 14, 1841.

8. By November 3 another recruit arrived: James William Donoghue, the first of many Irishmen to join. Donoghue was born in New Orleans and was seventeen years old. With the name Brother Thomas, he lasted with the Community until 1852. Michael Disser arrived next, on December 6, and took the name Brother Francis. He was one year older than Donoghue and born in Alsace. He remained only five years. Francis Rees was the fourth recruit that year, arriving on December 8. Born in Germany, he was twenty-nine, took the name Brother Anthony, but remained only one year, not even making it to Notre Dame.

9. Letter, Edward Sorin to Basil Moreau, December 5, 1842, qtd. in Moreau, *Circular Letters,* 1.60.

10. Letter, Brother Gatian to Basil Moreau, February 18, 1846.

11. Letter, Brother Gatian to Basil Moreau, April 20, 1847.
12. Ibid.
13. Letter, Brother Gatian to Edward Sorin, August 20, 1848.
14. Ibid.
15. Letter, Brother Gatian to Basil Moreau, March 30, 1849.
16. Edward Sorin, *Chronicles*, 90
17. His father would live on to die in 1872 at age seventy-two.

Chapter Nine
Theodulus Barbé: Reluctant Martyr

1. Bernard Gervais, CSC, *General Matricule* (Notre Dame: General Archives).
2. Benjamin J. Webb, *The Centenary of Catholicity in Kentucky* (Louisville: Charles A. Rogers, 1884), 434.
3. Letter, Peter J. Verhaegen to Benedict Spalding, December 5, 1849, qtd. Webb, 305.
4. *Life of Mother Theodore* (1846), 318-322, qtd. Aiden O'Reilly, *Extracts*, 496.
5. Edward Sorin, *Chronicles of Notre Dame du Lac,* trans. William Toohey, CSC, ed. James Connelly, CSC (Notre Dame: University of Notre Press, 1992), 69.
6. Curiously, in Webb's *Centenary of Catholicity in Kentucky,* there is no mention of Holy Cross at all in the St. Mary's coverage. Webb only mentions Julian Delaune as the first of many secular priests to head the institution until the Resurrectionist Fathers took it over in 1873. From Brother Aidan's *Extracts*, we get the following details about the educational plan for the school under Julian Delaune:

   > To afford those whose avocations in life render unnecessary for them a classical education, a better opportunity of devoting their time and ability exclusively to the acquisition of those sciences which are generally considered as the most useful, no classical course will be taught in the institution, but English and Commercial course divided into three years ...
   > Faculty: John Maguire, Julian Delaune, A. Saulnier, Richard Shortis.
   > Terms: Bed and Board, Tuition, Washing, Bedding etc.
   > Bedding per annum (pay half yearly in advance) $75.00
   > Day School, 1st year $16.00
   > Day School, 2nd year 20.00
   > Day School, 3rd year 24.00
   > Board the week during vacation $2.00
   > —*Catholic Almanac,* 1848, 129-31.

7. Letter, Brother Theodulus to Edward Sorin, February 18, 1848. All Theodulus letters before 1850 are found in George Klawitter, CSC, *Adapted to the Lake.*

8. Etienne Catta and Tony Catta, *Basil Anthony Mary Moreau* (Milwaukee: Bruce, 1955), 1.552-564.

9. It does not help the Cattas' text that they persistently refer to the "Louisville" affair when, in fact, it really was a "St. Mary's" affair or, by extension, a "Bardstown" affair.

10. *Annales*, qtd. Catta, *Moreau*, 1.465, n. 107.

11. Letter, Brother Theodulus to Edward Sorin, February 1848.

12. Letter, Brother Theodulus to Edward Sorin, February 18, 1848.

13. Letter, Brother Theodulus to Edward Sorin, March 1, 1848.

14. Letter, Brother Theodulus to Edward Sorin, July 9, 1848.

15. Ibid.

16. St. Mary's College closed in 1976. One of its famous alumni was Joseph Cardinal Bernardine of Chicago. The town of St. Mary today has a population of 1600, while three miles away Lebanon has 6000 people and is known for its Ham Days Festival and Tractor Show held annually in September. In the 1960's Lebanon was known for its nightclubs.

17. Or in 1887, according to his United States Province matricule card.

18. Letter, Edward Sorin to Basil Moreau, qtd. Marvin R. O'Connell, *Edward Sorin* (Notre Dame: University of Notre Dame Press, 2001), 230.

19. Letter, Brother Theodulus to Basil Moreau, April 16, 1849.

20. Ibid.

21. Aidan O'Reilly, CSC, *Extracts*, 496.

22. Letter, Brother Theodulus to the Chapter at Notre Dame, September 9, 1849.

23. Ibid.

24. According to the minutes of the Minor Chapter at Notre Dame.

25. Sorin did not think much of Gouesse. He wrote to Bishop Blanc July 16, 1853, in the middle of the yellow fever terror: "Father Gouesse is not a man of God, and he will succeed only in creating trouble and discord instead of peace. Sainte Croix has committed an unpardonable fault in identifying itself with such a man" (qtd. in O'Connell, *Edward Sorin*, 318). For Sister Mary of the Angels' negative reaction to Gouesse's treatment of the Sisters on a boat trip see Sister Georgia Costin, CSC, *Priceless Spirit* (Notre Dame: University of Notre Dame Press, 1994), 93. On the matter of Gouesse's possible alcoholism, see James Connelly, CSC, "Charism: Origins and History," in Sister Georgia Costin, CSC, *Fruits of the Tree, Sequicentennial Chronicles, Sisters of the Holy Cross,* vol. 1 (Notre Dame: Sisters of the Holy Cross, 1991), 111. All negative assessments of Gouesse must be filtered through their sources, all of whom may have already chosen sides in the Sorin-Moreau fracas.

26. Letter, Brother Theodulus to Edward Sorin, June 10, 1850.

27. See Connelly, "Holy Cross in New Orleans: The Crisis of 1850-1854."

28. Fitzgerald in *Juxta Crucem* names the June 1853, deceased New Orleans Brother Victor (150), but this is incorrect. The dead Brother was Theodulus.

29. Letter, Gouesse to Basil Moreau, August 31, 1853, rpr. Moreau, *Circular Letter #56*.

30. Ibid.

31. The second man in Holy Cross to take the name Eleazar, he was born John Dobson in 1818 in Ireland. He entered Holy Cross in 1850 at age 32 and became a novice in February 1851. He died of yellow fever two and a half years later on August 18, 1853, in New Orleans without ever taking vows.

32. Basil Moreau, *Circular Letter #59*, September 21, 1853.

33. Fitzgerald errs in claiming Moreau's Circular Letter #60 speaks of "five Sisters dead in New Orleans." See Gerald Fitzgerald, CSC, *Juxta Crucem: The Life of Basil Anthony Moreau* (New York: P.J. Kenedy, 1937), 152. Heston translates the information as "five Sisters are still confined to their beds at New Orleans" (Moreau, See Basil Anthony Moreau, *Circular Letters,* 2 vols., trans. Edward L. Heston, CSC (n.c.: 1943), 1.290.

Chapter Ten
Alexis Granger: Sorin's Softer Self

1. Joseph A. Lyons, *Silver Jubilee of the University of Notre Dame, June 23rd, 1869* (Chicago: Myers, 1869), 80.

2. See Sorin's letter to Granger, August 31, 1840. All quotations from Granger correspondence in this paper are reprinted with the kind permission of the United States Province Archives and the General Archives at the University of Notre Dame.

3. From his novitiate days we have a twenty-seven-page document of his notes on the religious conferences given by the Le Mans novice master. Even more interesting, however, is a list of "Recommendations" given by Moreau:
Keep strict silence in common areas.
Don't look from one side to the other.
Don't move chairs noisily.
Put everything back in its place ...
Pray according to the method of St. Ignatius.
Confess every week ...
Get spiritual direction every other week ...
Kiss the floor if you are late for an exercise ...
Never go into anyone else's bedroom. (20)
Anyone professed in Holy Cross for over forty years will recognize the injunctions as standard novitiate routine. Granger also includes the daily schedule from 5 AM to bedtime. (See Appendix VI)

4. Qtd. O'Connell, *Edward Sorin,* 47.

5. Granger's vow formula is extant in the United States Province Archives, Notre Dame. It is written in Latin in his own distinct hand. We also have the certificate of his ordination to the diaconate and the certificate of his ordination to priesthood, but those two documents are printed with relevant dates penned in. The vow formula is the earliest piece of his writing available.

6. Letter, Alexis Granger to Basil Moreau, October 1844, qtd. Moreau, *Circular Letters*, 1.94-95.

7. E.g., O'Connell, *Edward Sorin*, 623.

8. In addition to Edward Sorin, living in what today is the "Old College" building would have been Brother Vincent Pieau, Brother Lawrence Ménage, Brother Joachim André, Brother Marie (Francis Xavier) Patois, and Brother Gatian Monsimer. Some of the novices in October 1844 might have been living in the original log cabin found when the first colony arrived in November, 1842. Granger was made novice master as soon as he "could make himself understood in English" (Sorin, *Chronicles* 43).

9. The Sisters in Indiana grew so tired of Granger's refusing all their requests when Sorin was out of the country that they stopped holding council meetings (Costin, *Priceless Spirit*, 51).

10. Letter, Victor Drouelle to Basil Moreau, November 1, 1848, qtd. Catta, *Moreau*, 1.929.

11. Sorin, *Chronicles*, 55.

12. Letter, Theodore Badin to Alexis Granger, April 18, 1846.

13. Sorin, *Chronicles*, 59.

14. Letter, Brother Boniface to Alexis Granger, September 29, 1868.

15. Report, Peter Cooney to Alexis Granger, 1874.

16. Letter, Maurice de St. Palais to Alexis Granger, February 12, 1854.

17. Letter, Vicar-General Janssen to Alexis Granger, November 10, 1873.

18. Letter, Bishop Luers to Alexis Granger, March 2, 1863.

19. Letter, Bishop Luers to Alexis Granger, March 19, 1863.

20. O'Connell, *Edward Sorin*, 567.

21. Letter, Alexis Granger to Bishop Peter Paul Lefevere, February 13, 1853, United States Province Archives, trans. Klawitter. The typescript in the General Archives names Bishop Purcell of Cincinnati as the recipient, not Bishop Luers.

22. Arthur J. Hope, CSC, *Notre Dame: One Hundred Years* (Notre Dame: University Press, 1941), 73.

23. Notre Dame *Scholastic*, 1878-79 (561), qtd. Hope, *Notre Dame*, 187.

24. Notre Dame *Scholastic*, 1868-69 (68), qtd. Hope, *Notre Dame*, 149.

25. O'Connell, 623.

26. Thomas J. Schlereth, *A Spirit of Faith: The University of Notre Dame's Sacred Heart Church* (Notre Dame: Notre Dame Alumni Assoc., 1991), 20.

27. Hope, *Notre Dame*, 254.

28. Lyons, *Silver Jubilee,* 82.
29. Letter, Victor Drouelle to Basil Moreau, November 1, 1848, qtd. Catta, *Moreau,* 1.929.
30. Hope, *Notre Dame,* 253.
31. Ibid., 253.
32. Ibid., 254

Chapter Eleven
Rémi Mérianne: A Voice of Reason against Separatists

1. See the censure document on Leonard in Chapter Four (MS) of *Early Men of Holy Cross* by George Klawitter, CSC.
2. There is no record of the Brothers' staffing a school in La Quinte at the time.
3. Vigna Pia was a vineyard (donated by Piux IX) worked by Brothers who lived at the Santa Prisca orphanage, which was staffed by Holy Cross from 1850 to 1868. See Etienne Catta and Tony Catta, *Basil Anthony Mary Moreau,* 2 vols. (Milwaukee: Bruce, 1955), 1.816.
4. Frédéric François Xavier de Mérode, born in 1820 into Belgian nobility, resigned his military appointment and was ordained a priest in 1849. He was hired by Pius IX to run the prison system in Rome. He also supervised architectural projects. Consecrated an archbishop in 1866, he then supervised the distribution of papal alms. He sided with the anti-infallibility faction at the First Vatican Council, but accepted the dogma after its passage by the Council.
5. Piux IX (Pio Nono) was pope from 1846 to 1878, an extremely long pontificate (31 years). During those years, the Vatican lost the Papal States, and Pius IX thereafter considered himself a "prisoner" of the Vatican.
6. There is a curious item in this account because when Rémi asks the pope for blessings on various people, including one for his old father, he asks for a blessing for Brother Stephen, whom he identifies as "the first of the Institution," but Stephen in actual fact was not the first to answer Dujarié's call in 1820. He was the fourth. The first to arrive was Brother Ignatius (Pierre Hureau) who left the community twice, the second time (in 1830) for good. The second was Brother Louis (Louis Duchêne), who lasted only five years. The third was the great Brother André Mottais, who was dead by the time Rémi wrote this letter from Rome. Then came Stephen Gauffre, who was still alive at the time of Rémi's June letter but who died a few months later in Le Mans. He was probably sick at the time of Rémi's request to the pope. By calling him the "first" in the Community, Rémi undoubtedly meant "first in rank," which was true since André was deceased.
7. Holy Cross worked at La Souterraine only from 1855 to 1865.

8. Letter from Brother Rémi to Basil Moreau, October 19, 1847. Notre Dame: Holy Cross General Archives.

9. Letter from Brother Rémi to Edward Sorin, February 14, 1878, trans. George Klawitter, CSC. Putting one's hand on "the holy ark" refers to the incident of Uzzah in the Old Testament, 2 *Samuel* 6:1-7, 1 *Chronicles* 13:9-12.

10. 10. By 1887 one of the chief separatists, Brother Leonard Guittoger, would be dead, and his voice had effectively been silenced by 1871.

11. Bishop Claude-Madeleine de la Myre-Mory was appointed bishop December 5, 1819, and resigned December 22, 1828.

12. Moreover, the use of priests for secondary schools implies that the Brothers were reserved for primary school teaching.

13. See letter by André Mottais to Bishop Bouvier, November 14, 1834.

14. There is no February 1878 letter in the collected circular letters of Edward Sorin. Clearly there was one because Rémi references it specifically to February 3, 1878, in his own letter of March 23, 1878, to Louis Champeau. Sorin's circular letters were published in two volumes in 1885, eight years before his death. He was Superior General until his death. Sorin obviously supervised the publication of his own collected circular letters. Why the February 3, 1878, letter is not included is a mystery.

15. Rémi was not yet a novice but he arrived at Ruillé in January 1825 and was present for the news spread among the novices.

16. Rémi makes no mention here of Vincent Pieau, whom most sources include in the group of directors.

BIBLIOGRAPHY

Alerding, Herman. *The Diocese of Fort Wayne 1857-1907.* Fort Wayne: Archer, 1907.

Alerding, Herman. *A History of the Catholic Church in the Diocese of Vincennes.* Indianapolis: Carlon and Hollenbeck, 1883.

Anon., *Life and Life Work of Mother Theodore Guerin.* New York: Benziger Brothers, 1904.

Anon. *The Metropolitan Catholic Almanac and Laity's Directory.* Baltimore: Fielding Lucas, 1842.

Anon. *Sainte-Croix en France: Chronologie.* Notre Dame: Indiana Province Archives, n.d.

Bennoune, Mahfoud. *The Making of Contemporary Algeria, 1830-1987.* Cambridge: Cambridge University Press, 1988.

Bierne, Kilian, CSC. *From Sea to Shining Sea: The Holy Cross Brothers in the United States.* Valatie: Holy Cross Press, 1966.

Brown, Sister Mary Borromeo. *The History of the Sisters of Providence of St. Mary-of-the-Woods.* 2 vols. New York: Benziger Brothers, 1949.

Catta, Etienne, and Tony Catta. *Basil Anthony Mary Moreau.* Trans. Edward L. Heston, CSC. 2 vols. Milwaukee: Bruce, 1955.

Catta, Tony. *Jacques Dujarié.* Trans. Edward L. Heston. Milwaukee: Bruce, 1960.

Cedar Grove Cemetery Records. Notre Dame: Notre Dame Archives. MCEM, Reels 1-5.

Cheney, David. "Adolph Dupuch." *Catholic Hierarchy.* http:www.catholic-hierarchy.org/bishop/bdupuch.html

Cheney, David. "Louis Pavy." *Catholic Hierarchy.* http:www. catholic-hierarchy.org/bishop/bpavy.html

Chronicles of Notre Dame de Sainte-Croix. Notre Dame: General Archives.

Cleary, Hugh, CSC. "A Year of Rejoicing and Spiritual Renewal." Rome: Via

Framura 85, 2006.

Connelly, James, CSC. "Charism: Origins and History." In Sister Georgia Costin, CSC. *Fruits of the Tree, Sequicentennial Chronicles, Sisters of the Holy Cross.* Vol. 1. Notre Dame: Sisters of the Holy Cross, 1991.

Connelly, James, CSC. "Holy Cross in New Orleans: The Crisis of 1850-1854." Paper. Holy Cross History Conference, 1988.

Costin, Sister Georgia, CSC. *Fruits of the Tree, Sequicentennial Chronicles, Sisters of the Holy Cross.* Vol. 1. Notre Dame: Sisters of the Holy Cross, 1991.

Costin, Sister M. Georgia, CSC. *Priceless Spirit: A History of the Sisters of the Holy Cross, 1841-1893.* Notre Dame: University of Notre Dame Press, 1994.

Cullen, Franklin, CSC. *Holy Cross on the Gold Dust Trail.* Notre Dame: Indiana Province Archives Center, 1989.

de la Corbinière, Clémentine. *The Life and Letters of Sister Francis Xavier (Irma Le Fer de la Motte).* Saint Mary-of-the-Woods: Providence Press, 1934.

Dionne, Gerard, CSC. "Book Review" of Thomas Maddix, CSC, *Naming the Options: A Study of the Mission of the Brothers of Holy Cross During a Period of Comfort and Discomfort.* Rpr. George Klawitter, CSC, ed. *Brother André Mottais, Pioneer of Holy Cross: "Remove my name every time it appears."* Austin: St. Edward's University, 2001. 84-101.

Fitzgerald, Gerald C., CSC. *Juxta Crucem: The Life of Basil Anthony Moreau, 1799-1873.* New York: Kenedy & Sons, 1937.

Fournier, Jules. *La nouvelle Eglise d'Afrique. La conquête religieuse de l'Algérie, 1830-1846.* Paris: 1930.

Gervais, CSC, Bernard. *General Matricule.* Notre Dame, IN: Midwest Province Archives, n.d.

Granger, Alexis. "Novitiate Notes." United States Province Archives. Notre Dame, IN.

Hanners, John. "The Great Wizard of the North." *Traces of Indiana and Midwestern History.* (Spring 1990): 26-35.

Hope, Arthur J., CSC. *Notre Dame: One Hundred Years.* Notre Dame: University Press, 1941.

Klawitter, George, CSC. *Adapted to the Lake: Letters by the Brother Founders of Notre Dame, 1841-1849.* New York: Peter Lang, 1993.

Klawitter, George, CSC. *After Holy Cross, Only Notre Dame.* New York: iUniverse, 2003.

Klawitter, George, CSC, ed. *Brother André Mottais, Pioneer of Holy Cross: "Remove my name every time it appears."* Austin: St. Edward's University, 2001.

Klawitter, George, C.S.C. "Chronicle of the Brothers of Saint Joseph." Notre Dame: Midwest Province Archives, 2002.

Klawitter, CSC, George. *Holy Cross in Algeria: the Early Years, 1840-1849.* New York: iUniverse, 2007.

Lyons, Joseph A. *Silver Jubilee of the University of Notre Dame, June 23rd, 1869.* Chicago: Myers, 1869.

McAllister, Anna. *Ellen Ewing, Wife of General Sherman.* New York: Benziger Bros., 1936.

McKee, Irving. *The Trail of Death: Letters of Benjamin Marie Petit, 1811-1839.* Indianapolis: Indiana Historical Society, 1941.

Mace, Georges. *Un Departement Rural de L'Ouest: La Mayenne.* 2 vols. Mayenne: Floch, 1982.

Maddix, Thomas, CSC. "Breaking the Historical Amnesia: A Fresh Look at the Originating Vision of the Brothers of St. Joseph." In *Naming the Options: A Study of the Mission of the Brothers of Holy Cross During a Period of Comfort and Discomfort.* Diss., 1989. Rpr. *Mottais,* ed. George Klawitter, CSC, 67-83.

Mérianne, Rémi, CSC. *Recueil Documentaire.* Ed. Philéas Vanier, CSC. Notre Dame: Holy Cross Archives.

Metz, Helen. *Algeria: A Country Study.* Lanham, MD: Office of the Federal Register, 1994.

Monsimer, Urbain (Brother Gatian). *Chronicles, 1847-1849.* Notre Dame: United States Province of Priests and Brothers.

Moreau, Basil Anthony Mary. *Chronicles of Notre Dame de Sainte-Croix.* Notre Dame, IN: General Archives.

Moreau, Basil Anthony Mary. *Circular Letters.* Trans. Edward L. Heston, CSC. 2 vols. n.c.: n.p., 1943.

Moreau, Charles. *The Very Reverend Father Basil Anthony Mary Moreau, Priest of Le Mans and His Works.* Trans: anon. 2 vols. Paris: Firmin didot et cie, 1900.

Morin, Brother Garnier, CSC. *Holy Cross Brothers: From France to Notre Dame.* Notre Dame: Dujarié Press, 1952.

Notre Dame Scholastic, 1870-2013. Notre Dame: Notre Dame Archives, on-line.

Nowlan, Sister M. Emerentiana, CSC. Unpublished Chronicles. 2 vols. Notre Dame: St. Mary's Archives, n.d.

O'Connell, Marvin R. *Edward Sorin.* Notre Dame: University of Notre Dame Press, 2001.

O'Dwyer, Ephrem, CSC. *The Curé of Ruillé.* Notre Dame: Ave Maria Press, 1941.

O'Reilly, Aidan, CSC. *Extracts.* Notre Dame: Archives, n.d.

Sagan, Eli. *Citizens & Cannibals: The French Revolution, The Struggle for Modernity, and the Origins of Ideological Terror.* New York: Rowman & Littlefield, 2001.

Schlereth, Thomas J. *A Spirit of Faith: The University of Notre Dame's Sacred Heart Church.* Notre Dame: Notre Dame Alumni Assoc., 1991.

Scholastic. University of Notre Dame Archives, on-line. http://www.archives.nd.edu/Scholastic/

Smith, Charles Edward, CSC. *Documentation for Preserving the Memory of Canon James François Dujarie.* Private printing: 2003.

Sorin, Edward, CSC. *Chronicles of Notre Dame du Lac.* Trans. William Toohey, CSC. Ed. James T. Connelly, CSC. Notre Dame: University of Notre Dame Press, 1992.

Sorin, Edward, CSC. *Circular Letters.* 2 vols. Notre Dame: n.p., 1885.

Vanier, Philéas. *Canon Dujarié.* Montreal, 1948.

Veuillot, Louis. *Les Français en Algérie: Souvenirs d'un Voyage fait en 1841.* Paris: 1947.

Webb, Benjamin J. *The Centenary of Catholicity in Kentucky.* Louisville: Charles A. Rogers, 1884.